Die Schwersten Tage des Bürgerkriegs, 1864 und 1865

-

Der Feldzug unter Schofield und Thomas gegen Hood in Tennessee.
Die Schlachten von Franklin u. Nashville.

-

Die Erinnerungen von Fred. W. Fout.

CONGRESSIONAL MEDALIST.

The Darkest Days of the Civil War 1864 and 1865

The Campaign under Schofield and
Thomas against Hood in Tennessee
The Battles of Franklin and Nashville
Recollections of Fred. W. Fout

English translation of
Frederick W. Fout's
1902
Die Schwersten Tage des
Bürgerkriegs, 1864 u. 1865

Translation by Philip Graupner

Original copyright of the book in German
was in 1902 by Albert E. Fout

English Translation
© 2014 Philip Graupner.
 All rights reserved. This book and any portion thereof may not be reproduced or used in any manner whatsoever without the express written permission of the publisher except for the use of brief quotations in a book review or scholarly journal.

ISBN: 978-0-578-14547-1

First Printing, July 2014

Published by:
Philip Graupner
9066 County Road Q
Baileys Harbor, WI 54202

Translator's Foreword

Frederick W. Fout (1829 – 1905) was born in Germany and immigrated to the United States when he was fifteen years old. He lived with his uncle in Indiana, finishing his schooling and learning the carpenter's trade. In 1861 he volunteered for three months service in Company O, Seventh Indiana Infantry and saw some action, but was mustered out after the three months were up. He reenlisted a short time later in an Indiana artillery regiment, eventually joining the 15th Indiana Independent Battery, in which he served until the end of the war, being honored with the Congressional Medal of Honor for his bravery at Harper's Ferry in 1862, and achieving the rank of First Lieutenant by the end of the war. Later in life, he wrote a history of the war, "**Die schwersten Tage des Bürgerkriegs, 1864-1865**", appearing in 1902 in German, with his son Albert E. Fout as publisher. The main focus of the book is on the battles of Franklin and Nashville at the end of 1864. This was followed by "**The Dark Days of the Civil War, 1861-1865**" in English, published in 1904, the focus of which was Fout's experiences during the earlier years of the war, ending after the Battle of Atlanta in 1864. I am not aware of an earlier version of that volume in German.

I was asked to do a translation of some of the 1902 book for a Milwaukee man, John Busch, whose great-great-grandfather had been a bugler in an Indiana infantry regiment. He was interested in Civil War history and perhaps hoped to learn more about his ancestor's experiences in the war. I worked from a microfiche copy of the book from the Library of Congress that Mr. Busch had acquired years earlier and finished the translation in 2013.

I took the liberty of correcting the spelling of the names of officers, towns and geographical features, using the many resources that are available to us today. Otherwise, I did not do any editing. I do not know why the book wasn't translated into English by Fout or his son. He died in June, 1905 and is buried in St. Louis Missouri where he spent the last years of his life.

The illustrations in the microfiche copy of the book that I worked from were not in a good enough condition that they could be transferred to the translation manuscript. I copied the original frontispiece from a 1902 copy of the book in the Stanford University Library that had been digitized by Google Books. The other illustrations in the book were replaced by a few photographs of the important officers that were taken from Wikipedia life histories of the individual officers. All of these photos come from the Library of Congress archives. A copy of the original book in German can be downloaded from Google Books.

Information about Frederick W. Fout's life was gathered from a number of sources: Wikipedia, Find-a-Grave, Roots-Web and Antietam-on-the Web. What is missing in those biographies is more information about the writing and publishing of the books.

Philip Graupner

Table of Contents

Introduction   1
Gathering the Army at Pulaski   5
The Battle of Columbia   10
The Skirmish of Spring Hill   15
The Retreat from Spring Hill to Franklin   22
The Ford and Bridge Building on the Harpeth River   28
Southern Troops Prepare to Attack   36
Battle Formation of Hood's Army   42
Cheatham's Charge on Wagner's Forward Position   56
The Battle at the Center   59
The Battle at the Left Wing   70
The Battle at the Right Wing   76
The Battle at Sundown   82
Description from the Enemy Side   88
The Battle after Dark   99
Wilson's Cavalry Skirmish on our Left   109
The Work in the Field Hospital   115
Retreat to Nashville   120
The Horror of War   129
Results, Lessons and Comparisons   139
Wagner's Conduct during the Battle   151
The Battle of Nashville   157
Defending the Railroad   165
The Army under Thomas   1781
First Day of the Battle of Nashville   180
The Battle of Nashville under Thomas   190
After the Battle   202
Arrival of the 23rd Corps in Washington   225
The Ocean Voyage to Wilmington   230
The Bombardment of Fort Fischer   236
Sherman's March through Georgia   252
The Capture of Savannah   265
From Savannah to Columbia   277

Kilpatrick Overrun and the Battle of Averasboro   286
The Battle of Bentonville   292
Stoneman's Ride   301
General Wilson's March through Alabama   304
From Goldsboro to Raleigh - Johnson's Capitulation   314
The Causes of the Civil War   324

Original Preface

Having been encouraged on many sides, especially from comrades during the time of the Civil War, I present this book to the public. While writing it I relied first on my own memories and notes made during the campaigns. In addition, I used information gathered through extensive correspondence with veterans; but the most valuable help came from the official reports of the War Department which were most readily made available to me. I have steadfastly remained true to the facts and have represented the events of those memorable days in 1864 and 1865 as they really took place – favoring no one, misrepresenting no one – and my work can, as a result, claim to be a true representation of one of the most important episodes in the history of that bloody war which waged for nearly five years on the soil of this country. As such, the following pages form, although modest, an unembellished, unbiased, and as far as possible, exact contribution to the historical representations of the American Civil War. It is as such a contribution that I confidently put this book, the result of many years of work, into the hands of the reader.

The Author

Introduction

Almost 37 years have now passed since those important and memorable campaigns and many memories of that exciting time have been forgotten. However, the official reports from the War Department that have been released during the last years, as well as the many individual narrations from those who had taken part, now give us the opportunity to bring to light the truth about what took place during that time. We can't require more than the truth. This report will justly represent everyone who took part.

This narration will be of interest to many from St. Louis, especially the 15 Missouri (Swiss) Infantry Regiment, which under General Conrad took such a large part in the Battle of Franklin. The 44th Missouri Infantry Regiment, mostly youths from St. Joseph, Mo. recruited for just one year, lost more men in this battle than any other regiment on either side. It went into battle with almost 900 men and only 360 reported as capable of duty at the first count the next morning.

This campaign will forever stand as the most brilliant of the successes in the civil war. Wellington in Waterloo lost 1756 killed out of his army of 43,000 men. Hood at Franklin in a battle lasting only three hours, according to his own report left 1750 dead on the field out of the 24,000 men he led into battle. Nowhere in history has the question of attack or defend been answered so decisively as in those short November days near Franklin. Hood didn't take the time to dig trenches or parallels in order to have an advantage over us, but gave the command to advance. During the battle he had the saddle taken off his horse and used it as a pillow to get some rest. One shouldn't assume from this that the Southerners were cowards. He had lost his right arm in the Battle of Gettysburg in July 1863 and at Chickamauga on 20 September 1863 his left leg. The bravery of those under him in carrying out his orders can be seen in the number of his generals lost. Six died on the battle field; six were seriously wounded and one rode over a breastwork where his horse was killed under him and he was taken prisoner. Among the seriously wounded generals was also our present Senator Cockrell. The fierceness of the battle is demonstrated by the death of five brothers from a Mississippi regiment, who had all taken part in all the battles from Shiloh in 1862 to Franklin, but all five were killed there. General Pat Cleburne and his horse were hit by 49 bullets.

The history of the Civil War shows many bloody conflicts between the two armies, but it was at Nashville that General Thomas wiped out an entire army. Hood, in his report to the government in Richmond, reported to Jefferson Davis, the president of the Confederacy, that the Tennessee Army had been destroyed. He could have gone further and in truth said that the left wing of the rebels was now something that used to be; for after the campaigns of Thomas in Tennessee, the Confederacy only fluttered with its right wing in Virginia.

And as General Sherman himself told this author in Burnett House in Cincinnati in 1889, his march through Georgia would have been worthless without the successes of Schofield and Thomas in Tennessee.

It cannot be disputed that the leadership of armies on both sides in the year 1864 lay in the hands of the best generals. General Grant in his memoir gives Jefferson Davis and General Hood full credit for an excellently designed plan to destroy Sherman's lines of communication, the success of which might have been possible with the active sympathy of the northern "Copperheads", but after the sharp conscription carried out in the north, their sympathy for the "Knights of the Golden Circle" went to the devil. The collecting of recruits for Hood's army in Kentucky and Tennessee also failed. With that, every chance of Hood's campaign succeeding disappeared. Sherman pursued Hood on his campaigns back and forth to the border of Alabama. Up to that point, the war games of both sides were interesting. Hood's intention was to draw Sherman away from Atlanta and if possible, to move the battle area into Tennessee and northern Mississippi. So far, Hood had carried it out well, but his opponent, General Sherman, had other plans, which to be carried out only awaited the support of General Grant.

Grant's view tended in the direction; since Sherman had followed Hood so far, he should move the first of his armies to Tennessee in order to completely destroy Hood during his advance.

Sherman answered Grant, when he turned his back to Hood, Hood would follow him. Grant now agreed to Sherman's plan in which the defense of Tennessee would be turned over to General Thomas. He had already moved two divisions of the Fourth Army Corps under General Stanley from Georgia to Tennessee. Besides these, Sherman expected that together with Thomas's army and other troops already occupying Tennessee, with the exception of those in East Tennessee and Kentucky stationed under Schofield in the Ohio Department, would add up to 65,000 battle-ready troops with which to defend the state. Thomas thought that if he had Schofield too, they would be able to handle Hood. Sherman agreed to allow Schofield to remain with Thomas, but wanted the 23rd Corp to remain with his army. Schofield protested to Sherman however, that the 23rd Corp had shrunk to about 8000 battle-ready men in the campaigns against Atlanta and asked that they be allowed to remain with him in Tennessee, in order to bring it back up to full strength with new recruits. Sherman granted Schofield's wish and at Rome, Georgia, while on the march back from Gadsden, Alabama, we took our departure from Sherman's army, which now gathered at Atlanta while we marched on toward Dalton in order to be transported from there by train to Nashville.

As we saw above, it was Sherman's opinion that Hood would follow him. Grant took a different view and believed that Hood would march to Tennessee. As it appears, neither was right, for Hood was evidently very surprised by Sherman's bold move, for after the active campaigns in northern Georgia during October, he remained in camp near Florence, Alabama until 21 November, perhaps uncertain whether it would be better to follow Sherman or to break into Tennessee.

The great perseverance of the American as long as there is a shimmer of hope was very evident in Hood's army, for after the devastating blows around Atlanta as well as Altoona which only resulted in losses, many another army would have completely lost the courage to fight on. Hood himself was in a desperate situation.

After replacing General Joseph Johnston in Atlanta, the people expected successes which he could not offer them. The southern public was becoming impatient. In order to satisfy them, Beauregard was given supervision over Hood and Taylor (the latter was commander in Mississippi). Beauregard immediately roused Hood to more action. He excused himself however, that there weren't any provisions for the army. However, every comrade that took part in the campaign will still remember that if Hood had been as active in Tennessee in November as he had been in Georgia in October, he could have gathered all the supplies that he required before Thomas had been able to assemble his army.

In the following chapter we will describe the gathering of troops in Pulaski under the command of Schofield and the Battle of Columbia.

Gathering the Army at Pulaski

As mentioned previously, our army corps (23rd) separated from Sherman's main army at Rome, Georgia. We marched in the best fall weather to Dalton, a distance of 40 miles, which we accomplished in two days. Arriving in Dalton, the weather became wintery and raw. Since we had to wait for transportation by train, we sought shelter in nearby homes, because the tents for officers and troops had been taken from us by the still active (then very energetically so for the rebels) General Wheeler on the Hiwassee River at Charleston, East-Tennessee, a few days after the Battle of Chickamauga in 1863. Since then, during storms, rain and sunshine, only the sky had been our roof. In Dalton we found a German clockmaker. We asked him for lodgings, which we then received for money and good words. At that time a German officer from the Second Missouri Regiment who had been badly wounded in the last battle had been living in the house. The daughter of the clockmaker (whose name I have forgotten) was giving her undivided attention to the wounded man, whom she also later married. The old man was very talkative and complained first about the leader of the Union and then about the rebels. Complaining had become a habit for him. On the evening of the first day that we were there, the son of the clockmaker arrived home. He had been in the Rebel Army and after being captured by Union soldiers, had been sent to Palmyra, NY. There he had taken the oath of allegiance and afterwards had worked in the area, at the same time acquiring a girlfriend which ended with marriage. As we all waited for our evening dinner, the young man came into the house with his better half. After greeting his father, he introduced his wife. The old man stood there as if struck by lightning. The young man took his wife along and introduced her to his sister and the wounded Second Missouri officer and then went to his mother in the kitchen where he also introduced his wife. As this was happening, the old man brought forth the most vulgar insults against his son and his young wife. Until that point we had listened quietly, but among the artillery officers was an older man from Michigan who requested permission to say something and chewed the old man out for his shameful greeting of his son and daughter-in-law to such an extent that the old man just stood there like a wet poodle and afterwards never spoke another word to us. Our comrades from the Second Missouri Regiment perhaps remember this old clockmaker from Dalton. The same occupied the town for a long time and fought several skirmishes there.

The military railroad administration in Georgia and Tennessee was very good in spite of the conditions of the time and a short time later transportation to Nashville arrived for us. The stretch from Dalton to Chattanooga is 40 miles, from Chattanooga to Nashville 151 miles. It took two days and two nights to cover that distance by train during the worst November weather. The horses and mules were in the cars, the troops had to find room between the canons and one regiment, the 79th Indiana, had to ride on top of a cattle car. There we were exposed to rain, snow and ice, which required a lot more stamina sitting than marching. Having arrived in Nashville, we were immediately sent on to Franklin, 20 miles further south. We left the train there and marched 60 miles further to Pulaski, where the 4th and 23rd Army Corps united before advancing.

In order to hinder the gathering of a large army under Thomas, the rebel General Breckinridge marched against General Gillman in eastern Tennessee, who commanded the Union Cavalry there. Forrest had already carried out a similar raid in October and the beginning of November in western Tennessee and Kentucky as far as Paducah on the Ohio without lasting success. Breckinridge's action was also without success.

Around 15 November, Forrest and his cavalry were at Florence and guarded a new bridge over which Hood wanted to march to Tennessee. The weather delayed the advance of the enemy for several days.

The roads were almost impassable for artillery and wagons. Rain, snow and frost alternated regularly and the wheels sank in the muck to their axles. On 20 November, Beauregard ordered Hood to advance without further delay.

Schofield, who was personally in command in Pulaski, now had 20,000 men under his command. Hood intended by means of forced marches to attack Schofield from behind and immediately sent the General C. D. Lee-Corps to Columbia by way of Lawrence. General Hatch was in command of Schofield's cavalry and reported to him the advance of the southern army. In great haste, the remaining supplies were transported by train to Columbia and during the night of 21 November, we marched back to Lynnville, about halfway between Columbia and Pulaski.

Hood's intention to reach Columbia before the Union troops could arrive there was foiled by our troops being in possession of the crossroads at Lynnville, and the enemy was forced to continue its march forward with a detour without coming in contact with the railroad. The advantages of this campaign were all on the side of the South, for on 6 November when it crossed the Tennessee River at Florence, Hood's army numbered 41,185 infantry and artillery and 3544 cavalry; 44,729 battle-ready troops in all. To this came later Forrest with his cavalry of 9209 service-ready men, so altogether 53,938 officers and troops, while Schofield was unable to oppose Hood with more than 24,000 men.

General Thomas' instructions to Schofield were to hold up the enemy until General A. J. Smith could arrive with the 16th Corps. He even hoped that we would hold our position in Pulaski, which because of Hood's superior forces was quite impossible. But here the bad weather was a big help to us. On the 23rd we were again informed of Hood's actions and that Forrest with his cavalry was putting so much pressure on ours at Mount Pleasant that Hatch could no longer hold his position.

During the night, Schofield's little army started moving toward Columbia. Cox's Division, to which we belonged, led the march. As we got near the city at dawn, we already heard the noise of the cavalry battle between Forrest and Capron, who quickly retreated to the town. Cox's infantry marched in an opposing move, right across the field to that place. The three batteries (4th Ohio, 23rd and 15th Indiana) were brought at full gallop to the edge of town and faster than one can write about it, we greeted Forrest with rapid fire from 18 artillery guns, which immediately brought him to a standstill. But had we been even less than a half-hour later, the enemy would have been in possession of our connection to Nashville.

As Capron neared the city he divided his cavalry to allow us the opportunity for our fire to achieve full results. Forrest followed Capron and brought his own artillery into the fight but without meaningful success. Better than his artillery were his sharpshooters. Every southern infantry-brigade had a 20-man sharpshooter-corps armed with English "Whitworth" rifles. As soon the battle began, the sharpshooters would go to the front to shoot officers and artillery men. These had already made us very anxious during the campaigns to Atlanta. By about noon on the 24th, Schofield had placed his little army in a half-circle around the city of Columbia to defend it. Here too, one could see how much was at risk in order to be first in place. Had General Cox hesitated, the campaign would already been lost in Columbia.

Hood didn't make us wait long and on the morning of the 25th he and his entire army were across from us. During the entire day and again on the 26th, the outposts of both sides came in contact but without serious action.

Those residents that remained true to the Union started their retreat toward Nashville by whatever means were still available. Those that could, loaded up all their belongings, occasionally consisting of nothing but a bale of cotton, on a retired government wagon and with worn-out horses transported their meager possessions northward. Since the weather was now good, they reached the city of Nashville without further disturbance, where in the following days they could hear in the distance the thunder of the cannons and the rattle of small fire near Columbia and Franklin but were safe from attack. *(Cotton commanded a very high price then and a bale was worth several hundred dollars.)*

Schofield's position at Columbia was strong if the attack was made from the front, but it had the disadvantage of a small river (Duck River) behind him, which here made a bend like a horseshoe toward the city. The land in the bend was low and could be covered from the southern shore.

Schofield was certain that Hood would not risk an attack on our breastworks, although if possible would try to get the advantage over us by way of a flanking movement. Hood with his superior forces could easily have gone around Schofield's right wing, but the former was still in the dark whether our reinforcements under General A. J. Smith had already arrived or not and whether the assembled occupation troops from Tennessee were with us.

In the night of the 25th, Schofield led a portion of his command across the Duck River to a position from which he could cover the pontoon bridge. On the evening of the 26th, the rest of his little army followed and on the morning of the 27th Hood occupied the city which we had deserted.

Hood now placed his artillery under cover on all possible high points.

On our side nothing more was done on the 27th than to observe the actions of the enemy and to get into position.

General Wilson, who had accomplished excellent cavalry service under General Grant in Virginia, was sent to us in order to lead the western cavalry under Thomas, but Sherman had kept the best of the riders for himself. The few that were still capable of service under Capron and Hatch were inadequate to keep us exactly informed about the enemy's movements.

The Battle at Columbia

Wilson heard on the 28th that Forrest had crossed the river eight miles above at Heuy's Mill. The former tried to get his forces together as quickly as possible in order to throw them against the enemy. He didn't succeed in this until reaching the area around Hurt's Crossroads, between Springhill and the Lewisburg turnpike.

About 8 o'clock in the evening, it became apparent that Forrest was marching east instead of toward Franklin, as would have been expected.

Around 1 o'clock in the night, Wilson received a report that Hood's infantry had positioned a pontoon bridge near Heuy's Mill and that the enemy infantry was in the process of crossing.

Schofield was immediately sent a message of this movement but it didn't reach him until 8 in the morning on the 29th. The courier had to take a round-about way to make sure the message would be delivered, because Forrest's cavalry was already swarming everywhere behind us. Immediately Post's brigade, from Wood's division of the Fourth Army Corps, was ordered to Davis Ford to keep watch on our left. General Stanley received the order to march to Springhill with 2 divisions of the Fourth Corps. Wood's division remained for the time being as reserves behind Cox's line. General Ruger was instructed to block any possible way to the north by felling trees and then to march to Spring Hill. Our own position next to the river and the burned-down bridge was dangerous. The river was constantly falling and the superior enemy forces could already approach us at several places without having to use a pontoon bridge.

Shortly after daybreak on the 29th, the enemy opened heavy artillery fire on us from more than 30 guns in order to drive us away from the city. We returned fire with about 20 guns.

At the west end of the city was a stone fortress, which offered enough protection for a small group.

The superiority of the southern forces was so great that no one doubted the defeat of the northern army in the coming battle. To see this spectacle, the southern officers had invited the ladies of the city and surrounding region to the stone fortress. Our battery was in two positions; one half was in General Brown's flower garden under the command of Lieutenant Kuntz, the other half under my command was posted in a wooded area near the Franklin and Columbia Turnpike.

A little breastwork of about 36 feet served as our protection, just high enough that the mouths of our guns showed over the wall. The other batteries in the skirmish were posted in such a way that the caissons could be brought into safety.

It wasn't until about 10 o'clock in the morning that we noticed the ladies in the fort; they had cheered loudly when the right wheel of our second gun was shot off in a direct hit from an enemy ball. As soon as the wheel had been replaced on the crippled gun, we sent off three percussion bombs toward the onlookers. All three shots died against the stone wall without landing in the fort. As we were told later however, the ladies toppled over one another in an attempt to get out of the line of fire. It certainly wasn't a game for the ladies to watch.

During the day the positions of the enemy batteries were changed often in order to get an advantage over us. Other than the wheel, the enemy didn't cause us any damage. But had he been able to use hollow balls instead of solid balls, the results would have been different.

Toward noon, the cook brought us our dinner. Since I had this position alone, I invited our artillery boss Cockrell to dinner. I believe our table was better furnished than any other officer in Sherman's or Thomas's army, thanks to our black, who had been the cook on a Mississippi steamboat earlier, but through losses that his former owner made in a card game, had ended up in eastern Tennessee, from where we had taken him along with us.

Just as we were enjoying our meal most, a solid ball sailed about 6 feet above our heads through a tree and scattered bark and splinters into our coffee. The brave artillery boss thought that two balls would never take the same direction, so we remained quietly seated. But the comment was hardly out of his mouth when another ball hit the tree at its base and covered us with dirt and dust. Some of the team near us thought we were hit and came to help us. Col. Cockrell jumped on his horse and quickly led one of his reserve batteries into the fight and against the flank of the battery that had disturbed us at dinner. We had the pleasure a short time later to see one of the enemy caissons explode into the air, and then had time to finish our meal without further interruption.

After we had continued our artillery duel until 4 o'clock in the afternoon, the enemy brought a pontoon bridge to the bank of the river in order to speed up our already planned retreat with an attack by their infantry. The thunder of the guns on both sides indicated to the advancing enemy that Gen. S.D. Lee and his corps and the artillery remaining in Columbia were experiencing greater resistance than expected. Since the position of our guns was closest and in direct line north of the ferry, we directed well-aimed fire toward the pontoon bridge and the opposite shore in order to hinder any attempt by the enemy to march through the river. We succeeded at this too, until darkness, when we once again blasted the enemy with several loads of "canister" (grapeshot) which made an advance impossible. During our position in the bend of Duck River, we used about 364 shots; 40 of which were canister. The other batteries in the skirmish were not sparing in using ammunition either, although none had used canister. As it got dark, the enemy sharpshooters wounded several of our drivers and horses. We now marched to Franklin and left the defense of the ferry in the hands of our infantry snipers, who followed us after midnight.

Stanley with Wagner's division of the Fourth Corps reached the neighborhood of Spring Hill about 11 o'clock in the morning. Kimball with his division stopped about eight miles from Columbia at the crossing over Rutherford Creek. Wood's division halted four miles from Columbia in line with the battle. Cooper's brigade at Beach's Ferry was sent to Franklin. A procession of supply wagons, as well as the artillery of the Fourth Army Corps, was all on the way to Spring Hill. At about noon on the 29th, Schofield received news that the enemy was moving from Davis Ferry about five miles north of Columbia.

At about the same time, the rebels realized that we still had a significant force in the bend at Columbia which caused Hood to be uncertain whether we would risk an attack on the troops and artillery that he was leaving behind under General J. D. Lee. This was because many reserve troops, mainly new recruits, had joined us in the last few days; the 40th Missouri, mostly consisting of men from St. Louis, the 44th Missouri from St. Joseph, as well as the 181st and 183rd Ohio Regiments with many veterans from the 9th Ohio German-Regiment whose service-period had expired.

As mentioned above, Forrest and his superior forces were causing Wilson some confusion by sending Beauford's division on the Lewisburg Turnpike, having Chalmers' division cross the river at Huey's Mill, while he himself with staff and a small brigade crossed the river somewhat east of Chalmers at Davis Ford, which awakened the impression that he intended to march to Shelbyville, Tullahoma or Murfreesboro. Wilson had to split up his divisions into smaller groups in order to lead them against Forrest's varied and larger divisions. He was only able to offer significant opposition to Beauford at a crossing. Forest now occupied all the roads beyond Schofield's forces now at Spring Hill.

On the evening of the 28th, Wilson gathered his entire corps at Hurst's Crossing and made Beauford's further progress along this road impossible. But during the night, Beaufort and Forrest united and early in the morning the entire enemy cavalry advanced against Wilson. The latter defended every step of the way to Franklin with Johnson's division. Capron, who had suffered serious losses the evening before, marched forward on back roads, while Hatch's division moved in the middle.

Forrest, with his superior forces, was always able to drive Wilson out of any position using flanking movements. In this way, Mount Carmel was reached, where the Murfreesboro and Spring Hill Road crosses the turnpike on which all of the enemy movement had so far taken place. Here Coon's brigade from Hatch's division had erected breastworks and defended the same, while Wilson's cavalry marched through.

Forrest made two different attempts to attack this little defensive position but was forced back each time. Wilson slowly pulled himself back toward Franklin because Forrest was now in possession of the road behind us toward Spring Hill and no longer made any effort to follow Wilson. He marched straight to Spring Hill and arrived at the same time as Stanley's infantry. With this move Forrest separated Wilson from Schofield's infantry, as well as two brigades of cavalry that were in position below Columbia. Mistakenly, Wilson had held to the Lewisburg and Franklin Road after Forrest had taken possession of the Rally hill Road. Had Wilson marched over Mount Carmel, he would have been in Spring Hill ahead of Forrest.

Hood did not get his infantry over the Duck River during the night as expected, but in the early morning Cleburne and his division crossed over the pontoon bridge and the rest of Cheatham's corps followed right behind, as well as Stewarts' and Johnson's divisions from Lee's corps. Hood was himself in the first division and led this as quickly as possible to Spring Hill in order to attack whatever should be in his way. But General Post's movements on the River Road and the dull drone of the guns in Columbia, as already mentioned, made him so anxious, that he believed that we would try to split up his army and destroy it one piece at a time.

The Skirmish of Spring Hill and Schofield's Exemplary Withdrawal from Columbia

Due to a delay which the First Division of Hood's Army at Rutherford Creek suffered because of having to rebuild a bridge that was carried away in the high water, he was forced to form up Stewart's corps in a battle line parallel with the road along which he marched in order to repulse an expected attack by Schofield, who was marching as fast as possible on the Franklin Turnpike toward Spring Hill. Schofield had also brought Kimball's division into a battle line at Rutherford Creek in order to resist Stewart's advance. At the same time, Ruger's and Wood's divisions were near enough to be able to offer support in case Kimball should be attacked. Hood must certainly have been of the opinion that any resistance at Spring Hill would be insignificant and that Cheatham and his troops could soon reach the Franklin Turnpike and then push our troops south on that road if Schofield's army got itself into a situation at Rutherford Creek in which it could easily be wiped out or taken prisoner.

But the prospects of Hood successfully attacking us from behind at Spring Hill disappeared through the prudent and masterful moves of General Schofield, who so advantageously positioned his little army against his opponent that Hood was completely misled.

The Union line at Rutherford Creek was solid for several miles and an attack by Stewart here would have perhaps been thrown back as bloodily as it was on the next day in Franklin. Stewart didn't move until Cheatham was turned back at Spring Hill, and then was led, as we will see later, to give support to the latter.

By the time Stanley reached Spring Hill, Forrest already was in possession of parts of the village. The former positioned Wagner's division, consisting of Opdycke's, Bradley's and Lane's brigades, to protect the village. Bradley's brigade (later Conrad's) was set about ¾ mile ahead of the other parts of the division in a wooded area on the east side of the road, where they could cover an attack from the Rally Hill Road on which enemy was advancing.

One battery was now with Wagner's division, another with Wood's, and artillery chief Captain Bridges (*better known in the army as "Leather Bridges"*) of the Fourth Army Corps brought 6 batteries back to Spring Hill in order to send them on to Franklin as soon as possible. But since Forrest's Cavalry was already in possession of the road to Franklin, Capt. Bridges took his guns to a hill west of the Columbia Road, where they could cover a charge from the east, and where they later were extremely effective.

The enemy cavalry tried very hard to get possession of our supply wagons, which were gathered nearby along the paths of a park, and at the same time Forrest also wanted to destroy the railroad station near the Columbia Road and the Franklin Turnpike. Protection of the wagons and railroad station required the full efforts of Opdycke's and Lane's men. Bradley was also of help, but the skirmishes weren't of importance until Cleburne's enemy divisions arrived. He formed his detachment of soldiers parallel to the Rally Hill Road and advanced the right wing in order to possibly reach the Columbia and Franklin Turnpike. He was however uninformed about the presence of Bradley on his right, because only one of his brigades under Lowrey was in contact with Bradley on the right wing. Cleburne was so strongly attacked that he suddenly turned his whole division to the right in order to meet Bradley full on. Bate's division followed Cleburne and reformed itself in the same direction. Bate had almost reached the Columbia and Franklin Pike when he realized that Cleburne had changed his position. Since his orders were to join Cleburne to the left, he needed much time to change his position.

Brown's division, which Bate followed, was supposed take position forward to the right of Cleburne, but with Cleburne's position change was also delayed.

Bradley's position was too isolated and too far forward for a single brigade against such a wide battle-front of three divisions and after a sharp confrontation with Cleburne, he had to retreat to the other two brigades. Bradley was himself wounded here, which caused some disorder in the retreat.

Col. Conrad of the 15th Missouri Infantry (Swiss-) Regiment was now put in charge of this brigade, which quickly took a position in the southern part of the town to the right of Lane's Brigade and received for support a regiment from Opdycke's brigade, made necessary here for a line of defense.

Wagner's division now stretched like a half-moon around the city from the Columbia Road to the south, then eastward, and then northwest to the train station, so that it was hardly a strong "skirmish" line. Even the 103rd Ohio Regiment, which was guarding the supply wagons, had to join the fight, and every strong position that offered some protection was taken over.

Cleburne and Brown followed Bradley's retreat but were greeted by such continuous fire from the whole line that they believed they were being opposed by a mighty force. They hadn't expected the concentrated artillery fire which poured over them from all (about 30) guns of Capt. Bridge's batteries and thought that it could not be from a single division and this kept them from advancing further. They evidently came to the conclusion that Schofield's entire army was confronting them.

The well-aimed shrapnel and grapeshot fire had done a good job of cleaning up and they suffered huge losses. It was now getting dark and Hood was convinced that if he was to expect success, he would require Steward's entire corps. He ordered this to join him quickly, including Johnson's division from Lee's Corps. Jackson's cavalry division had possession of Thompson Station about three miles north of Spring Hill and Forrest's other riders were active in the same area. It was night by the time Steward arrived at the battle scene and he was posted to the right of Cheatham.

Schofield had ordered Cox to hold his position at Columbia until it got dark, and then to march to Spring Hill with his division, leaving pickets in his place. Wood's and Kimball's divisions were to follow him.

The pickets were told to operate until midnight and then were to follow the army as a "rear guard". The various divisions were ordered to march on the left flank in such a way that if they had to stop they would already be in battle formation and would be ready to fight. In this way they could use the fence along the road as a barricade in case of an attack.

By this arrangement, every confusion or mix-up could be prevented. The whole army, when it halted, was ready to fight and the columns of marching troops were considerably shorter.

When Schofield heard that Stanley had been attacked at Spring Hill by the enemy infantry, he hurried with Ruger's division, which at that moment was the nearest that was available, and personally led the two brigades of that division in a fast march to Stanley's aid.

As he got closer to the village, he found the outposts of the enemy in possession of the road. These were driven back and by 7 o'clock he had joined Stanley. Whitaker's brigade from Kimball's division also had orders to follow Ruger. When these reached the battlefield, they were set up right of Wagner's line in order to cover the remaining groups of the troops marching from Columbia.

When Stanley reported to Schofield that the enemy was in possession of Thompson Station, three miles in back of us, Schofield marched to that point with Ruger's troops in order to keep the turnpike open from the enemy. As he drew nearer, Jackson with the enemy's cavalry withdrew and Ruger took over the position without further bother. Schofield rode back to Spring Hill, reached the village about midnight, just as (our) Cox's division made its appearance there. The Union commander now had his troops in good positions, for attack as well as for defense.

When we withdrew from Columbia, the enemy artillery was very active. The 104th Ohio, as well as the 12th and 16th Kentucky, suffered losses even late in the evening from solid cannon balls, which we could not return because we were out of ammunition. On the withdrawal we didn't stop until we had reached Rutherford Creek. The night was pitch black and the procession moved without the least sound. The gunners marched alongside the guns, ready at any moment to unlimber them, in order to respond to any attack with the last few grapeshot shells that remained after we had been in Columbia.

At Rutherford Creek the bridge was gone but caused no great delay. About three miles from Spring Hill, we were ordered to leave the stone road and to march forward on the grass or on side

roads in complete stillness. In a northeastern direction, the reddish sky from camp fires showed us that troops or an army was camped there. Naturally, we all believed it must be the Fourth Army Corps that had gone on ahead of us and had set up quarters and that we too, at least until early morning, would also be enjoying some rest; for we hadn't had the least opportunity to rest in the last five days and nights. But as we came closer to the glow of the fires, to the right of us camped
and stood our enemy around the fire, here at quiet midnight, so quiet that one could hear a falling leaf drop, while our comrades from Wagner's division and the Fourth Corps batteries to our left marched past without lights in deathly quiet, watching every movement of the enemy not even a half-mile away from the road where we were marching. Here and there a figure moved in order to stoke up the fire with a fence rail or other burnable material. The southern veteran sat or lay down again to enjoy the warmth of the newly stoked fire and didn't seem in the least to notice or be disturbed by our being near.

It wasn't just occasional outposts here and there, but the divisions of Cleburne and Bate, along with the regiment from Cheatham's corps, who all sought rest here, so near to the path of our retreat that we could count them. Behind these, about another half mile further, was Stewart's corps from the same army, and to their right camped or swarmed Forrest with his almost invincible riders. Certainly the southern commanders believed that Schofield's little army at Spring Hill was as good as lost already, but he and no other would dare to march past an enemy camp at such a short distance from the road, especially since the road in many places was already in the control of enemy outposts and further north the rebel cavalry had already established solid positions.

Schofield had risked much by remaining so long in Columbia; but he was a soldier and the duty of a soldier is to obey. Thomas had ordered him to remain in Columbia as long as possible in order to win more time to move General A. J. Smith and his Sixteenth Corps here. The rebel leaders, earlier colleagues and pupils at West Point, couldn't believe that their teacher of the "Philosophy of War" (Schofield was for a long time a teacher at

West Point and several of the higher rebel officers had studied under him.) would dare to make such an audacious move to get out of such a disastrous situation. But Schofield took the risk in order to get out of his terrible and disastrous position, with his veterans from eastern Tennessee, Chickamauga and Atlanta and their well-tested leaders. His undertaking was then also crowned with the greatest success, for which he gave his full measure of gratitude to his troops and their officers; for if there had been the slightest error by one of his subordinates here, everything would have been lost and Hood's intention to march to Louisville while Sherman marched to Savanna could have resulted in the independence of the south.

General John M. Schofield, the officer in command during the Battles of Columbia, Spring Hill and Franklin, November 1864

The Retreat from Spring Hill to Franklin – The Choice of Positions in Franklin – Schofield's Disappointment at the lack of a Pontoon Bridge.

Schofield, his staff and guards marched with Ruger's division in front and drove the enemy cavalry out of Thompson Station, where Ruger's division then stayed.

Our (Cox's) division moved on the same highway to Franklin, following the orders of the leading generals. As we marched past Thompson Station, some wagons that had been set afire by the enemy were still in flames, as well as the deserted campfire of the southern cavalrymen. One of our artillerymen was so overcome by tiredness that he fell asleep in the ditch during our brief stop and didn't notice that our division had moved on; but not much later he was awakened by the enemy cavalry that was chasing after us. They took him prisoner and he was ordered to march without a guard back to Spring Hill, which the enemy believed was already in the hands of the southern infantry. He followed their orders, but as soon as he could, he turned into the fields and meadows and by roundabout way headed toward our position and a short time later had the pleasure of finding himself with our troops again, so that by 2 o'clock in the afternoon he had rejoined our battery. On the whole march to Franklin we had been constantly pestered on the right or from behind by the enemy cavalry.

The wagon train moved on the left or grass side of the road on which we were marching, and on the right side next to us, the infantry was moving forward as cover. The battle line was to the right.

Wood's division, which served as the reserves for Cox while in the Columbia area, was to follow Cox, and Kimball was to follow Wood. The outlying pickets that were posted at Columbia under Rousseau and White were also withdrawn around midnight and the latter reached Spring Hill in good order around 4 a.m. Around this time, Wagner's division was still in the battle line in the same place. Rousseau marched without further ado forward and reached Wood's division, which he joined. At Thompson

Station, still in the company of his troops, he provided valuable and bloody resistance to the enemy cavalry, which always made use of even the smallest opportunity to try to capture or destroy the wagon train. As Wood's division passed that of Ruger's, the latter followed Wood and Kimball; from here on Ruger's troops followed all the way to Franklin.

Wagner's division covered the retreat and it wasn't possible for these troops to leave Spring Hill until 6 o'clock in the morning.

The biggest delay was caused by the stragglers from our own army. As mentioned earlier, several thousand new recruits had reached us while stationed at Duck River that hadn't yet acquired the stamina or gotten used to the strains and dangers, and when marching still held fast to their full knapsacks.

It was hard work bringing the recruits forward in order to save them from a shameful imprisonment. For those who suffered from swollen feet or weren't fit for battle for some other reason, their packs were either carried or thrown away. The completely disabled were taken forward by ambulances or wagons. All this caused delay; but without great losses the last of them reached the camp in Franklin.

We marched at a comfortable pace and without disturbance from Spring Hill so that we wouldn't get too far ahead of the wagon train and its guards and arrived in Franklin after 4 a.m., still a few hours before daybreak.

After Schofield had issued orders to the various divisions for the withdrawal from Spring Hill, he rode at a fast pace ahead to Franklin, because his presence there was of greatest importance to investigate a possible encampment position north of the Harpeth River, as well as seeing or obtaining the means by which he would be able to get his army over the river. At the same time he wanted to get in touch by telegraph with General Thomas, his superior commander in Nashville.

At his first appearance at Spring Hill before midnight, he had ordered his chief engineer, Major Twining, with a small guard of cavalry to Franklin, in order to inform Thomas of his situation and movements, and also investigate by which means and where the army could cross the river. He (Twining) was also supposed to guide any reserve units that might have arrived with General A. J.

Smith to Franklin. Twining arrived in the town at 1 a.m., and right away telegraphed Gen. Thomas about Schofield's situation; that it wasn't expected that the army would be able to march backwards in the night further than Thompson Station and that before evening that same day, a decisive confrontation with the enemy would take place or Schofield would lose his wagon train.

As the first house in the town was visible at dawn to the northward marching troops, the infantry of our division had to move off on both sides of the road, so that the road stayed open for the wagons to pass through. The troops of the division immediately made their coffee, for they were tired and hungry after marching 26 miles since 7 o'clock the evening before. The division's artillery also pulled off to the side but we were not allowed to unhitch. We also weren't allowed to make coffee, but the good-hearted infantrymen were kind and shared their quickly prepared breakfast with us, for the artillerymen were just as hungry as they were.

Schofield was very eager to find out if the pontoon bridges that he had urgently requested in his telegram to Thomas on the 28th had arrived and immediately rode on to Major Twining, from whom he learned that Thomas had not sent them, but ordered Schofield to use those that he had used at Columbia. However, the boats that served us as bridge boats there were heavy wooden boats for which there were no wagons available on which to transport them, so they had been destroyed and left behind. Thomas sent another telegram to Schofield at 11 a.m. on the 29th, but it didn't reach him because the enemy had control of the road at Thomas Station. Since Schofield didn't hear anything further on the morning of the 30th, he believed that he would reach the bridge in Franklin. General Cox rode with his staff to the house mentioned earlier, woke up the family and informed them that for the time being he had to use a portion of the house as headquarters. A large room was cleared for them. Here they lay down on the floor and all were soon asleep, until Schofield's return roused them from their sweet slumber again.

General Schofield was terribly upset over the disappointment of not finding the expected pontoon bridge or the usual ferry boat at the Harpeth River. For two days and nights he had had no peace, but had been extremely active during that time and had carried out the most wonderful maneuver against the enemy, which perhaps will stand out for centuries in our history.

In this mood, he informed General Cox that no pontoons were there, that the county bridge had also been torn down and the railroad bridge was unusable, that he and Major Twining were looking into what could be done in order to cross the river, while General Cox should take over the command of the 23rd Army Corps and get into position in order to hold the enemy back until they could get the supply wagons over the river. Later that day General Cox received the a written order from Schofield's adjutant repeating the vocal order, and at the same time an order to move the batteries of the Twenty-third Army Corps to the north side of the Harpeth River, while placing the batteries of the Fourth Corps, as soon as they arrived, at designated positions in the line.

The intention was to get as many vehicles and horses as possible over the river right away. When General Schofield met Major Twining in Franklin, the latter handed him a telegram from General Thomas in which Schofield was informed that General A. J. Smith's troops had arrived at the landing by riverboat, but that it was impossible to send him Smith's troops on that day. Under the circumstances, Schofield should try to hold Hood back and take position on the north side of the Harpeth River.

Schofield insisted however, that General Smith and his troops march to his assistance immediately, in order at least to be of service in guarding the wagon train. The correspondence took place about 5 o'clock in the morning. At the same time, Schofield telegraphed Thomas, that he hoped to get his troops, as well as his wagon-train over the river yet that morning and would try to get Wilson's cavalry in position on his flank. Somewhat before 10 o'clock, Thomas was again informed that half of Schofield's troops had arrived in Franklin and the other half still had five miles to march. For that reason, he asked whether it would be better to remain where he is, or to form a new line further north.

Schofield hadn't received any news from his cavalry since the morning of the 29th, so he was relieved when he arrived in Franklin to get a telegram from the commander of the Union horsemen, which informed him that they were nearby. Schofield had begged Thomas to order Wilson to cover him with at least a portion of his cavalry, for Schofield believed that Thomas must be in contact with Wilson. The absence of the cavalry had only increased Schofield's danger during the entire retreat from Columbia to Franklin.

Another telegram from Thomas reached Schofield at 10:25 a.m., which reported that the unloading of Smith's troops would require the entire day. But he would send them to Franklin or Brentwood, unless it was necessary to keep them in Nashville. Wilson feared that Forrest would make a dash to Nashville and had impressed that idea on Thomas. It was for that reason also, that the Union's cavalry leader had held so tightly to the Lewisburg Turnpike and was, as a result, separated from Schofield's army at Springhill. Schofield was told to hold Franklin until the enemy movements had developed more, unless the risk for his army was too great. The question for Schofield was: "What is too great a risk?"

At about noon, Schofield answered that he had already exposed himself to great risk and that the slightest error by one of those under him could lead to great losses; but he promised Thomas that he would with pleasure carry out the wishes of his superior as soon as he was clearly and comprehensively told what they were. Schofield indicted to him that he should bring all his forces together as soon as possible, if not at Franklin, then someplace further back. Shortly thereafter, Thomas telegraphed Schofield that a division of Smith's Corps hadn't arrived yet and Schofield should hold Hood back until those troops could also reach Nashville. Then he would get all the forces together, and would reorganize and strengthen the cavalry, and then try to destroy Hood. For that reason he asked Schofield if it would be possible to hold Hood back for three more days. Since Schofield had already reported that Hood with Forrest's cavalry could cross the Harpeth River at any moment, he answered at 3 p.m. that he wouldn't be able to hold the enemy back for another three days. One day might be possible; for the enemy would need about that much time to bring its army into position in order to carry out new flanking actions. It appeared that the enemy had already made preparations to cross the river, Forrest's cavalry above and

Chalmers' riders below the city. For several miles during the retreat, Wilson had already been skirmishing with them. Schofield's idea was to make a stand at Brentwood Hills (halfway between Franklin and Nashville). A portion of Smith's corps and well as Steadman's troops from Chattanooga and Murfreesboro should join him. Thomas agreed to this plan, and the wagon trains from Smith and Steadman were to start out right away. But Hood's attack at Franklin came sooner than these connections could be carried out and the battle of Franklin changed everything.

The Ford and Bridge Building over the Harpeth River and Preparations for the Terrible Battle at Franklin

The correspondence discussed in the last chapter show the mood of both Generals and the main emphasis placed on the necessity of holding the enemy back until the wagon train as well as the army could be brought into a safe position.

The house which served the Twenty-third Army Corps now as headquarters and later as the center of the attack and defense, was the property of an old man who lived there with several grown children. One son, who had served in the rebel army and had been taken prisoner by our troops, was now at home on his word of honor. The house was built of brick and was quite large, although not tall. Several outbuildings were made of the same material and as we will see later, served us as a kind of fortress or citadel and provided much cover for us.

At soon as it was dawn, the surroundings were inspected in order to choose stations for the troops. The village of Franklin with about 2000 inhabitants was perhaps ¾ mile from the headquarters and separated from it by low terrain. This valley-like low spot served excellently as cover for the ammunition wagon trains, as well as for the caissons, as if divine intervention had created the spot for us. The hollow served the citizens of the towns during peacetime for gardens and fields and surrounded the village from the river above to below it in a sort of half-circle. The Harpeth River bordered the town on the east and north in the form of a right angle. The river valley ran southeastward from the town and north of the village it wound its way to the northwest, until it flowed into the Cumberland River 50 miles away.

At the right angle of the river northeast of the town was a hill known to the inhabitants as Figuer's Hill. On top of this hill was Fort Granger, which had been built two years before as a bridgehead to protect the railroad bridge. As we will see later, our battery was stationed here during the battle. The railroad bridge on the river at the foot of the hill was completely covered by the artillery in the fort and the over 1000 yard straight stretch of the railroad roadbed also had good protection from the citadel.

The layout of the town can be best described by looking at an open hand, in which the inner surface would be seen as the town; then following the left finger after the pulse to the thumb we have the river around the town; the middle three fingers show the three turnpikes that run to the town from the south; in the center the Cumberland Road, in the East the Lewisburg and in the West, the Carter Creek Turnpike. They all come together at the courthouse.

The line of defense was created at the already mentioned place about a half mile south of the town in the form of a Turkish saber, the handle of which would touch the river, then curve around to below the town where the point would touch the river again.

The breastworks consisted of 8' wide dug trenches that were similar to those earthworks we used during the Atlanta campaigns. The point furthest west reached a little hill from which a large portion of the field could be overlooked. The Carter House, now the headquarters of the Twenty-third Army Corps, was also situated on a prominent high point; from that point one could keep the entire line to the northwest in view. About a half mile southwest of the Carter House, was another rise next to the Carter Creek Road. Here stood the house and outbuildings of the wealthy plantation owner Bostick with the beautiful whitewashed huts that formerly had served the slaves as homes. Bostick's Hill would probably have become part of our defense line, but Schofield's little army didn't have enough troops for us to spread out so far and taking possession of this hill would have left our right flank "up in the air", where it could easily have been gotten around.

Our defense line curved in the aforementioned half-circle in the valley of the little Carter Creek below the city toward the Harpeth River. The terrain lying before us, the future battlefield over which Hood's Army would have to march in order to attack us, extended out two miles south of us and three miles from east to west without any feature (with the exception of the Bostick plantation) that could have provided the enemy any kind of protection. The wave-like low areas from east to west were the only things that could save the columns attacking our defenses from annihilation before they could get close to us. Two miles further south of our line was also a half-circle formation starting in the east from the Harpeth River...the wooded Winstead Hills served as the southern rim of the bowl in which the town of Franklin lay. It was here that the southern commander had the desired cover under which to prepare his divisions for the attack. Since the wooded area bordered on the Harpeth River, it could be expected too, that it would be from there that the attack would be started.

About halfway from our line to the Winstead Hills, rises an isolated hill locally known as "Privet Knob". It was from this point that the Southern corps commanders overlooked the attack and the retreat of their troops. If one stood on a hill in our line and looked out at the field with the white highways visible here and there, he would see a splendid view that the viewer would not soon forget. About 100 yards east of the turnpike in the defense line was the now historic "cotton-gin", which had been partly taken apart to provide materials for the structure of our breastworks.

At the point where the Lewisburg Pike crossed the defense line, the road had been torn up to use as embankments for a battery. The cotton-gin caused the engineer of the breastwork to lay out a half-corner in the breastwork with just enough room for a battery of six guns, from where later ruinous destruction was delivered into the flank of the enemy advancing on the Columbia Road. In the line from the road to the railroad tracks there were about 24 such alcoves or places for a similar number of artillery guns with fairly good cover. In front, east of the road was a strong, dense Osage-thorn fence. This was "thinned out" somewhat and as far as it lasted; the cut bushes were used as abatis. But for more than 300 yards east of the Columbia Turnpike there wasn't anything to protect the breastwork. Although the line in this part of the field had been very well constructed, the desired "head logs" were missing. There weren't any trees nearby from which they could be made. The troops standing in the defense line had to expose their most vulnerable body part (their head) to the murderous fire of the enemies. For that reason, the majority of the dead and wounded had been hit in the head.

The Third Division of the Twenty-third Army Corps, consisting of Henderson's. Casement's and Reilly's brigades, with the exception of the 12th and 16th Kentucky Regiments, filled the stretch between the railroad and the Columbia Pike, as well as the already mentioned 24 artillery guns. The crossing between the highways through the defense line was open, but further back about 30 yards, this opening was blocked by a double barricade. In order for the approaching wagons and troops to get around the barricade, they had to march to the right first. On each side of this opening batteries of six artillery guns were brought into position to provide extra protection at this spot. So we can see that our center was very well provided with a very strong defense, for behind the front line and the aforementioned batteries, were reserve troops; on the left the veterans from Kentucky and Tennessee under Col. White and Rousseau and on the right and behind the Carter House was the proud and iron brigade of Opdycke; both of which, as we will see later, shed enemy blood with the cold steel of their bayonets.

Just west of the turnpike was the aforementioned Carter House, which even before evening served as a sort of citadel between the front line and the barricades in the opening for the highway.

Although the house was the focal point of the main battle, it still served the entire day and night as the headquarters of our army corps and our General's (Cox) banner was not taken down until the withdrawal started around midnight. It was from here that all orders for the defense were issued until the battle had ended.

The defense line west of the highway was led by Ruger of the Second Division of the Twenty-third Army Corps. These troops reached Franklin about 7 a.m. and were immediately moved into position, although only consisting of two brigades, Strickland's and Moore's.

Cooper's Third Brigade, which had guarded the ford through the Duck River at Centerville, was unable to reach us and only rejoined us in Nashville by a roundabout way. Cooper also had two of Strickland's regiments with him. As replacements, Strickland received the 44th Missouri, a new one-year regiment. Later he also received the 183rd Ohio Regiment, a new regiment of which many were veterans from the 14th and 9th Ohio (German) Regiments. So, Strickland's brigade only had one regiment of his old troops. The two veteran regiments, the 50th Ohio and the 72nd Illinois, were placed in the front line. For support they had the 44th Missouri and the 183rd Ohio in the second line. Since these troops accomplished the most and held out the longest, it is appropriate to describe their position in more detail. Moore's brigade, which Strickland put on the western part of his line which followed the right wing, had to spread out in the front line to the Carter Creek turnpike and the following regiments...from left to right...were defenders here; the One Hundred Eleventh Ohio, 129th (German) Indiana Regiment, 23rd Michigan, 118th Ohio and 80th Indiana opposed the attack of Bate's division in Cheatham's Corps here, without having a single man in reserve to cover the Carter Creek Road, because there weren't enough troops. The breastworks in Ruger's line were similar to those in Reilly's 3rd Division, but not yet completed. The area to the right and southwest of the little valley between Carter Hill and the Bostick Plantation was covered with young locust trees. These and the nearby apple orchard provided Ruger with material for the structure of his breastworks; also for an abatis to protect same; but as "head logs" (for head protection) the trees were too small. The line of defense west of the Columbia Pike was not nearly as strong as that to the east, but the outbuildings of the Carter plantation offered more protection here than did the "cotton-gin" (cotton mill) to the east of the highway.

  The protecting walls for the batteries on the west couldn't compare with those on the east end of the line under Reilly's command. Ruger's line ran perfectly flat for more than 100 yards and then sank in a northwesterly direction. Right in the bend was an excellent spot for a battery of more than 12 guns, from which very effective shots could be fired over the heads of the frontline defenders at the attacking enemy, while the Bostick plantation gave our guns free play on three sides.

  Another battery found a spot next to the smoke house of the Carter plantation. Here the reserve infantry, as soon as they could get tools, also built a short line of earthworks which ran to the west directly in line with the barricades across the Columbia Pike. This second line really was a disadvantage for us because troops left the front line when the enemy attacked in order to find protection behind. But one really can't blame the warriors in the second line if they tried to find cover, for they were following their natural instincts and the largest part of these troops had only been in the service for 30 days. The protection offered by the little barricades wasn't much, but later when the enemy attacked, the thick clouds of gun smoke during the battle, strengthened the defense significantly.

At 12 noon the Fourth Corps' batteries reached camp and a portion of them were immediately moved into positions on the front line. The other portion remained in camp until the enemy attack developed, because we believed until the end, that since the day was already ending, no attack would take place. Those batteries, still resting in camp, were then also moved into position in prominent locations where the infantry had to make room for them, they being moved back as cover. Inspection of the line showed that the west end was not strong enough, and Kimball's division of the Fourth Corps, just arriving from Spring Hill, was moved there. These positioned themselves on Ruger's right flank, following the half-circle toward the Harpeth River below the city. Kimball's division consisted of three brigades, under Generals Gross, Kirby and Whitaker respectively. Their position was on the first rise northeast of the little Carter Creek, which here runs from the Columbia Pike from southeast to the northwest. Kimball's breastworks hardly deserve to be called that, for there was no time in which to build them.

It is without doubt, that if Hood had attacked from the west, he would have had a better chance for success and the result of the battle could have changed. The time required for such a change of plans was too short, because the sun was already starting to set. Therefore, he had to attack before it got dark, because by morning we would have already deserted the town.

The placement of Kimball's division on our right flank completed our line of defense in front of Franklin. The troops behind the breastworks busied themselves with their dinner. All morning the Columbia Road had been packed full with processions of supply wagons and canons side-by-side, hurrying to get through the opening in the front line in order to find cover behind the barricades. The commander General Schofield and his chief engineer focused their personal attention on building a bridge. We and our battery reached the river at dawn. Immediately, the first gun went into the ford, where the water reached over the axles. Six horses could barely haul it out on the other side and the entire team of artillerymen had to help. The second vehicle required 12 horses, the third 18 and the fourth 24. That is how all the canons and supply wagons were brought to dry land. Later, to reduce the struggle, the banks on both sides of the ford were shoveled in and driving through was much easier. Right away we drove into camp. After unhitching the horses and feeding them, we slept the "sleep of the just", from which we were awakened at 10 o'clock in order to fill our empty caissons with bombs and grenades. At the ford there was still lively activity because neither of the two bridges could be driven on yet. But around noon, Wood's infantry marched over the repaired county bridge, the result of superhuman efforts by the well-organized units of Pioneers and "Pontonniers" under the Chief Engineer.

An old veteran would find the reports, about the destruction of bridges in South Africa by which one side or the other wanted to delay their enemy, laughable. At the beginning of the Atlanta Campaign, Sherman had a duplicate for every bridge from Chattanooga to Atlanta ready in a construction yard in Chattanooga. When Sherman wanted to get over the Chattahoochee, he told Col. Wright, his bridge builder, that he had to have that bridge ready to get a locomotive over in three days. The intelligent railroad administrator Wright informed Sherman 24 hours later that the bridge was ready for traffic. "Cheers to American engineers!" When we were still dealing with Johnson's Army in Kennesaw, the bridges over the Etowah River behind us were destroyed by the enemy cavalry. A short time later, the leader of the "Bush Whackers" went to General Johnson's headquarters and reported that he had destroyed the bridges and that for a long time the Yankees would suffer from lack of provisions. As he was still reporting his heroic deeds, the shrill whistle of a locomotive down below could be heard. The "Bush

Whacker" didn't continue. As quickly as he could report his deed, the ruined bridge had already been repaired.

Several houses near the county bridge were torn down for materials so that the railroad bridge could be made usable for wagons and troops. One can imagine that Schofield was in a different mood now that the bridges were strong enough to get the wagons over, which also meant that the struggles at the ford also ended, and the prospect was that all the vehicles would reach the north side of the river before sundown, and that the troops could then follow in the event that the enemy didn't attack us, which was most desirable.

Now was a time for the officers and troops to rest and recover. Quiet followed the rattling of wheels on the cobblestone streets of the town which had been heard all morning. The noon meal in camp was over. The horses had been fed, brushed and harnessed again. The artillerymen lay in groups on the grass, smoking or sleeping as they wished; for the day was bright and warm, a taste of a real "Indian Summer", which is usually followed by the first frosts or snow as winter begins. The air was somewhat humid, nothing disturbed the peace, other than here and there a straggler looking for his troop, or an occasional canon shot which showed us that Wagner's division of the Fourth Corps, as rear guard, was still several miles away, keeping the enemy from advancing too quickly.

Wagner covers the Retreat – The Southern Troops under Forrest and Hood Prepare to Attack

Wagner's division of the Fourth Corps had carried out the difficult task of covering the retreat very well; two brigades, Bradley's (now Conrad's, after Bradley was wounded at Spring Hill) and Lane's marched alongside the wagon-train as guard with the same composure as all the others in the two corps (Fourth and Twenty-third). Opdycke's brigade, which made up the other part of Wagner's division, retreated in lines, and when they were pestered too severely by the enemy, they halted and drove the pursuing cavalry apart. The arduous task of bringing the stragglers forward was harder than holding the enemy back. At about 11 a.m. the rearguard under Wagner reached the Winstead Hills, which, as indicated earlier, were about 2 miles south of our main line of defense, running in a circular fashion from east to west. Following the orders of General Stanley, Wagner had to form his entire division into battle formation and stop. Opdycke's brigade was in the gap of these hills. One section (two artillery guns) from Battery G, 1st Ohio Artillery, was with him. The brigades of Lane and Conrad spread the line east to the Lewisburg Turnpike. The division's men put down their weapons and were allowed to enjoy their breakfast. At the same time, Whitaker's brigade from Kimball's division occupied the hill west of the highway with a section (two artillery guns) from Battery M, V. St. Artillery. This brigade had orders to follow the other parts of the division (Kimball's) as soon as the road was free. It didn't take long before the enemy advance guard made their appearance. Wagner ordered his troops into formation, but noticed that Whitaker's brigade was marching straight toward Franklin. Since he himself did not have any special orders, he followed that brigade with his division. As a result of that movement, Opdycke's brigade, after resting for an hour and a half, ended up at the rear again. Wagner and his First brigade had approached to within a half mile of the line of defense, when he received the order to return to the hill that he had just left.

In his report, Wagner said that one of General Stanley's staff officers had handed him the written order to march back to the hill and to defend it unless he was pressed too hard. Obeying the order, he marched back to the hill near the Winstead Hills that he had just left, except for one regiment that he moved to the hill on the right side of the highway that Whitaker had been defending. Since Wagner's position played such a large role in the history of this battle, we give the actual order which almost caused the ruin of Schofield's little army:

"Headquarters of the Fourth Army Corps, 30 November 1864, 11:30 a.m., to Brigadier General Wagner in command of the Second Division of the Fourth Army Corps.,
The commanding General orders that you occupy the hill until it gets dark, unless you are pressed too hard by the enemy; that you relieve Opdycke's brigade and leave him, as well as the other brigades under your command in reserve, and that after dark, you will cross over the river to the north side, where you will be given a new orders.
Your faithful servant
J. S. Fullerton
Assistant- Adjutant-General of the 4th Army Corps."

Around 12 noon it was recorded: *"Opdycke reached the hills two miles south of Franklin and General Wagner has orders to hold and support him there, until threatened with being overpowered."*
The Generals Stanley and Schofield were consulting together in the house of Dr. Clift, which up to that point had served as headquarters of the army. About this time, Schofield made the decision to lead all of his troops over the river when it got dark, since there was no prospect that the enemy would attack. Headquarters was immediately moved over to the other side and set up in the house of a Mr. Truet about a half-mile from the railroad bridge. Generals Schofield and Stanley rode together to the north side. Schofield did not wish that any part of his army should get into a serious conflict with the enemy on the south side of the river.
The wagon train was, now that the bridges were repaired, gotten over to the other side in good order and without problems,

and if Hood didn't attack before dark, the army would reach the north side of the river in good order during the night. The enemy that Opdycke had the skirmish with, turned out to be Forrest's Cavalry, and the first infantry showed up as Wagner was marching back to the Winstead Hills. It was to be expected that Hood would try, as he had at Columbia, to maneuver us out of our position, for both Schofield and Thomas point that out in their correspondence, and neither of them thought that Hood would still attempt a "Coup de Main"...an all-out assault.

The order to Wagner was most likely written in the belief that he was still in his position in Winstead Hills; but the meaning of the order was that he should withdraw after it got dark, unless he was pressured too hard. Except for Wagner, this order had no urgency for the other division commanders, for it had first been delivered to General Cox at 2 o'clock.

The orders to Kimball and Wagner were written; they were ordered to pull back as it was getting dark, Kimball over the foot bridge and Wagner over the railroad bridge. Kimball was ordered not to bring in his outposts until midnight. This was in line with the order to the division; but when Opdycke reached the Winstead Hills again, everything had changed. The enemy now marched forward in quickstep in two columns alongside each other. The section artillery was still with the division and opened fire with hollow balls and shrapnel. The two highways to Columbia and Lewisburg came close together here. Wagner noticed the enemy was going around his left flank and quickly pulled his troops back again and sent a staff officer to the corps commander (Stanley) to inform him of this movement.

He followed the order which he received and left Lane's brigade as rearguard with Conrad and Opdycke for support. The artillery section was with Lane on the hill (Privet Knob, as described earlier), from where one could better observe the advancing enemy. Captain Whiteside delivered the notice to General Stanley and at the same time informed him that the brigade commanders were very much against keeping their troops at the front any longer. But no other orders were sent back to Wagner. This was about 2:30 p.m., just when Stanley and Schofield were riding to the north side.

Stanley's answer wasn't necessary, for in that situation, his silence was also an answer, and approval for what Wagner had done. The latter had fulfilled the intent of the order. He should have followed the order literally and brought his troops back to the main dense works behind the bridgehead in Cox's lines.

Around p.m., Col. Fullerton noted in the journal of the 4th Army Corps: *"Wagner reported two columns advancing; they are nearing Opdycke's position. The enemy troops are marching on the Lewisburg and Columbia Pike. Since his troops can't provide any resistance to such superior forces, he is bringing his divisions into Gen. Cox's Line, which surrounds the city of Franklin."*

From this one can see that Wagner should not have kept his troops on the front, but should have brought them behind Gen. Cox's line as reserves. That Wagner understood the order as such is evident, since he himself brought Opdycke's brigade inside the line of defense, and placed them as reserves in the regiment's column on the west side of the pike.

In his conversation with General Cox, Wagner informed him that his orders were to keep the other two brigades of his division on the front line until they were forced back by the enemy, and then giving skirmish, pull back into the main line.

General Schofield, in his public report, wrote that Wagner's terrible losses were caused because he kept the two brigades of Conrad and Lane too long as outposts, when they should have been pulled back sooner and have taken their position in the reserves.

All of these matters indicate that Wagner should have pulled back sooner and, as he evidently himself understood, placed himself in reserve, just as Opdycke's brigade had done, which he himself led into position.

The commanding general had informed General Cox (the commander of the battle front) at the very last that Wagner's brigade should only be kept in the trenches at the front as observers until the enemy's intentions were evident.

But, as it seems, the relationship between the division commander Wagner and Corps Commander Stanley was not a friendly one, for Major General Stanley sent Wagner a written order to relieve Opdycke's regiment from service as "rear guard", where it had so bravely served all morning. This intervention by a corps commander in the authorities of the division generals shows that not everything functioned properly or was in agreement.

Wagner had positioned Lane's brigade with one section of artillery on Privet Knob, halfway between the Winstead Hills and the main line of defense. With Opdycke and Conrad he marched north to within about a half-mile from the main line. Opdycke received orders here to form his brigade into battle formation. Since he was familiar with the terrain from earlier years, he resisted staying in that spot any longer and he was allowed to bring his brigade into reserve. Wagner's last words to Opdycke, as he left him in the reserves, "Now Opdycke, grab on and pound away where-ever you think best or can. Perhaps we won't ever see each other again!" With those words, Wagner rode to the headquarters in Carter House.

Privet Knob was a mile from Carter House and about the same distance from the Winstead Hills. Conrad had formed his line about 450 yards from the front line. Later, Lane formed his brigade here on Conrad's right. Wagner's intention was to pull the brigades back to the front line in the form of an echelon. This movement would also have been a good one, if the battle hadn't started and the brigades had not been overrun by the enemy.

Lane should have vacated his hill sooner and followed Opdycke into the reverses. Wagner's preparations indicate that was what had been intended. Steps had already been taken to carry that out and no change of plans followed. In the headquarters of the 4th Army Corps and in the army, everyone believed that Wagner's well planned retreat was in progress. We will now question and exam why this intelligent plan got interrupted in its execution and turned into such an indelible mistake.

Col. Lane reported at 2 o'clock that the enemy was advancing and going around his flank, but that he had been able to hold the enemy back with his sharpshooters and the two artillery guns on Privet Knob until he was ordered to pull back his command to 400 paces in front of the front line, "where I brought my brigade in line to the right of Conrad." The lieutenant in command of the two artillery guns reported that he had pulled back his canons from Privet Knob around 2:30 and positioned it on the turnpike about a 1/3 mile in front of main line between Conrad's and Lane's brigades, and again fired on the advancing enemy. Wagner himself reported that Lane had stopped on Conrad's right, and should instead have pulled his men back behind the line of the 23rd Army Corps.

The Southern Array and Battle Formation of Hood's Army - Magnificent Advance of the Enemy Troops.

We don't want to list the various regiments as they appeared in the battle line, but just mention that the 15th Missouri (Swiss Regiment) was positioned on the right or west side of the highway, right where Cockrell's enemy brigade made its irresistible charge against the regiment. The courageous St. Louis troops of Swiss birth received the first and deadliest attack in our lines.

During Wagner's visit in headquarters of the 23rd Army Corps in Carter House, he was made acquainted with the main defense line. The entrenchments, barricades and embrasures for the artillery were topics of the conversation. Wagner's own experiences in building such breastworks stemmed from the Atlanta campaigns and he knew that the lines were strong enough to resist an enemy attack. In his own corps-headquarters, he reported that he was bringing his brigades back to the defense line.

Conrad's formation with one regiment (the 15th Missouri) west of the turnpike, leaving the road open, shows that his presence in the front was only temporary. The barricade on each side of the turnpike at that point for the length of one regiment was stronger than further east or west, but as a whole, was just a half-finished trench. When the enemy spread itself out in a battle formation at Winstead Hills, Conrad sent someone to ask Wagner if he expected them to hold the line with the two brigades. But just as Conrad's adjutant wanted to go to Wagner's headquarters, Wagner himself rode out to Conrad and told him to hold the line as long as possible, and if necessary, to have the sergeants mount their bayonets in order to keep their troops in the trenches.

The pitiable troops had barely a half-hour to shovel a bit of dirt for cover; in Lane's line even less, until the enemy made its irresistible charge.

It seems almost as if General Wagner was so upset by Opdycke's unwillingness, having ordered his brigade into the reserves, that giving no heed to the rapidly advancing enemy, he threw himself with two brigades against Hood's entire army. Such impulses are not unusual with brave and heroic officers. But usually what they lack is quiet reflection. It was this that led Wagner to issue orders which brought the two brigades into a disastrous situation.

But in his official reports, Wagner insisted that his orders to Conrad and Lane were to hold the line until the enemy prepared to attack. This report places Wagner in agreement with his superior General Stanley. Wagner thus refutes Conrad's statement.

From the barricades at Carter House, one could watch the colorful line of the enemy, which marched forward on the wavy white lines of the highways. But two miles is too great a distance to tell the difference between a group of men and a moving column. Here and there the sunlight sparkled and glittered off the gun-barrels of the approaching enemy. At the base of the hills, the ground was not only lower, but also covered with trees. The trees and low area provided enough cover for the formation and preparation of the attack.

For an army of 30,000 men, this would definitely take more than three hours before a column could be formed into a battle line. The reserves and guards also had to get into position, and the artillery placed in their assigned positions; for in the battle line, the exact arrangement is of more importance than in a parade, especially if the success of a large battle with combined forces depends on which forces make the attack.

The commander of the front line, General Cox, once again inspected his defenses and informed his subordinates that his headquarters would be in Carter House. Ruger, who expected the attack from the Bostick-House farm; had his command post in the right wing of his (the 2nd) division on the Carter Creek Road. Reilly, in charge of the 3rd Division, could be found at the cotton-gin throughout the whole battle.

Since Ruger's regiment at the outermost western point was vulnerable to crossfire from the Bostick farm, the troops there had thrown up a kind of hook or traverse, hereby gaining some protection for the right wing. The trees in the locust grove had been, as mentioned, cut down and Ruger had free play for his infantry and also a clear view. This was also the case for Reilly's Division, as long as the cloud of gun smoke didn't obscure it.

The troops in Wagner's line focused their eyes and ears on the advancing enemy as soon as it was reported that it was being readied for the attack. From the headquarters of the army, the corps, the lines, divisions and brigades...everywhere, officers were in movement to deliver the last orders. It was now about 3 p.m. Since the shortest day of the year was only a few weeks away, the sun would set already at 5 p.m. Hood therefore did not have much time to lose before he made the attack. Wagner was once again warned to bring his two brigades, Conrad's and Lane's, into the reserves.

Schofield had established himself at Fort Granger, from where he could oversee everything. At a quarter after 3 o'clock, Wilson reported that he was being attacked by the southern cavalry and a lively conflict was in full action between Wilson and Forrest for control of the ford above the town.

This will all be clearer and better understood in what follows about Spring Hill.

Not until dawn on the morning of 30 November was Hood informed of Schofield and his little army's retreat over Spring Hill. Forrest's, along with Buford's and Jackson's cavalry divisions, were immediately sent after us on the Columbia and Lewisburg turnpikes, while Chalmers with his division of riders scoured the region around the Carter Creek turnpike for us. Hood couldn't believe that during the night, Schofield's troops and wagon trains had marched right past his camp which was next to the straight Columbia-Franklin Road. Late in the evening of 29 November, he had halted further action at Spring Hill in the belief that Forrest and his cavalry would prevent us from using the road to Franklin, and that Schofield would certainly surrender himself and his army the next morning. Chalmers must certainly have expected that our columns, which at twilight were still engaged in the fighting in Columbia, would have had to leave the Columbia and Franklin Road and try on some side road west to find a new road to Franklin.

He was astonished at the audacity of the Yankees, that they had moved their army so close past the enemy camp, and for that reason marched west on the crossroad until he reached the Carter Creek turnpike. Here he turned to the north, despite knowing then that no part of Schofield's army had marched on that road.

Hood's infantry at Spring Hill consisted of Stewart's and Cheatham's divisions along with Johnson's division from Lee's corps. He also had two batteries of field artillery...Guidor's and Presstman's...each with six guns. He started moving his troops as soon as Forrest had moved his riders out of the way.

The cavalry had run out of ammunition and his supply wagons were still back in Columbia with Lee. Forrest then had to borrow ammunition from Hood's infantry; his troops were infantry horsemen and had weapons of the same caliber as Hood's line troops. General Stephen D. Lee's Corps, after the loss of Johnson's division, consisted now only of Clayton's and Steven's divisions; but he still had almost all of the artillery as well as Hood's supply wagons. It wasn't until 3 a.m. that he became aware that we had left his front at Columbia.

The distance from Columbia was twice as far as that which Hood's other troops had to cover. In spite of beginning his march before daybreak, he could not reach Franklin before the attack and came too late to take part in the battle. The audacious front of Wagner's divisions at Winstead Hills made the enemy cautious and caused him to spread out his troops in battle formation. The failure at Spring Hill discouraged him to attack with the forward point of his troops. He said in his report that the telegrams from Thomas to Schofield (that he had tapped at Spring Hill) seemed to indicate that Thomas wanted to hold Franklin and bring all of his forces together there. Therefore, Hood would have to attack Schofield before he could protect himself with defense barricades.

It would certainly have been best for Hood to get Schofield into battle as long as he was still alone, and to chase him away or destroy him before he could join Thomas and the other troops. At the least, he didn't want to lose more time with flanking movements and for that reason, attacked the opponent directly from the front.

He had followed us so closely that one can't blame him for wanting to attack us before our defenses had been prepared. But his experiences in the Atlanta campaigns should have taught him that we didn't wait around and didn't need much time in which to construct a defense line to repulse an attack once we decided to make a stand. His desperate frustration over our (as he thought) hair-breadth escape out of his net at Spring Hill in which he had already trapped us, muddied his thinking. He also blamed his subordinates for holding back, although he himself was responsible for that. And now in his frustration he was led astray and wanted to risk everything with a dangerous attack.

Forrest had such a reputation as a cavalry commander that he never restricted himself to support work as part of the army. Either advancing or retreating, he showed that he could protect the movements as if he was carrying out one of his brilliant independent expeditions against the enemy. Forrest gave Hood excellent support through his flanking movements, and now on the 30th, with his two divisions, he opened up the path for Hood's infantry, pressured our rear guard, sprang against our wagon train, and stayed constantly at work, helping Hood move forward and didn't think of independent expeditions as long as Hood could make use of his services. At about 1 o'clock, Wagner left the road over the Winstead Hills open and pulled his divisions back. Hood's infantry immediately advanced on the Columbia and Lewisburg turnpikes, while Forrest's cavalry covered the hills further east and made room for the infantry, now in battle formation, to advance.

Jackson had Forrest's right wing and stood opposite Hatch's division of our cavalry near Hughes Ford. Buford on Jackson's left stood opposite Croxton of our riders near McGavock's Ford. Both enemy divisions halted while Hood's infantry organized itself into battle formation. Buford was ordered to move closer to Steward's right wing as soon as the army-corps of the latter advanced to attack. Chalmers marched with the other cavalry divisions forward on the Carter Creek Road and according to his orders, had to protect the left wing of Hood's army and to attack the enemy (Schofield's little army). Around noon, Ruger's troops could already see Chalmers' cavalry, whose sharpshooters were quite far forward, but focused on the movements of Wagner's people at Privet Knob. As soon as Chalmers' troops appeared on our right side, Cox requested, as already mentioned, more troops to cover Ruger on the right and Kimball was sent to provide support. Hood could see, as could we, that an attack by his right on our left would provide the best results if they were successful and if Forrest could drive Wilson back, which was certainly expected with such superior forces; our lines of communication could then have easily been reached.

The enemy commander kept not only the two divisions of Forrest's cavalry on the right, but Steward's infantry had to move into that area and it was necessary to leave room for Cleburne's division of Cheatham's corps between the Columbia turnpike and Stewart's left. In this way, Hood had placed four divisions between the Columbia turnpike, which was our center, and the Harpeth River above the city, while only two divisions were positioned west of the Columbia Pike. Johnson's division of Lee's corps was being held in reserve and Lee's other divisions didn't reach the battle field soon enough to take part in the battle.

The battle formation of the southern side was an array of two brigades in the front line with a second line of two brigades for support of each division and enough room between the divisions for the artillery. The battle field was somewhat funnel-shaped as the enemy approached. Reilly's 3rd Division of three brigades in our line had to hold out against four divisions of the enemy. Ruger, although first only having to defend himself against two divisions of the enemy, afterwards also had to repulse the attack of Johnson's division from Lee's Corps, was therefore also against three enemy divisions. The attack on Ruger collapsed, but Kimball's left brigade did too, during Chalmers' cavalry attack on Kimball's center and right.

Hood's orders to Johnson were that his infantry should stay to the east of the Carter Creek Road. The space was too narrow for that and his lines spread out as far as Kimball's Division.

With the expansion of his battle line, Steward had Loring's division on his right. The latter was put together with Scott's, Featherston's and Adam's brigades. Walthall's division was the center and consisted of Quarles', Shelley's and Reynolds' brigades. French's division was to Stewart's left. This division had only two brigades, Cockrell's (Missouri) and Sears'. Ector's division was serving elsewhere at that time, guarding the southern pontoon train. General Cleburne's division of Cheatham's corps was east of the Columbia turnpike and its left wing used this as a guide. The brigades of Govan, Polk and Granbury belonged to this division.

Brown's division of Cheatham's corps was the first unit west of the Columbia turnpike. Its right wing used this road as a guide and it was made up of the brigades of Gordon, Strahl, Carter and Gist. Bate's division of the Cheatham Corps was the left wing, with orders to join Brown's line and end it on his left at the Carter Creek Road and then to attack from Bostick Plantation. His division was made up of brigades under Finley, Jackson and Smith.

Johnson's division in reserve from Lee's Corp opened the battle but didn't begin firing until the other parts of the corps had reached the battle field. The brigades under Brantley, Deas, Manigault and Sharp made up this division. We will mention the arrangement of this division in the battle later as soon as they move to attack, as well as the other divisions named. In Steward's corps there was still space between each division for an artillery section (two guns) from Guibor's Missouri Battery. Presstman's Battery of six guns went into battle together, first on the slopes of Privet Knob and later on the hill of the Bostick Plantation near the Carter Creek Road in Bate's division.

Chalmers' cavalry had orders to go around Bate's left. Shortly after noon he had already tangled with our outposts on the Carter Creek Road but later he moved further to our right. When he then moved forward to attack, he came out of a low area almost at a right angle to Bate's line. During Bate's attack, he was in the low area and knew nothing the former's movements and wasn't exactly informed about Bate's position. He himself thought that Bate had not proceeded according to the battle plan; that he should have positioned himself to the right of Chalmers. Bate himself was unaware that Chalmers had taken part in the battle, for he reported later that his left wing had suffered terribly because Chalmers' cavalry hadn't given him the support that he had expected. We will look into this again later, when the battle proceeds.

Hood set up his headquarters at Neely House on the Columbia turnpike, not far from the Winstead Hills. He could not overlook the battlefield from there and had to be satisfied with the reports of the generals about how the battle was developing. Whether he could see the battle personally or not is unimportant, for the thick gunpowder smoke obscured any view. He was so exhausted from the work and difficulties of the last two days, being crippled as well, (he had lost an arm and a leg in earlier battles) that he lay down on the ground with his saddle as a pillow and a few blankets underneath. In that position he received reports and issued orders during the battle.

At about 2:30 p.m. our sergeant reported that the ammunition that we expected had not arrived yet and that so far only 100 shots per gun (other than the hand grenades that had been left over from Knoxville) had been loaded into the caissons. I immediately got on my horse and rode to the ford, where I met Stanley and Schofield. On the other side of the ford, I galloped to Carter House, our headquarters, to find Col. George W. Schofield, the corps artillery chief. He had just ridden to the front to Wagner's and Lane's line and I followed. Arriving there, the most wonderful picture and most awe-inspiring sight that I had ever seen in my years as a soldier unfolded. Just then, to our left, the divisions and brigades of Stewart's corps moved forward in quickstep out of the wooded area to organize the battle line, with flags flying and music sounding, in the form of two brigade columns aimed at the furthest right wing of their enemy. When they had reached their assigned positions, they halted. This division was followed by the second, third and fourth; the latter came straight forward on the highway toward us and soon as they were in range of the two guns that were positioned on the road between Conrad and Lane, the artillery lieutenant opened fire. I talked to the officers of the 15th Missouri Regiment and asked whether they were going to hold the front line in the trenches.

He answered, if they stayed in the trenches until the enemy got there, it would likely be their grave. At that time the sound of enemy drums on our left, the music band in the center and trumpets on right of the enemy line could be heard by everyone on the front. Col. Schofield gave me information about the ammunition and I galloped back to my battery. Had the southern army wanted to make a parade for us, they couldn't have offered us a better sight. Everything on their side took place in such military fashion, and presented such a magnificent sight that one could hardly believe that in a few moments we would try to exterminate each other. Artillery, officers and orderlies sprang in great hast from one spot to another in order to deliver the last orders and warnings to the troops.

When I reached our line, Col. White from the 16th Kentucky, asked whether the enemy was really marching toward us. When I affirmed it, his people commented, that it had never happened before in all the time they were in the service that the enemy had attacked our breastworks. I rode quickly through the city to the ford. Before I arrived there, the shots of the artillery stopped and were replaced by terrible rifle fire. Gen. Stanley met me and galloped on to Carter House. I crossed the river and found our horses hitched to the guns. An officer, Col. Wherry, from Schofield's staff, brought the order to immediately move the battery to Fort Granger and into the fight. I had the teamsters and gunners mount and in full gallop, as fast as I could get the horses to move, we headed to our assigned position.

The troops in the main line were most likely informed about the expected attack, but they still thought that the enemy would set up camp for the night outside the range of our guns, and then try with flanking movements, as at Columbia, to drive us out of our positions. From the elevated portions of our line, as well as from the barricades of the main line, the battle formation of the advancing Southerners with flags flying could be seen clearly on the lower terrain, running from southeast to northwest, as mentioned before. This low area in front of both of Conrad's and Lane's Brigades gave the enemy the advantage of getting close to the weak forward defense line without having to expose themselves to danger until they were so close to Wagner's line that the brigades (Conrad's and Lane's), after firing, didn't have enough time to reload; faster than they could do so, the enemy was in their midst.

The sun was going down and already so low that in the west a kind of haze darkened its beams on the weapons and leather gear of the enemy, then still over a mile from the front line. The most beautiful picture was that of Steward's corps marching forward toward our line out of the wooded area to our left.

Nothing stood in their way and their march was unstoppable and quick. In the center, where Gen. Cleburne advanced with his division, he was stopped by our advance guard, still standing shoulder to shoulder. In spite of Cheatham having already driven Lane's Brigade from Privet Knob a half hour before, he still found strong opposition from our sharpshooters in that part of the battlefield. Our cavalry on our left...above the village at the ford of the river...was quite far forward of our infantry line, and was already engaged in a fresh, lively skirmish with Forrest's people.

Conrad's and Lane's people were still working with pickaxes and shovels, in order to strengthen their trenches; such work had become second nature for our men, for as soon as the enemy was seen halting in the field, and the necessary tools were available, they started digging again in order to at least have some cover in combat, unless they knew that they would have to march again right away. Conrad's people were still working on it, as I said, when I arrived to consult with our artillery chief, Col. George W. Schofield, at the front line. This brigade made use of the fence crossbars to strengthen their barricades, which were filled with the dirt thrown up. Conrad's line, starting from the Columbia Road, ran from the southwest to the northeast, while Lane's line ran from southeast to northwest, the two lines forming a wedge with the point on the turnpike. But one couldn't view the trench as a bulwark. For that it was too weak.

The long lines of the Southerners soon moved out of the low area, in which they had gone into battle formation, and marched in quickstep forward with brilliant and splendid composure to the attack. For everyone who saw it, it was an uplifting sight that he will never forget. A charge of such masses of troops is actually very rare and had never been seen in America before; for in our wooded and thinly settled southern states it was uncommon to find a battlefield on which the opposing sides could see each other. Our battles usually took place in forests and wooded districts where we could only estimate the extent of the battle by the roar and thunder of the artillery or the rattle of small arms fire between the opposing forces.

That the show presented to the Northern troops was just as imposing to our opponents, we learned through many reports; but an especially lively description is given to us by Col. Capers from the 24th South Carolina Regiment in his memoirs. He provides us the opportunity to see the battlefield from the viewpoint of an officer in Brown's division of Cheatham's corps. When this body of troops went over Privet Knob and was pushed forward to attack our breastwork behind the Carter House, this brave Colonel from hot-blooded South Carolina was himself badly wounded during the charge, and we can certainly imagine why he describes the beautiful landscape and brilliant parade, which made such an unforgettable impression on him, and how it looked as he plunged fearlessly in the face of death into the smoke cloud of the battle's chaos. He said: Brown's division marched in best formation on the right flank of the regiment's column toward the Winstead Hills and through the low terrain before the first ridge toward us. Then they formed themselves forward into a line with Gordon's and Gift's brigades in front according to the length of the brigades, with Strahl's and Carter's as support.

As we marched forward, Col Capers says, the Union troops opened with deadly fire on our front. We marched forward in spite of that without stopping. The enemy pulled back as we approached. Just before the charge was ordered, our brigade passed over a hill, from which we had the most uplifting view of the battlefield panorama. Our music played, generals and staff officers rode in front of and between the lines, hundreds of flags fluttered in the powder-smoke of the battle. The dying hollow shells screamed like wounded eagles through the air; on exploding they were like Saturn with many cloud-like rings, while over twenty thousand brave Southerners gave the "Rebel Yell" and thinking only of death and destruction, stormed into the fight.

It probably isn't exactly fashionable to be emotional in military things, but the result of this battle with the terrible picture of the field has always brought out such a strong impression from the southern officers with incredible power, so that many in their reports cannot hide the sorrow in their hearts and feelings, while others who had witnessed the terrible brother-murder let it pass over without involvement. Later we will have an opportunity to return to Col. Caper's report, but first will touch on the advancement of the enemy on our left.

Stewart's corps had formed the attack column in a double line with two brigades in front, and one brigade as reserve for each division. The rapid narrowing of the battle terrain also required squeezing together the attacking troops to such an extent, as far as we were able to differentiate from our position, it was one column of brigades in quickstep, holding their rifles in their right hands, getting ready to charge.

In the space between the various divisions, their artillery galloped forward, unlimbered and kept firing until their infantry had passed them and then the same maneuver with the artillery was repeated. One section of two guns was with Wagner's division and they were the first of our artillery in action. They held an effective, well-aimed fire at the advancing enemy. The battery under Col. Cockrell in Fort Granger, with their far-reaching rifle-guns, and our battery (also rifle canon) which was positioned along and outside his soon after the battle started, were the next artillery in action. From this position we could strike the entire left front of our army and could see almost every gun and troop from both sides involved in the battle from one flank to the other. The batteries on both flanks also opened a sure and deadly fire as soon as the enemy came within range. As already mentioned, we were in gallop, as fast as the horses could run, on our way to our position on Fort Granger. Here we unlimbered and using shrapnel, opened fire in the same direction toward Stewart's advancing columns. But, although we were the battery the furthest left in our line, we received the command right away to hold fire, until Forrest's Cavalry, which most likely was awaiting the success of the infantry, attacked us, and then to shoot them down with grapeshot and rapid fire. If the sight of the advancing enemy, as I described as seen from Conrad's and Lane's positions was an uplifting one, so unfolded here before our eyes on this hill a picture of indescribable immensity, that no pen or brush could reproduce, which was changed in a short time into one of the greatest tragedies of all times. We were only allowed to see this show in all its immensity for a moment. The guns in the fort and on the front had hardly fired their shots when Conrad's and Lane's brigades were overrun by the overwhelmingly superior forces of the advancing enemy, and these troops, now intermixed, were followed by the southern veterans to our main line. The storming enemy troops who were now pushed through our main line mixed with the remnants of Wagner's two brigades in a tangle with some of the defenders under Reilly and Strickland, and now moved on the road toward town. It caused the commanding General Schofield, who had seen the whole movement, to believe and fear that our line had been breached. He said that his heart had almost stopped beating when he saw the movement of the dark mass through the streets toward the river, and he believed that for certain all was lost; but right away he saw how at the crossing of the breastwork and the second barricade, both armies fought like blind giants for their existence. This gave him the certainty that the victory was ours, for after a lively fire was opened at the trenches and barricades, he would have seen that our columns had held fast and the growing dark column going through the city was made up for the most part by prisoners. But the fear that he felt in those few minutes could not be described in words.

General Jakob D. Cox, commanding officer of the Federal defense-line in the Battle of Franklin, 30 November 1864.

Cheatham's Charge on Wagner's Forward Position

General Cox, the commanding general of the battle front, positioned himself on an elevated spot at the far left end in Henderson's line in order to be in a better place to observe the movements of the enemy than was possible at his headquarters in Carter House. He became anxious when he saw that Conrad's and Lane's brigades were not moving back while the enemy was advancing and he sent his adjutant (Coughlin) along the line telling the troops in the center to hold their fire until Wagner's people were safely behind the breastworks in our front line. At the same time, Opdycke was ordered to prepare to attack the enemy, should they be able to break through our line. The 12th and 16th Kentucky Regiments received the same orders. Lieutenant Mitchell's two artillery guns in Wagner's line between Conrad and Lane opened the battle. As soon as they were within range of the enemy guns, he trotted his guns back behind our lines in good order. The last shots, with which he had greeted the enemy, were grapeshot. His losses, as long as he was in position between the two brigades, were two dead and five wounded.

Since Mitchell had pulled back, it was expected that the two brigades would come too, but to everyone's astonishment, all opened with well-aimed and rapid fire on the enemy. For a short time they held Cheatham's advancing corps back, but the enemy went around them on the left and right and they were overrun. Although they stood fast, the enemy was soon over the light barricades and in amongst them. It was then that they collapsed and the survivors struggled in great disorder to get back to our hill line. General Cox, seeing the hand-to-hand fighting, again sent an adjutant (Capt. Tracy) to Col. Opdycke and reminded him to be ready to attack, for Wagner's line had broken. He himself went to tell Henderson and Casement to hold fast under all circumstances.

In gallop Cox then rode to his headquarters in the center but was thrown from his horse when the harness to a caisson burned through and delayed him somewhat. As he passed the cotton-gin, Reilly's reserves (the 12th and 16th Kentucky Union troops) were already attacking from the east with lowered bayonets between the front and rear barricades. At the same time, Opdycke's well-organized brigade moved forward. All hell broke loose as the "rebel yell" sounded from the throats of 25,000 enemies, answered by the musical "hurrah" from the 20,000 Union troops now confident of victory, combined with the thunder and rapid fire of 50 canons and the rattle of rapidly repeated rifle fire. Many from Wagner's two brigades tried to flee at first, but when they noticed the well-organized Kentucky Union troops and Opdycke's brigade charging forward in splendid military form, most of them gathered around their officers behind the protection of the Carter outbuildings and directed well-aimed and deadly fire at the storming enemy. Generals Cox and Stanley proved themselves to be the bravest of the brave, and both remained at the focal point of the battle. The Kentucky Union troops under their hot-blooded leaders, Rousseau and Col. White, used their bayonets against the brave Southerners, because there was no time to reload. Opdycke, at the head of his brigade, which with composure fought all through the battle side by side in closed rows, used his revolver and when that was empty, grabbed a club and encouraged his brave comrades by his personal participation.

Every officer tried to overpower the enemy with closed ranks. Stanley was always with his troops as they "cleaned up" among the enemy with bayonets as never had been done before. The sight was astonishing. The enemy had possession of some empty places around the Carter House and on the highway, and right in front of the buildings he tried to reform his broken lines. The two batteries, one on each side of the road, were in advantageous positions and they tried to use them against us; but the horses were uncontrollable because of the noise and bolted with the caissons. Many of our people, especially the young recruits, were taken prisoner; but there wasn't any time in which to get them back. The noise and thunder of the canons was terrible. The setting sun turned blood-red in the cloud of smoke as if it was ashamed to see such terrible, bloody butchering going on. The rattle of the rifles sounded here and there. Hood had ordered his corps commanders to attack and drive us into the river. At his camp he could now hear from all the noise that this wasn't so easy, and as he later said, it reminded him of the violence of the battles in the East. The slaughter at Carter House was violent but brief. The Southerners were driven back and left their dead and wounded in our hands, as well as a large number of prisoners.

Opdycke's people now joined Reilly's on our left and Strickland's brigade on our right. Both batteries were brought back into their position and the fight was continued anew, since the Southerners still thought they were the victors. General Stanley was wounded in his neck and his horse lay dead on the road; several bullets had made holes in his jacket. He had to retire to the military hospital, where Dr. Hill of the 45th Ohio Regiment bandaged the wound. The time from the first charge of the enemy against Wagner's divisions, until the line was reformed, lasted barely 20 minutes.

The Battle in the Center at Franklin

Much of my commentary above was based on my personal experiences, so I naturally had to leave out much of what happened in the center. We therefore would like to take up again what happened during the clash between the enemy and our forward position.

That the brave sharpshooters of Col. Lane's brigade held fast, supported by Lieutenant Mitchell's two artillery guns, had a remarkable effect on the advance of Hood's army. The delay of the center of the enemy's line caused by Conrad's and Lane's brigades defensive position, turned into a great disadvantage for the southern general on that short day.

The two brigades were placed in the form of a wedge. The columns of the Southern attackers had to deal with that. When the charge was made, the right wing of the enemy was closer to our left wing than to our two brigades further forward. Stewart's center had held back and reached Wagner's brigades at the same time. Conrad told us that the enemy had for a short time recoiled from the first fire from his front, but then in the protection of a little hill, had reformed and recharged in closed ranks. In this second attack, Cleburne's troops stormed the barricades and Conrad's and Cleburne's veterans ended up in hand-to-hand combat with rifle butts and bayonets. Conrad's and Lane's people were surrounded by the superior forces and now fled back to the main defense line.

After Wagner had issued his last orders to Conrad and Lane to hold fast, and encouraged his troops to fight with some personal words, he rode back through the opening in the main line where the troops were still working on strengthening the breastworks.

Captain Schofield, the engineer-officer in charge of the works, commented to General Wagner that the enemy infantry fire was coming ever faster and closer, and that both artillery guns were in action. At the same time, a staff officer of one of the brigades on the front reported to Wagner in an excited voice that the enemy on the entire front was getting ready to charge. Wagner answered; "That's good! Remain where you are and turn the attack back!" (The officer was from Lane's brigade.) Wagner commented further: "And the frizzy-haired Dutchman (Conrad) will, if he has a chance, take on Hood's entire army." Soon thereafter another officer came with the same message. Hood gave him the same answer as the first. The officer noted further that Hood's entire army was marching forward. Wagner, who had a stick in his hand, hit the ground with it and said in a gruff tone: "That doesn't make any difference, hold fast and defend yourselves."

Wagner's corps had held back both enemy corps under Stewart and Cheatham at Springhill and had covered themselves with honor; now it went for Wagner as for any other mortal. When things go well, one gets the fixed belief that it will always be so. The staff-officer had barely returned to his brigade when the artillery section trotted back and without warning...said Schofield...all hell broke loose and Conrad's brigade stormed through the opening in the breastworks and over the entrenchments between the road and the cotton-gin in complete disorder, pursued and mixed together with Cleburne's and Brown's enemy divisions. Wagner jumped on his horse and rode toward the collapsed brigades, tying to bring them to a halt. But in vain! His scolding and curses didn't help. The broken mass pushed him and his horse through the opening in the breastwork and his expletives had no further use than to give vent to his anger, which had caused his mistake in the first place. The regiments of his divisions had received many new recruits in recent days. Naturally these loosened the cohesion of the veterans that had fought in all the campaigns from Shiloh to Atlanta, earning honor everywhere. In spite of the bad position in the front line, they still held fast until they were overrun by Cheatham's Corps. It was not possible to expect more. The American soldier, no more than the African Boer, can never be made into a military machine like his colleagues are and must be in the European military states. The common soldier in our army knows as quickly as any officer when a huge mistake has been made, but even then, he is always willing to do his duty and fulfill his obligations.

If the line is broken, the body of troops can only end up in a wild pile, for the panic and terror of the men allows nothing else.

The only remaining healthy comprehension that is available to an officer in order to lead them back to their command is to get them together behind the main line and reorganize them; before that they are of no use.

To cover for such cases, one has well-organized reserves that can jump in right away. This was the service that Opdycke's brigade, which was resting on the west side of the highway, had to carry out. While the disorderly mass of Conrad's and Lane's brigades fled past, this reserve grabbed their weapons, formed a line...a wall of shining steel...and marched forward to attack. The trusty Kentuckians under Rousseau and White joined them on their left. Some of the former carried self-loading Henry rifles and their rapid fire made terrible holes in the enemy ranks. The soldiers under Col. White (16th Kentucky) mounted their bayonets and with bare metal cut down anyone that wouldn't surrender. Over one thousand prisoners fell into the hands of Opdycke's and White's troops and over 100 enemy dead lay inside our lines at the center. The actions of the reserves under Opdycke, White and Rousseau completely reestablished Reilly's and Strickland's lines, with the exception of a short stretch behind the Carter House, where Strickland's reserves, as mentioned earlier, had built a breastwork as a second line. It was here that the largest portion of Lane's brigade went after retreating over the breastwork. A large group of the 15th Missouri also took a stand here and provided...with the main line and the reserves...deadly resistance. It was here in the line of Strickland's brigade that the fight was the bloodiest and lasted the longest. After Wagner was pushed back through the main line by his own troops, he screamed at them to pull back behind the main line and reorganize. He was somewhat successful at this but not in good enough order that he could lead them into the fight again that evening. After the best troops in the world had, by the obstinacy of their division leader, been held in such a bad position, one can't expect anything else than that their courage for further action had sunk quite low.

When Wagner visited Conrad's line, Wagner had been reminded by Conrad, that the position of both brigades would be a very dangerous one if the enemy advanced. Wagner had responded that the 2nd Division (his) could beat Hood's entire army and drive the devil out of hell on top of it...and he (Conrad) should for that reason hold fast. Conrad answered that he would try. Wagner came to his senses in the last moment and tried to soften his remark. Conrad reported, "Just when we could reach the enemy with our fire, an officer from Wagner's staff rode up and said that the general had ordered that if the enemy was too strong and I could be overpowered, I should pull my troops behind the main line"..."But", Conrad continued, "our opponent was already so near, and half of my men were new recruits, draftees or proxies. To bring them back under fire without them bolting was impossible. So I decided to stay and ordered the men to open fire."

Captain Bridges quickly moved the reserve artillery next to Opdycke's brigade and brought it into the line west of Carter House. The short stretch from the Columbia Pike to Carter Creek Pike in Ruger's division had 24 guns, well served by artillery-veterans.

When Wagner's brigades fled through the opening in the main line and over the breastworks, they carried with them the First Kentucky battery and a section of the 20th Ohio battery. The horses on the caisson and wagon couldn't be stopped until they found some protection in the low area behind our line. The eight guns were in enemy hands and they were turning them around to use against us, when Rousseau, White and Opdycke and their troops either took them prisoner or sent them to eternity; no retreat for either side was possible in this spot. The artillery men of these batteries were on hand as soon as the guns were recaptured and before the end of the battle, made up for lost time with rapid fire in spite of enemy rifle fire. The Kentucky battery fired almost 200 shots before the battle ended. For a while, the enemy held tight to the breastworks, but in the end had to surrender.

A misunderstood command by Col. Hayes of 100th Ohio Regiment, who was guarding the battery, was probably responsible for the retreat of the teamsters of the guns. He had screamed to Conrad's people to regroup behind the line. The artillery men thought that they were meant and went back. If the Southerners had had the caissons by the check-lines, they most certainly would have been able to make good use of the guns and Opdycke's veterans would have had a hard time getting out of it as the victors.

But just as a brigade or a few regiments protected the army here, we also like not of forget the bravery of individual soldiers.

When everything was falling apart in the center, Sergeant Baldwin of the 100th Ohio Regiment grabbed the flag and planted it on the breastwork next to the drive-through. It cost him his life. Captain Hunt with a few faithful gathered around him and were, to the last man, also killed. But the flag stayed there and waved until the withdrawal at midnight.

Col. White with his regiment, four men deep, made the attack to recapture the batteries. His losses were great but he was victorious because, as mentioned, everything was cut down by bayonet if it didn't surrender. The 8th Tennessee and 12th Kentucky Union Regiments under Col. Rousseau also formed a line, four men deep, with the 104th Ohio Regiment and a portion of Reilly's brigade that couldn't be shaken, although the enemy in that corner near the cotton-gin tried desperately to break through. But these were worked over so hard with crossfire from east and west of the cotton-gin that every visible "Johnnie" was either dead or a prisoner.

Lieut. Baldwin, who commanded the 6th Ohio Battery in that corner, said that the enemy had several times taken possession of the gun placement enclosures and fired on the artillery men, and one time the artillery men had to defend themselves with wipers, axes and picks, until they finally got the fuses into some grapeshot shells and, instead of hand grenades, rolled them down on the enemy in the trenches. Not until then did the "Johnnies" cry, "Enough, we surrender". The hand-to-hand fighting was worst at the two batteries in the drive-through. As soon as some of the enemy was led away as prisoners, the replacements were there again, for Cleburne had attacked with his regiment eight men deep. Poor Pat! He was so excited about the coming attack, and as he thought, a certain victory, that he told Hood before he gave the order to attack, that he was more certain of a Southern victory than he had been since the beginning of the war. He requested Hood's permission to attack in mass columns. Hood granted him to attack in whatever form he wanted as long as he drove the enemy into the river. With this order he rode back to his division and gave the order to advance. When his division was resisted at the opening of the breastworks, he rode forward himself in order to see what was wrong, and about 20 paces from the cotton-gin, he and his horse were felled with 49 bullets.

"Yesterday still on his proud horse,
Today shot through the breast....
Tomorrow in the dark grave."

So it was with General Pat. Cleburne...the "Stonewall" of the West. But we are getting ahead of ourselves. We will come back to Pat. Cleburne when we describe the battle from the view of the Southerners.

It was not possible for the Southern commanders to evaluate their own situation because the cloud of gun smoke made it impossible to see if the attack had been successful or turned back. Since they believed it was certain they would be victorious, they kept pouring reserve troops in, which only made the list of dead ever larger. And the Southerners were so close to the batteries positioned between the cotton-gin and the Columbia Pike that several times they tried to disrupt reloading the canons by shoving fence rails into the guns. The earthworks were the only thing that separated them from our people. Two wing companies of the 12th Kentucky Union Regiment, which were provided with revolving rifles, never made better use of them as right here in our great time of need, and cleaned up the enemy horribly. Human courage can't withstand such fire. An officer watching the movements of the enemy through the powder smoke said that after jumping over the trenches, they were crowded together like sheep in a stall. At every salvo they fell together in a tangled pile. The enemy strength to resist was so diminished that Captain Brown of the 12th Kentucky Union Regiment climbed up on the breastwork with the flag and with a "hurrah" waved it in the faces of the enemy and was able to spring down again unhurt.

With such rapid fire, ammunition was running out, so some of the line officers started to carry ammunition, still packed in cases in the wagons in the ravine, on their shoulders to the soldiers under fire. The boxes were broken open here with axes and picks and the officers carried them to the troops in the line in their caps or hats. Everywhere in the line something similar was taking place as was here at the cotton-gin, and the tension, courage and enthusiasm was everywhere the same.

Col. Sterl of the 104th Ohio Regiment describes the situation in his front as follows: The angle of the line allowed me to give cross-fire in either direction from the cotton-gin. The three companions on my left opened fire first, while the enemy advanced on Casement and Stiles. Loring's enemy division was somewhat further ahead than Walthall's Mississippian (Southern) (we will describe this in more detail later). So Loring received our first fire. At the same time, Wagner's men fled on our right and before we could fire on the enemy, all the trenches from the angle next to the cotton-gin to the Columbia Pike were filled with the enemy, many of which were already on the breastworks trying to drive us out.

He continued: The noise and confusion and screaming of officers to the men of Wagner's brigades almost got us in a muddle, because many of my men thought the orders applied to them. But when we saw the second line with mounted bayonets advancing, we knew they intended for us to "stand or die". So we kept up a steady and deadly stream of fire and hundreds of the enemy in trenches and in front of the line were cut down. He continues: The energy and bravery of the enemy was indescribable. The enemy officers planted a large number of flags on our breastworks and many of their people kept a steady fire at our line from on top of the entrenchments. Bayonets and rifle butts where in use until they were shot down and fell back into the trenches. The officers urged them on shouting; Boys, we'll have the Yankees beat if we each do our part!

In his report, General Reilly speaks very highly of his regiment commanders; especially the colonel of the 175th Ohio, a new regiment, who just been made its officer that day. Unfortunately, the colonel of this troop didn't hand in a report of his services, but General Reilly does these brave "Buckeyes" full justice in his own report. He says: When the danger was the greatest and the fight was at its bloodiest, this regiment, which had never yet opposed an enemy with weapons, moved forward in almost parade-style closed ranks without firing a shot until they could see the "whites of the enemy's eyes". Then they gave fire and attacked with bayonets mounted. Up to that point the brigade had only served guarding bridges and was already on its way to the north side of the river, when Col. McCoy asked permission of General Schofield, to keep the regiment in the line so they would have the opportunity, in case there was a battle, to prove their ability as troops. Schofield granted his wish and these troops share a rich portion of the glory of the victory.

The 44th Illinois Regiment under Col. Russell of Opdycke's brigade also took part in a brilliant bayonet attack with others in Reilly's line and also provided valuable service in bringing the Kentucky battery back into our hands. The artillerymen of that battery went back into battle as soon as the guns were recovered and opened rapid and effective fire on the enemy that was still attacking.

Many of Wagner's people, under their officers, had joined Reilly's line and still delivered valuable service, even though their entire division had dissolved. Although Reilly was commander of a division, he was personally in command of his own brigade and subject to the most violent attacks and dangers of the battle. His own example repeatedly encouraged his people to glorious action.

Col. White of the 16th Kentucky Union Regiment had his upper lip with a fine mustache shot off while he was leading his troops in an attack. In his report, he doesn't mention his loss, but on the second day after the battle, when we met each other in Nashville, he heartily laughed at his close call. In spite of his wound, he remained in command of this regiment.

The losses in Reilly's brigade were 233 men, not counting the 175th Ohio and 44th Illinois regiments, which served under him briefly. The largest portion of the deaths can be attributed to the collapse of Conrad's and Lane's brigades. We will mention this later when we present the battle from the viewpoint of the Southerners.

In the fight at the cotton-gin, our division lost one the best comrades in our army, Lieutenant Coughlin of the 24th Kentucky Regiment. A son of poor Irish immigrants, he had worked himself up to officer and served at the beginning of the Atlanta campaign as a staff officer under General Cox. He possessed a natural military talent and could quickly comprehend the large picture, his judgment was clear, his soldiery demeanor worth emulating; his love of the truth won him the trust of his superiors and true friends. He carried the first orders to Opdycke to ready himself for attack. On his return, he rode through the thickest tangle of the battle in order to encourage his old comrades in Reilly's brigade to retake the breastwork, but in the moment of victory was shot through the heart. The comrades from staff buried him at dark midnight near the cotton gin, right where he had fallen.

James Merrifield, from St. Louis, then of Company C of the 88 Illinois Regiment (who earned a medal of honor by capturing a flag), took part in the charge with Opdycke. It is almost impossible to give every regiment that took part in this action enough credit, for all stormed and streamed toward the opening where the enemy had captured the aforementioned batteries, just in time to recapture them before the rebels could use them against us. The 125th Ohio, which recaptured the battery on the right wing, found here only one single corporal from the artillery men still alive. After the recapture, he aimed one of the still loaded guns at the enemy still pouring through the opening, and seldom, if ever, has the firing of a shot had a greater result then this one. He opened the drive-through, giving the infantry a chance to reorganize the line and the rest of the guns to renew firing. The 20th Ohio Battery was to the right of the turnpike and the Kentucky Battery in the line. Further west were Bridge's batteries and to the right of these, near the Carter Creek turnpike, Ziegler's Pennsylvania Battery.

During its advance, Opdycke's brigade took the form of a wedge with the point on the turnpike. The buildings of Carter House prevented an advance in a straight line. Between the buildings, in several places the troops were eight to ten men deep; but the buildings served our troops, as soon as they were reached, as a kind of citadel where they could get themselves reorganized and from there provide strong resistance. Although the brigade under Lane went over the breastwork of Strickland's line in better order than did Conrad's people in Reilly's brigade, the enemy was able to briefly take over a short section of Strickland's line, and Hood's officers tried hard to make use of that advantage by pushing their troops more, in spite of heavy losses. But crossfire from the cotton-gin from Reilly's brigade made it possible to recreate the line here again. The losses of the 44th Missouri Union Regiment here were almost unbelievably large. This regiment had just signed up for one year, and had hardly any practice using the weapons, so it was kept in reserve here until the front line collapsed. As mentioned, they had built a second breastwork, but it was very thin. In defending it, they led 900 men into the fight and on the next morning, only 360 reported at roll call. Colonel Barr, their commander reported that in spite of the heavy losses, no man fled the place and they held their post until midnight when the retreat was started. The 50th Ohio Regiment, which formed the outer left of Strickland's line, was pushed back to the Carter Plantation buildings, but when Opdycke's people moved in they joined them and recaptured their position again. The 72nd Illinois Regiment was positioned on the right end of the line, but managed to hold the breastwork, even though the left wing had been destroyed. It was here that the 183rd Ohio Regiment first joined the fight and drove the enemy, which was now storming the second line, back bloodily. A nearby fence furnished material to strengthen the second line somewhat. Since the right wing of the regiment was still holding the first barricade and were vulnerable to enemy crossfire, they were pulled back to the second line. Here a large group of Wagner's people gathered too. These veterans held their position; never leaving the place.

  The evidence shows that the opening in the front line west of Carter House was open longest and it was there where the fighting was the most violent. General Cheatham, of the southern corps commanders, said in his report that the next morning he had found his dead 50 yards behind the main breastwork in our line. As they marched ahead, they had Opdycke's and Reilly's storm-regiments on one side and the 44th Missouri on the other side, with the 72nd Illinois and 183rd Ohio in front of them. This crossfire made the enemy cautious and gave our troops an opportunity to storm them in closed ranks with mounted bayonets, which cleared out the field in greatest disorder and from then on, the enemy didn't risk going over the barricades. Because of this, our line between Strickland and Reilly was able to be completely reestablished.

The softening of Strickland's brigade in the front line gave the left flank of Moore's brigade the opportunity to attack, and in one of those fateful moments, the chief of staff of Moore's brigade, Captain Dowling, led two companies from this flank and swept the area captured by the enemy with crossfire, so that the rebels in that region no longer dared go forward, and those that did, surrendered as prisoners. Moore's troops didn't retreat one inch from the first barricade, but the 44th Missouri, as already mentioned, had more losses than other regiments in Strickland's brigade. The lines were very close to one another. The troops in the buildings of Carter Plantation were better protected, but even their lines were broken. They fired from doors and windows and every opening and groups collected at the corners of the buildings and delivered crossfire from that protection until the line was reestablished. It was not possible to survive the crossfire from Reilly, Strickland and Moore. From general down to the common soldier, everyone tried hard to do their duty and the result was not what the southern officer shouted in the trenches in front of Reilly's position: "They could have had us if they really wanted to." but if the "Johnnies" had realized it, they had been beaten harder than in any other army since the invention of gunpowder. But the smoke of the guns didn't allow the Southern officers to see how bad their losses were, and since they believed our line to be hopelessly broken, they kept sending new victims to the butcher-block. The line being reestablished in the center was the first step to complete victory.

The Battle at the Left Wing

We have already described how Hood's army in the center of the battle was held back and resisted by the fire from Conrad's and Lane's brigades while still holding their positions in their forward line and how the right wing of the enemy marched toward our left wing. So it happened that the rebel corps under Steward collided against the two Union brigades under Stiles and Casement from Reilly's Regiment in the main line. Wagner's two helpless brigades were almost a half-mile in front of the main line and their unnecessary resistance allowed Stewart to march ahead of Cheatham. We followed Wagner's brigades, which are the key to this battle, until the danger in our center passed by the breadth of a hair.

It would have agreed more with the actual situation, had we started our history of the battle at the outermost left end of our line in Stile's brigade. It was here that Steward's infantry first came into contact with our main line. However, the connection between cause and effect is of greater value than the exact point at which the attack took place. The forward position that Wagner's brigades had taken, gave the battle its unusual character and we can only understand what happened in other parts of the battlefield, when we consider the results of the enemy attack on the two brigades, who through their collapse and flight, opened the way for the enemy into the very heart of our line.

Now we can go back and follow the attack on our two wings, one after the other; first to Stiles' and Casement's brigades in Reilly's division and later to Moore's brigades and Ruger's and Kimball's divisions on our outermost right flank, where Chalmers' enemy riders stubbornly tried to drive back our right flank near the river and to get around us. At these two ends, the Southern army attempted to conquer these barricades, such as we had erected, by a frontal charge over flat ground without the advantage of the disorganized and fleeing troops, such as was the case behind Wagner's division. The results of these charges were not encouraging for the Southerners. The formation of the Southern corps under Steward, as we have seen, was a battle line of three divisions; each division had two brigades in the front line and a third marched behind in reserve. The exception was French's division; here one brigade marched in front and one in reserve. The third brigade was guarding the pontoon train and hence was not present. The right wing of the enemy corps kept to the Harpeth River, which runs northwest, until it reached the left flank of our line. As Stewart's troops advanced, the width of the battlefield narrowed. Incidentally, there were a few conditions that the enemy did not become aware of until confronted by them. The main delay was caused by the field surrounded by the Osage thorn thicket previously mentioned.

Walthall's division was the center of Steward's corps and he alone of this corps wrote a full report of this battle, (at least as far as official documents are available in Washington.) He described in detail this thicket of bushes and the hedge which made it necessary to lead his left brigade (Reynolds') around the Osage thorn-thicket by crowding to the left. But this prevented him from getting into the correct position. In order to fill the gap, he brought Shelly's brigade from his reserves forward. A short pause naturally resulted before the line was fully in order again. Since the enemy's right wing still had the river as its border, both Loring and Walthall had to seek space on the left as they advanced.

This brought Walthall ahead of the front line of Cleburne's division, since the latter had been delayed by Conrad's holding fast. When Conrad noticed that Walthall already was at his back, he had to give up and his men had to flee, and a portion of Conrad's left wing was taken prisoner by Walthall.

So it was that Loring's whole division, as well as Walthall's right wing, attacked Stiles' and Casement's brigades of Reilly's Division. As soon as the enemy line was demolished in front of our eyes, the two batteries in position on the hill in Stiles' line, as well as the two batteries (the 4th Ohio and 15th Indiana) from Fort Granger, opened with devastingly rapid fire on the storming enemy, now eight men deep, first with shrapnel and then with grapeshot. The position of the 120th Indiana Brigade was at a sharp angle to the main line, parallel to the railroad tracks, which here made a deep cut through the aforementioned hill. This regiment was exposed to enemy artillery and rifle cross-fire but held fast to their position. The center of Stiles' brigade was protected by a thorn-hedge, and when the enemy ran into it, it despaired and doubted being able to advance forwards.

At the same time, the little bushes offered no protection from the batteries or the devastating rifle fire from Stiles' front line. At the right end of this brigade, Loring's attack was bloodily repulsed. The second line then advanced and reached the barricades in front of the 128th Indiana Brigade. Here they planted their flag on the parapet and some scrambled over the breastwork. The flag bearers were shot and those that came over the barricades were taken prisoner. The bravado and determination of the Southerners was matched by the courage of our people and the attack on all portions of this brigade was repulsed. The rebel officers tried hard to lead their people toward the river so that they could get them to attack and advance on our left. One heard them shouting: "Soldiers, as you love your fatherland, push to the right, push to the right." But the terrible fire from the regular Battery M 4 U.S. Artillery and the rifle-fire of the brigade, didn't give the enemy a chance to carry out the desired movement.

This artillery, under the command of Lieutenant Samuel Canby, swept the field in front of Stiles' Brigade until the enemy got near our barricades. Then the right section was moved to the left and from there opened crossfire on the enemy, who was trying to reach our left flank through the railroad cut. Colonel Henderson, usually in command of Stiles' Brigade, but had for several days been too ill to lead, pulled himself together in order to be with his men during the battle. He said about Lieutenant Canby and his battery of regular gunners, that their performance and such excellent service in this wing had won his admiration. But not Canby's battery alone deserved the honor of being of service at this end of the line. When Mitchell's section of Marshal's battery returned to our line, it was sent to this wing. Not much later, the other four guns of Marshal's battery near the railroad were moved into the battle. Just when the attack was its peak, both batteries simultaneously started to greet the enemy with grapeshot and kept up crossfire toward the railroad gap where the enemy was trying get around our left flank on hands and knees.

The rifled cannons in Fort Granger (Battery D 4th Ohio and 15th Indiana) on the other side of the river were in rapid action and the uninterrupted rattle of rifle fire combined with the thunder of the cannons tell us why Scott's and Featherstone's enemy brigades from Loring's Division were having such terribly bloody losses. The fight was bitter and stubborn. It is difficult to determine how long it lasted, but the enemy sent its reserves forward and repeated the attack several times, until it finally gave up and retreated into a low area out of range of our guns, where the survivors regrouped. Many, who had reached the trench in front of our barricades, came over the breastwork and surrendered. Others lay down flat in front of the thorn hedge and waited until it was dark before they pulled back.

About an hour after the beginning of the battle, no enemy columns could be seen in front of the front line of Stiles' brigade that were in any condition to attack and at twilight the sharpshooters were moved into position and were not pulled back until after midnight. During the attack of Loring's Division, Guibor's enemy Missouri Battery caused our batteries and the 120th Indiana Infantry Regiment problems, but since they only had smooth-bore guns, they were forced to retreat from our fire from the rifled guns at Fort Granger.

The battle in front of Col. Casement's brigade was just as hot as in Col. Stiles' front. Casement had the advantage of a straight line without an angle on its flank. For that reason, the fighting here was more even. No single regiment was more stressed that another. But Casement's line also didn't have any advantages, such as Stiles' brigade had through the thorn hedge at its center. But his entire line did have a light palisade which had been made of the bushes cut down in the thorn thicket. These palisades were not buried in the ground and served more for show than as resistance to the attacking enemy columns. The 65th Indiana Infantry Regiment, positioned on the right flank of Casement's brigade, was supplied with Henry repeater rifles. The head-logs of Casement's barricades were also more consistent than in any other portion of our breastworks. But the greatest advantage in Casement's front was the clear path for his artillery and rifle fire. Also, no part of his line was affected by the flight of Conrad's brigade over the breastworks.

No officer in our division, I would like to say in our army corps, had greater influence over his men than Casement. He was impulsive by nature, but with a clear head, he had his eye on everything. During the battle, he was everywhere with his men. His sonorous voice could always be heard above the hellish noise of the battle. He had full control over his men and made them hold their fire until the enemy was close enough to be most effective. The left portion of Featherston's enemy brigade, which attacked first, was thrown back on Walthall's Mississippians with heavy losses. Once united, they attacked again and again, each time being bloodily repulsed.

The plain before Casement's front was covered with the wounded and dying. Casement reported that he didn't stop firing until it was dark night, because the enemy kept trying to conquer his line; only adding greatly to the list of casualties.

During a brief pause between the charges, which allowed one to recognize objects through the cloud of gun smoke, the officers in the front line took the opportunity to cast a look over the barricades in order to have a better understanding of the situation. In the enemy line they could see an officer on a spooked horse trying to organize his troops for another attack. Some shots from our side felled the rider and the horse, but suddenly the horse got on its feet again and made a wild gallop toward our breastwork, where it collapsed with his front hoofs in our front line.

The officer who had been shot through the hip, tried to crawl away. Casement, who at the moment was in the right wing of his brigade, called to him in a loud voice that he should save himself by surrendering. But the officer paid Casement's well-intentioned words no heed; perhaps he couldn't hear them in the noise. So he was hit by several flying bullets and lay helpless on the spot until his brigade was completely wiped out by our men. After dark, Casement sent his snipers out and they brought back the wounded officer. It was General John Adams, who commanded the left flank of Loring's Division. He was still alive, but in spite of the best medical attention, his wounds were too serious and he died a short time later. Since Adams was in the reserves, this shows that three brigades ahead of him had already charged, and his was the fourth column trying to storm Casement's line. Casement's one brigade had defended itself against four; his reserves were not brought into the fight here.

Stiles' reserves weren't moved forward either, but on the enemy's side, everyone fit to serve had gone into the battle. They often sent the attack columns in eight men deep, since one brigade would push ahead of and between the others. Attacks of this kind lasted as long as there was daylight.

Casement's losses were light and he attributed the real reason for that was because his troops stood fast. In his report he said: "No man left his post during this battle unless he had been ordered to do so." The experiences of this brigade teach us and offer proof, that although almost all of the troops were only armed with front-loaders, the protection of a common earth wall is sufficient in order for a line of two teams to turn back an enemy advancing over an open field, even if it is several times stronger, and this defense can be accomplished without great losses.

The Battle at the Right Wing

The right wing of Ruger's division (Moore's brigade) was not attacked as early as Strickland's brigade, for the situation here was somewhat different. The wedge form of Conrad's and Lane's positions made it necessary for the enemy divisions under Cleburne and Brown to position themselves parallel to the two brigades, since the attacks were made head-on to both as long as they managed to hold their position. The retreat and the chase after them, after the line broke up, led along the highway toward the opening in the breastwork.

All the enemy regiments that made the attack on Lane, turned their line forward and in this way reached Moore's left half of the line. As soon as Lane's men were out of the way and the rebels were close enough for our troops to reach them, Moore's brigade opened with rapid and well-aimed fire which resulted in terrible destruction. None of Lane's men fled to Moore's line, but, as mentioned earlier, the 72nd Illinois Regiment in Strickland's brigade was the center point of their flight.

Moore's teams proved that, as had Casement's and Stiles' troops on the east side of the turnpike, wherever they had room for their fire, and wherever the fleeing troops didn't provide the enemy an advantage and protection, they were completely able to defend their position.

When Strickland's front line retreated, it brought Moore's left into a very dangerous situation, but the bravery and stubbornness of the officers and men were completely adequate to hold their position. Colonel Sherwood of the 111th Ohio Regiment ordered his men to mount their bayonets and to prepare for bloody hand-to-hand combat as soon as the enemy reached the barricade. Captain Dowling, the Inspector of the brigade, with the courage of a hero, gathered up some of the runaway troops and led them into position to protect Moore's flank.

Somewhat later, the enemy made repeated attacks in trying to break through a part of the line of the 101st Ohio Division. At the same time, extra support was moved to Ruger's line from Kimball's division. With this it was possible for Captain Dowling to form a short defense line in the left flank perpendicular to Ruger's line. This allowed Dowling to bring crossfire in front of Strickland's line and sweep the enemy from the barricade right next to Sherwood's flank. Dowling was seriously wounded during this operation, but his work had already been accomplished, for the line that he supported could no longer be shaken.

Ziegler's Pennsylvania Battery on the Carter Creek Pike was commanded to keep crossfire going to the left where the enemy in full view of our troops was preparing an attack on the south side of the little low area mentioned earlier. Bridges' (Leather Bridges) Illinois Batteries, which were posted on a little elevation in Strickland's lines, crossed their fire with Ziegler's and the infantry between these two batteries aimed directly at this elevation where the enemy line, as reported by Ruger, rapidly melted away like snow in sunshine.

The first attack on Ruger's division was made by Brown's division from Cheatham's Corps, which marching forward had been guided by the Columbia Turnpike, but as mentioned before, was forced west of the road due to lack of space. Gordon's brigade from Brown's division had the pike as its center and stormed our breastwork in that position. Gift's South Carolina Brigade was on Gordon's left and attacked Moore's brigade in our line. Strahl and Carter supported Gordon and Gift. These were the troops which, after they were repulsed, regrouped on the other side of the low area already mentioned for another attack, this time near the spot where Lane's brigade had originally stood, and where now our infantry and artillery fire were causing ghastly destruction among them.

Bate's division from Cheatham's Corps was placed on Brown's right and rear, with two brigades in their front line: Jackson on the right and Smith on the left and Bullock in reserve. Presstman's battery was with this division. Bate, in order to reach his position to attack, had to march significantly further than Brown and because of this made his attack somewhat later. His advance was focused on the Bostick Plantation and Carter Creek became the center of his line. Presstman's battery opened fire from the home of the Bostick farm. Advancing, Bate ran into a very strong forward front line with both Union divisions under

Ruger and Kimball. For that reason, Bate immediately brought his reserves into the battle. He found however that his left flank was being harassed by terrible fire from Ziegler's batteries and Ruger's infantry so that he had to move his position somewhat and in so doing, broadened his front line. He expected Chalmers' cavalry to join him on the left, but Chalmers was much further forward on his left in front of Kimball and was almost marching at a right angle to Bate. The latter thought he was completely without support and knew nothing of Chalmers' position.

The fight was stubborn and in several places the enemy managed to get over the breastwork in Moore's line and ended up in hand-to-hand fighting with our troops. At the center of Moore's brigade, two companies from the 183 Ohio Regiment shoved in to close a gap which had been caused by the spreading out of the line. These men were new recruits and weren't able to hold back the enemy attack. Moore ordered two companies from the 80th Indiana Regiment on his right into this opening. On Ruger's orders, a regiment from Kimball's division, the 101st Ohio under Colonel McDonald, was also sent to this week spot in Moore's line and gave brave and valuable service.

In Moore's center, where the enemy had gained some advantage, the latter tried desperately to retain a hold and his death-defying attack on the flag of the 107th Illinois Infantry Regiment that was fluttering on the barricade somewhat left of the center of Moore's brigade, was so bravely repulsed by our troops, that the majority of the attacking enemy column lost their lives on the breastwork, and anyone who grabbed for the flag fell lifeless on the wall before they could carry out their intention.

The enemy planted several of their battle flags on the earthworks, but the 23rd Michigan Regiment gave crossfire to their left and every enemy flag bearer was swept away. The spot that was filled by the two companies of the 80th Indiana Infantry Regiment completed the line again and from that point on, there was no danger that Moore's line could be disturbed. The right of his line had an elbow or angle and was not reached by Bate's enemy troops, since Bate used his left wing to support the bloody fight against Moore's center and left wing.

Bate's left wing on the Carter Creek Turnpike didn't get within 150 yards of Moore and losses on our side at this road, where the 118th Ohio and the 80th Indiana were posted, were insignificant in comparison to the other regiments in this brigade. The 111th Ohio, which was on the flank near Strickland's post, suffered the most in Moore's brigade. General Bate's enemy division however, reported terrible losses, of which very few were prisoners.

Bate's attack was significantly later then the action on the left and in the center. He had his troops march to our right, while Brown stormed our center. Bate also had a much longer distance before reaching our right wing. This could have been a mile. Stopping and organizing, as well as moving Bullock's brigade forward on his left, took time, which is why it wasn't possible for him to keep step with Stewart on our left, for the day was too short to allow everyone to attack at the same time.

Chalmers' cavalry battery had bombarded our right wing from noon on, but since Bate's troops couldn't see them because of the hilly terrain and hindered by a little wooded area and orchard, the latter thought that the cavalry hadn't been able to reach its position. Actually, the cavalry was ahead of infantry on that flank. The low spot with the little creek which faced Ruger's line at a 45 degree angle, made a curve in Kimball's division between Gross's brigade positioned next to Ruger, and Kirby's which held the center of Kimball's division and Whitaker's brigade on Kimball's right flank reached the Harpeth River. Kimball's entire division faced west and the next hill in that direction. In the next low area there, Chalmers prepared to advance against Kimball. His horses were left behind with the usual team that took care of the horses and his line advanced on foot.

The country road that branched off the Carter Creek Turnpike to the northwest touched Ruger's right and ran in the same direction as Kimball's line until it connected with the Charlotte Pike. Kimball's brigades in the form of an echelon were positioned about 100 yards east with that road on his left. This distance increased as one followed Kimball's line to the right, so that in his center, the road was 150 yards away. Here in the center, this country road was crossed by a street running out of the city, and at this crossing the 77th Pennsylvania Regiment was posted as an advanced guard. This line extended left and joined Ruger's line. It was about a half-mile from Kimball's main line and extended all the way to the river by connecting with the sharpshooters of the other brigades.

Bate's advance pushed these sharpshooters under Colonel Rose of the 77th Pennsylvania Regiment back among our reserves. Rose used a ravine for protection and from this location, held Bate's troops back for a while. But when Chalmers' dismounted troops marched forward, Rose was exposed to dangerous crossfire on his right flank. The movement of the advance guard under Rose lifted the veil from a Pennsylvania battery and the left wing of Gross's brigade. Both opened fire on the now advancing enemy 100 yards away. These sought protection on and behind the hill of the Bostick Plantation. This attack was only made by two regiments from Bate's division, so it only reached the flank of Gross's brigade. Further left and toward our right, the enemy formed a skirmish line in front of the 9th Indiana regiment, but a salvo from the 75th Illinois and the 9th Indiana was enough to prevent the enemy from making further progress in that line. Our losses here were insignificant, but the 77th Pennsylvania regiment was badly beat up. The enemy did not make any further attacks on Gross's front. The skirmish here only lasted 15 minutes.

The brigades under Kimball in the center and on the right, under the command of Kirby and Whitaker, had to deal with the attack of Chalmers' cavalry men. The division generals on the Union side looked on Chalmers' troops as infantry, for most of the rebel riders relied in battle on guns and bushes more than on their saddles, and seldom or never on their sabers. Forrest's troops were usually dismounted in a battle. Toward the end of the war, we followed the same method.

The thunder of field artillery and the rattle of rifle fire were heard from Kimball's left flank for more than an hour. Around sundown when the troops under Kirby and Whitaker became aware of the enemy approaching, they gave fire and after two or three salvos, the enemy retreated. The advance guards moved back into forward positions and carried on lively fire until late in the night. In spite of that, they maintained control of this position without much trouble and the main line in this part of the battle field was no longer active in this fight. Special efforts were made by the enemy on the extreme right against Whitaker's brigade in order to test the strength of our line. As Whitaker reported, the enemy attacked three times, but each time was bloodily repulsed until it finally fled. A portion of Kimball's reserves were, as mentioned, sent to help Ruger. Chalmers told us that he had advanced at about 3:30 and driven our sharpshooters back until he was about 60 yards from our breastwork. He had then seen that his troops were not strong enough to make a charge. He reported his losses as 160 dead and wounded and insists that he held his position opposite Kimball. This was probably at the little elevation from which he made his attack on us, for Kimball maintains that after driving the enemy back for the last time, he no longer saw them, and the same hadn't shown themselves again before our troops withdrew at midnight. For that reason, it is possible that the enemy actions in this part of the battle field were only a kind of reconnaissance. Kimball's line was so stretched out that he didn't try to post his men tightly together. The barricades too, were only in such places where the troops could support each other and protect each other by their fire through the openings. When the fight started, many troops had no protection at all. The reports from the various regiments indicate that the breastworks hadn't been built yet when the battle started. The troops had to drop their shovels and grab their rifles when the enemy showed up. This caused Hood and Bate to regret not attacking more seriously with their left flank. But the focus of the attack had always been the Columbia Turnpike, which was the same for our officers. Kimball's division was more a reserve than a part of our main line.

The Battle after Sundown

Until now we have stuck to the description of the battle from about 3:30 to 5:00 o'clock in the afternoon. Between those two times, the enemy was completely repulsed by both wings. In those parts of the battle field, the outlying pickets were sent forward again and held their positions until our withdrawal was set in motion. The snipers were very active during this time; the rattle of rifle fire was continuous from our line in both wings. But a massed charge by the enemy was never carried out again as it had been in the center. When a new attack was made along the Columbia Turnpike, Stewart's division on our left and Bate's enemy troops on our right went into action in an attempt to divide our forces in the center if possible. Our batteries maintained fire then with grapeshot, and the rolling thunder and lightning of the rapid fire of our well-served 52 guns made a noise as if the battle was still in full action. But the stubborn attacks of the enemy were restricted to attacks on the two brigades of Reilly and Strickland near the drive-through, between which Opdycke's brave regiment had shoved itself in a solid column. This line of three brigades was strengthened and supported by groups of Conrad's and Lane's men that (it can be said to their honor) had regrouped in the front line.

After General Stanley was wounded and had to go to the hospital in order to have it bandaged, General Cox remained at the center and encouraged the various troops to new action and stubborn resistance. As soon as he saw that the Kentucky battery was back in our hands and in action again, he set out to learn how the line in Strickland's brigade was communicating with Moore's. We will here let him tell it in his own words.

He said that from the highway he couldn't see what was going on behind Carter House and the collection of plantation outbuildings. The comfortable home of the owners was surrounded by shade and fruit trees in a garden near the house. The line of trees along the road north of the house were still mostly standing, while to the south of the house, the group of locust trees near the breastwork had all been cut down. For that reason, the house and the outbuildings and the orchards hampered a free view to the west. As soon as he was free again after the initial collision of the enemy on Reilly's line and the highway, he turned his attention in another direction and personally rode to the center of Strickland's brigade to investigate the situation and conditions there. He had seen Opdycke's troops at the second barricade in line with the Carter House. This line was extended by the smoke house and outbuildings of the plantation. It was about 50 yards from the opening in the front line, through which arriving troops and wagons had to pass.

He couldn't see how this second line connected with Strickland's right flank. The smoke of the guns obscured the view somewhat, but he could see far enough to know that not everything was under control and that the enemy was still in possession of a significant stretch west of the turnpike and south of the plantation buildings. He said, when he had gone around the group of trees and buildings that covered the southern slope of Carter Hill and had a free view again, he had seen that his doubts about the second line had been confirmed and that our people had formed a second line here which was an extension of the smoke house which stood south of the family house and offered the enemy the best opportunity for a break-through, and indeed was being used by them again and again. The pause between the attacks was short and the time for further investigation too short. For that reason, General Cox sent a staff officer to Strickland with orders to get, by all means, his troops back into their original positions in the front line. Directly west of and near the smoke house in the second line, there was an enclosure for a battery, which the 20nd Ohio battery had taken over. The infantry extended the line left and right between the buildings and these guns. Just west of the battery was the breastwork that the 44th Missouri Regiment had built. When the front line collapsed, this became the collection point for the troops that were driven back. Opdycke's brigade on the left and Strickland's on the right, reformed here. When the reserves moved forward during the worst of the chaos, officers and troops of both brigades were pushed together, although Opdycke's troops stayed fairly close to the highway and Strickland's were shoved more to the right. Afterwards, both brigades still overlapped each other somewhat. But Strickland always managed to hold tight to one half of his original line and in the short pauses between attacks, the men moved right or left to get into a better position and to separate the two brigades from each other. Both reinforced the barricade of the second line behind which they had regrouped.

General Cox said further, that Strickland had reported to him that the line in the front barricade had been reestablished, but from the highway he observed that the enemy was making rapidly repeated attempts on the outer barricade, so that there still was a problem there. So he rode to Strickland's position a second time and just as the sun was going down he met Strickland at the west end of the Carter House. This was in the center and behind what was Strickland's original line at the beginning of the battle. In this spot now, Opdycke's and Strickland's troops were next to each other. Cox said he had pointed out Strickland's error concerning the front line as well as the cloud of smoke allowed, making clear the difference between his present position and the place where his men had first been stationed and that the enemy was still firing from the outside of the barrier. He ordered him drive the enemy away from the outer side of the barricade as soon as possible.

Cox now passed Moore's brigade and visited Ruger, the division commander. He found that Moore's troops had held fast and that not one man had moved from his post. Ruger reported that the battle west of the Carter Creek turnpike was not as heavy as in the eastern part of the front line. Cox therefore felt justified in moving a portion of Kimball's reserves to Ruger's division in Strickland's brigade in order to give him support in reestablishing possession of his front line, where the enemy continued to have an advantage which it hoped to make use of. With these personal visits, Gen. Cox intended to become informed about the forces in his defense line and then, with unified forces to make their already won victory a certainty.

He found that his right wing was in the best order. The same could be said of Ruger's division, with the exception of Strickland's brigade, which was as mentioned in the second line. Opdycke's brigade was spread out across the Columbia Pike, tight against Reilly's right and Strickland's left. Out of Wagner's troops, about 800 men had stayed at the front line. Wagner himself was back near the river with Conrad and Lane, trying to reorganize the rest of his troops; this was also the place which their duty required them to be, and where they could offer the most valuable service. General Cox stated further that he had described his visits to Ruger and Kimball in such detail, because the claim had been made as if Wagner and his two divisions had remained in the front line. General Cox now visited Reilly's line east of the pike and found here that the enemy attacks on our outer left flank had let up, while on Reilly's right wing near the pike, there continued to be repeated enemy attacks with fresh troops.

Since Strickland still needed help badly in order to retake possession of his front line, a portion of Henderson's and Stiles' reserves from the left wing, were sent to Strickland. But by the time they reached the new position it was completely dark, since these reverses had to march almost a half mile before Strickland could put them in place. Around 5 o'clock on that short winter day, the sun had disappeared. But the battle in this part of the battle field continued on without interruption until 9 o'clock.

When Cox returned to his headquarters in Carter House, he received a message from his quartermaster, that the bridges and the ford had been taken over by Wagner's fleeing troops and were disturbing the movement of wagons and ambulances. General Cox sent his adjutant to Wagner and ordered him to deal with the problem. Wagner, who had now regained some control of the troops under Conrad and Lane, posted guards on the bridges and prevented further disruptions.

The reserves from both flanks that were sent to Strickland were under the command of Major Dow, our division's inspector. He tried his best to reach the first barricade with repeated charges, being bloodily repulsed each time. Not until he was bravely supported by crossfire from a battery, and his troops bravely advanced on hands and knees, were his troops successful in crossing the short, but body strewn distance between the second and first barricades. As soon as the line was back in our possession, Reilly was ordered to sweep the enemy out the trench in front of his breastwork with artillery fire from the corner at the cotton-gin in order to make another attack on Strickland impossible. But Major Dow still had to retreat once more. Casement too, kept his troops in action in order to call the enemy's attention to his position. This all took place in order to help Strickland.

After General Cox had completed his inspection tour, he remained in his headquarters at Carter House, where the reports of all of his subordinates could reach him. The battlefield was soon obscured by twilight and pitch black night. During this time however, the enemy continued the battle without interruption with terrible intensity and desperate courage, because Hood's troops thought and believed that with the few advantages they still possessed, they could still turn it into a complete victory. They continued to make charges again and again with renewed courage in order to fulfill their intention. The battle was unusual, in that it started late in the day and therefore lasted deep into the night.

The weather helped too. After almost two weeks of continuous snow, storms and rain, there were a few days of sunshine. The air was still with some haze. The gun smoke didn't lift and didn't blow away, but lay in an impenetrable cloud over the battlefield and obscured the view more than normal. It has been said that Hood led his generals to the mistaken belief that they would have more advantages attacking the center than actually proved to be the case, and these led to heavy losses for the Southerners, even after every hope of success had vanished.

From our post at Fort Granger, we could see every troop and every gun in our line, as long as it was day and the cloud of gun smoke allowed it. But after sundown, the sparks of rifle fire and the lightning, thunder and groaning of the heavy canons was splendid and awe-inspiring for eye and ear.

John Bell Hood, Supreme Commander of the Southern Forces at the Battles of Columbia, Spring Hill, Franklin and Nashville, Tennessee in November and December, 1864

From the Enemy Side

The consensus of the officers and men, which made up our defense line in the center, was that the enemy marched forward to attack in deep columns, which then charged one after the other, perhaps a dozen times or more in all, with the intention of breaking through our line at the Carter House. He thought that with repeated attacks, he could certainly accomplish that. The evidence for that is the way the attacks were constantly renewed even long after our flanks on the right and left had been freed from heavy fighting. But this deep and repeated action was the result of chance and not their plan, for the official reports of the enemy which are now available to us in Washington show that their first battle plan was the same as ours. That is, a battle line in which every division's front was made up of two brigades in the front line and one brigade in the second line as reserves, with the exception of French's division in Steward's corps, from which one brigade was absent and resulted in one brigade in the front line and one in reserve. The reason that Hood held on to his intention to either go around us or break through our line on the left, was because he would then be considerably closer to the bridges and the ford, which would have to become our retreat route, should we be beaten.

But since Hood's first action against us was made with eighteen brigades against our five brigades between the Carter Creek Turnpike and the railroad tracks, it turned out that he had to attack with one after the other; the enemy attacks were all made with just one brigade, since this was the tactical organization of his troops, over which he had easy and complete control. The narrow space to advance in made it necessary for one brigade to overlap the other, and the unexpected obstacle of the thorn hedge forced them toward the Columbia Road. When it was loudly proclaimed that our line had been broken through and that they were in possession of the breastwork and the parapet at the Carter House, everybody pushed toward the center.

Since every division had its own support or reserves, as soon as our line was reached, they carried out a double attack, which ended then with repeated retreats and regroupings as long as their troops were willing to undertake them. The divisions of Loring, Walthall, French and Cleburne were all east of the Columbia Turnpike, and their left line followed this road, whereas Loring's right bordered the river and railroad tracks.

Because of the resistance caused by Wagner's two brigades, the enemy right flank advanced more quickly, Walthall moved in a staggered formation toward Loring and overlapped behind him for the length of a brigade, while French similarly overlapped behind Walthall. With the same movement forward, Cleburne's division was led behind French. This created a column of five brigades on the highway and to the east, one behind the other. This is confirmed in Walthall's report, which says that Shelly's brigade was still east of the highway when it attacked and furthermore, that Shelly was one of his generals that reached our breastwork in Reilly's line. This must certainly have been between the cotton-gin and highway, for east of the cotton-gin, no enemy reached the parapet in Casement's line. Reynolds' and Quarles' brigades were forced further east and attacked Casement's line, while Cockrell's (the present Senator from Missouri) and Star's brigades from French's division and another two brigades from Cleburne (that makes four brigades one after the other) stormed our center. But this wasn't all. Gordon's brigade from Brown's division also advanced on the highway and Gordon himself was taken prisoner on Reilly's breastwork.

So we see that in a short time, six different lines, one after the other, charged Reilly's and Strickland's line, without counting the various repeated attacks which followed each retreat and regrouping. It has been claimed that twenty-seven different attacks were made. If we add in the individual attacks on our left flank, we find that Loring's division in two lines made a brave but bloodily repulsed attempt at getting through or around us at the railroad cut. Featherston's brigade attacked further to the west and was blown up on Casement's line.

This attack by Featherston followed Quarles' and Reynolds' brigades from Walthall's division that attacked Reilly's and the Kentucky Brigade's front line unsuccessfully, one after the other. General Walthall delivers in his own report about these attacks the best description of these terribly bloody fights, so we let him follow with the main points.

He says, "His officers and men were completely aware of the importance of this battle; that the enemy (the Yankees) had to be beaten here. Paying no attention to losses, my line moved evenly and steadily ahead until it was near the barricades, and here we attacked the enemy without any doubts that they would have to retreat without being able to stop us. There they fell apart and pulled back to the stronger breastwork.

It was however, an extended open area between the enemy's (our) outer and inner lines over which my troops had to march in order to reach the latter. This was done under the most deadly and damaging rifle and artillery fire that any troop or attack column had ever been exposed to. We were torn apart by the crossfire of batteries that the Yankees had advantageously situated. (These were Battery D, 1st Ohio-Art. and the 15th Indiana Battery at Fort Granger). No less devastating was the fire of both types of weapons in front of us, but my line continued forward and wouldn't be bothered. Just to the right of the turnpike we reached the abatis in front of the enemy barricade, over which no troops could go in formation. Here my main line and the reserves were bloodily repulsed and scattered in a tangle. Even though it was impossible for an organized line to get over this obstacle, many officers and men (including General Shelley) were able to reach the trench in front of the enemy barricade. They were either taken prisoner or shot; in making their attempt to take the breastwork there was no chance of escape or retreat. Many reached the earth-wall beyond the trench which separated them from the enemy and they kept on fighting until far into the night, or until they were incapacitated and led off as prisoners."

The brave and humble Division Commander tells us nothing about his own experiences, but his corps commander, General Stewart, informs us in his report that Walthall had two horses shot from under him and himself was severely wounded and had to leave the battle field. (General Walthall represented the

State of Mississippi for many years in the Senate and died a few years ago after reaching a very old age.)

General Quarles, who commanded a brigade in Walthall's division, was severely wounded in the attack and all of his staff officers remained dead on the field. We are told further, that losses in his command were so numerous that when the battle ended, his highest ranking officer surviving was a captain. It is too bad that so few reports have come down to us from the Southern side; but Walthall's report shows us what the contents would have been.

On the west side of the turnpike, Brown's division advanced in two lines. In the first were Gordon's brigade touching the Columbia Pike and Gist's brigade touching Gordon's left. In the second line, Strahl's brigade backed up Gordon's first line and Carter's brigade was Gist's reserves.
Cockrell's brigade covered Gordon and Strahl during the advance.

Later, when the fighting was the heaviest, Bate's division overlapped Brown's division by the length of two brigades. Then Bate advanced in a single line with the other three divisions that reached all the way to the Carter Creek Pike. So it was that more than two of Bate's brigades attacked Strickland and Moore. As we can see, this made the third double line that attacked the center of Strickland's brigade. But that isn't all. An hour after it got dark, Johnson's division of General Stephen D. Lee's corps arrived on the battlefield and moved forward west of the Columbia Pike to support Cheatham. This strong division of four brigades made the fifth and sixth double attack columns that moved against our center near Carter House, where Opdycke's men, half of Strickland's line, and Moore's left flank defiantly resisted the enemy advance.

A regiment from Stiles' division on our left and one from Kimball's on our right arrived here just at the critical moment in aid of their pressured comrades. Concerning the report about the attack of Johnson's division, we will have to rely on the official report of General Stephen D. Lee, the corps commander. His division, he said, moved against the enemy breastwork under heavy artillery and rifle fire and brilliantly drove the Yankees from a portion of their line. The brigades under Sharp and Brantley (Mississippians) and Deas (Alabamans) were especially effective. Their dead were mostly in the trench in front of the enemy barricade, where they had found a hero's death in hand-to-hand combat. Sharp said that he had captured three enemy battle flags. Brantley was decimated by crossfire but this brave brigade did not retreat an inch in this night battle.

Brigade-General Manigault commanded a brigade of Alabamans and South Carolinians. He was severely wounded while bravely leading his men into fire, and two of his colonels that followed him in command of his brigade, were put out of action. Colonel Shaw remained dead on the battlefield and Colonel Davis was severely wounded. Lee said, that he had never seen greater bravery and steadfastness of service during the war than what the troops under the capable and brave General Johnson provided that day.

Here, as well as on the east side of the highway, the heavy loss of officers is the reason there are so few enemy reports; but all that exist show how bloody and fierce the battle was at the center. Hood himself said that this battle was the most terrible and bloody that he had been part of during the war (and he lost an arm at Gettysburg and a leg at Chickamauga.) Our people, he said further, took possession of the outer face of the barricade, while the enemy held on to the inner side, and many of our troops that reached the inside of the barricade were either shot or taken prisoner. The battle lasted until midnight. His dead and wounded remained in our hands. Never have troops fought more bravely.

Naturally there are errors in the above reports but these last ones show the actual character of the battle very well. General Lee also told how it came to be that he had Johnson's division attack. He said that about twilight, General Cheatham informed him that the enemy was giving him stubborn resistance and that he needed help. But since it was then already dark and he wasn't exactly informed about the location, it wasn't possible to make his attack on the enemy until an hour after sundown. ...

Then his report continues, he was a witness to the most desperate hand-to-hand combat that he had ever read about in history. Dark night made the flashes of the Yankee cannons and rifle-fire seem spooky and terrible, for the troops on both sides fought like real demons. The enemy barricades for the infantry were the best he had ever seen. General Clayton, also a division commander in Lee's corps, reported that his division reached Franklin late in the afternoon. The bloody and devastating battle was already in full force. We were brought into position so that we could also attack, but merciful nightfall saved us from the terrible fate that befell the comrades who went before us.

From General Brown's division of Cheatham's corps we have a report from Col. Capers of the 24th South Carolina Regiment (who we mentioned before), the only one available to us. He told how General Gist's horse was shot down from under him and he then led his brigade into the fight on foot, where Gist himself was shot through the heart and fell dead. At the abatis in the grove of locust trees they were held up and took several of Wagner's men prisoners. It was lucky for us, he said further, that the Yankees held their fire, in order to allow the fleeing men from the forward line to get over the breastwork, and we made use of that advantage to work our way to the trench. Here we climbed up on the breastwork and fought hand-to-hand with the enemy. We set up the battle flag of the 24th South Carolina Regiment on the parapet and defended it. The enemy retreated a short way but was able to reorganize itself quickly and charged us again without being able to drive us from our position.

At sundown there was a pause in the fire west of the Carter Creek Pike. Brown's division had taken hold of the trench in front of the barricade in the center for the length of Gist's brigade. But shredded and tired after they had lost every staff officer and almost every field officer, they were only strong enough to hold the position but not to attack.

Strahl's and Carter's brigades stormed forward to support Gist and Gordon, but the Yankee fire from the buildings of Carter Plantation in back of their front line, combined with the rapid advance of the Union reserves and the crossfire from the batteries on the north side of the river (Battery D, 1st Ohio and 15th Indiana Battery), tore Strahl's and Carter's front lines to pieces before they could reach the locust abatis.

Colonel Capers was badly wounded and wasn't able to be an eye witness to entire fight. After the war he became a preacher for the Protestant Episcopal Church and in the 90s became the bishop of South Carolina. He composed his report from the testimony of his subordinates. It too, contains errors, but it generally confirms the larger reports. He informs us, that at the end of the battle, Captain Gillis of the 46th Georgia Regiment was the highest ranking officer in the brigade still able to serve and that the soldiers in the trench in front of the barricade loaded the weapons and handed them up to their comrades on the barricade that were able to fire them. The bloody fight continued this way until it was completely dark.

The few reports from the Southerner side have to some extent been added to in the memoires of its officers, which they occasionally tell in their reunions. General George W. Gordon, who was taken prisoner by us, gave a talk at the unveiling of the memorial to General Patrick Cleburne in Helena, Arkansas in 1891. His talk included many valuable memories of his personal experiences in this battle, which are as follows. He told us how Hood's army advanced on the Columbia highway and how Cleburne and Brown's divisions from Cheatham's corps made their charge on both sides of the highway, Cleburne on the east side and Brown on the west. General Granbury's brigade was Cleburne's left flank and Gordon's own brigade was Brown's right flank. Both brigades went forward at the same time, separated only by the road. He said:

"When the two army corps (Stewart's and Cheatham's) moved forward in battle formation, they had spread out for a distance of two miles. The march went forward calmly, in almost parade-like, confident steps. He led them from the hill into the valley. The flags fluttered, the drums rattled and combined with the shining gun-barrels, it offered a splendid and magnificently awe-inspiring picture that is unforgettable. When we got about 400 paces from the first enemy breastworks, we halted and reformed the columns into brigade front lines before receiving the order to charge. The first barricade of the Union troops did not extend the whole length of their complete second line, but was only two brigades wide, one left and one to the right of the highway, about 450 paces ahead of the main line, which was very regularly and solidly built and offered considerably more protection for the Union troops. These first provisional barricades (Conrad's and Lane's) were ahead of Cleburne's left and the right flank of Brown's line in Cheatham's corps. When everyone was ready, the command, "forward to attack" was given. With a wild "rebel yell" we stormed their first line; the enemy (Conrad and Lane) fired a salvo against our brave, attacking veterans.

At first it stopped us, but then without any further pause, we chased the now fleeing enemy toward their second and main line. The officers shouted, "Boys, let's follow the enemy to the barricade." This call was soon repeated by thousands of troops as we followed the enemy after driving them out of their first position. Some were of course shot, and others that weren't so fast on their feet, were taken prisoners. Until that point we only had a few losses. But when we got within about 100 paces of the main line where the enemy stood fast and strongly defended itself, it was as if the ghosts of hell had been let loose against us. Our enemy had held his fire so that their fleeing comrades could reach the protection of the barricades. But these had barely reached safety when the entire front line became a sea of fire, and those union troops that were still engaged with the Southerners were exposed to the fire of their own comrades, which were now throwing a veritable hail-storm of solid ball, grenades, shrapnel, grapeshot and musket balls down on us. The thunder of the cannons, the explosions of the bombs, the rattle of rifle-fire, the banging of shots from rifled cannons, the whistle of rifle bullets, the "rebel yell" and the Union "hurrah", the falling of dead and wounded...all made this a show of the most terrible of the terrible, and one of gruesome grandeur.

This isn't the tale of a fiction writer, who tries to prettify his own experiences with the brilliance of poetry, but the words of a brave soldier at the grave of a comrade, giving us the purest narration of his personal experiences as leader of his brigade and what actually took place then. He had won his position as officer on the bloody battlefield at an early age and had taken part in the struggles on many battlefields. But of all his experiences in attacking and defending, he gives Franklin first place as the bloodiest of all bloody battles. It was in the storm of this battle that Cleburne lost his life, and it was in his memory that his friends had come to honor his name.

But with Cleburne's death, the attack and battle were nowhere near being over. Although my brigade had been almost completely demolished, Granbury's quickly moved up behind us, so that the remainder of my troops was mixed in with Granbury's and together they renewed the charge until they reached the enemy earthwork. But we were so exhausted and so few in number that we stopped in the trench. This was filled for the most part, by the dead and wounded of both friend and enemy. Some climbed up to the top of the barricade but were felled there by bayonets or rifle butts. In spite of that, he says further, we continued the fight over the barricade for a long time. Both sides used the protection of the earth-wall as much as possible to protect their heads, both making use of the head-logs, so that body and head were protected from the fire of the battle front. In this way a rapid but wild fire was maintained, for nothing was endangered other than the hands holding the weapon.

A crossfire through the trench from the left and right however, made it impossible for us to hold the trench and we repeatedly shouted that we would surrender. Finally they heard our shouts and understood. Their fire stopped and we crossed the breastwork and surrendered. To leave the trench and retreat meant certain death. Everyone that tried it (and there were many) put himself in danger of being shot down immediately, and all, without exception, were shot.

He continued; the left portion of his brigade had been successful in breaking through the Union line; Col. Rice and many of his brave men had gotten about 50 yards or more inside the line when they were shot, just as a Union brigade (Opdycke's) with mounted bayonets and rapid fire were lightening our ranks. Those that could sought protection in the trench as we had, but eventually were forced to surrender.

This detailed description from General Gordon shows with which eagerness everyone on the Southern side pushed toward the center and to the opening in the main line at the highway. Every division, brigade or regiment wanted to be the first. When General Cleburne noticed that his troops were getting mixed up and being held up by Brown's division, he rode to the place to find out what was holding his men back. This cost him his life as soon as he was exposed to the crossfire from the cotton-gin. This also was the reason later, why Gordon and his men that had found protection in the trench were forced to surrender.

Captain Joseph Boyce, then commander of Company D of the 1st Missouri Confederate Infantry Regiment, describes the array of the Southern Army as follows: He said, the preparations for the murderous attack had provided a grandiose picture, as far as the eye could see. The manly youth of the South moved in best discipline and order to their assigned positions in the attack columns and offered the onlookers a show as if it were a military parade. Troops moved back and forth, this way and that, until all were in their positions. As Nelson had at Trafalgar, an enthusiastic Southerner had shouted; "England expects that every man will do his duty." The 1st Missouri Confederate Regiment was made up of Irishmen. One of them remarked that if England had no better protection than the 1st Regiment it would soon fall, since none of them would be willing to shed a drop of blood for John Bull in order to keep his monarchy intact. The remark caused laughter in the area, but it was a kind of forced laughter, to take their minds off the coming bloodbath. Just before four o'clock in the afternoon, Cheatham's corps was in line. Stephan D. Lee's corps was just coming into view. Forrest was in position on our right. The setting sun poured blood-red light over the battlefield and down on the enemy line. It seemed to be an omen, as one comrade remarked, that a terrible slaughter was ahead of us before midnight.

Our brigade (the Missouri) was in reserve. General Cockrell ordered us to march directly at the enemy barricade without firing a shot until we reached the top of the breastwork. The general gave the order in a strong voice: "Shoulder arms...right shoulder shift arms...Brigade ahead...Guide center march." The band played a fast march and the well-trained warriors, all looking ahead at the front in order to see the movements of the enemy, marched in time to the music from the band now playing "Bonnie Blue Flag" and then "Dixie". It was an enthusiastic beginning. But when the brigade reached the expected point in front of the enemy, these opened up with such terrible rifle fire from their front line (Conrad and Lane), along with crossfire from their artillery north of the Harpeth River (Battery D, 1st Ohio and 15th Indiana Battery) on our right, that we halted for a few minutes still holding our fire. We had marched about 900 paces now and during that time our flag had gone down three times. Joseph T. Donovan (of St. Louis) was that first that fell with the flag. He was wounded by a dead grenade. John S. Harris and Robert Bentley were Donovan's replacements as flag bearers and both died on the field. Sergeant Dennis Callahan, a brave Irishman, successfully placed the flag on the enemy barricade but was wounded and he and his flag were both conquered in bloody hand-to-hand fighting by James. K. Merrifield, who had already been mentioned earlier in these memoirs. At the same time our brave boys were driven back by the enemy to Cleburne's line just to the right and east of the Columbia Pike. Once again we crossed the first barricade of the enemy and with a "rebel yell" again charged the second and main barricade of the enemy with an unquenchable thirst for revenge, to destroy the enemy. We now gave fire and we, the survivors, rolled with empty guns and wounded into the enemy earthworks. But it was only four men from our company that had to surrender to the enemy here; the rest, dead or wounded, covered the field from the beginning of our attack to the trench of the barricade. The enemy retreated, but our strength to follow him was gone before we reached the barricade. For in that fateful moment the guns, of the few of us capable of shooting, were empty and without an officer to lead us, we were not capable of resisting the enemy reserves (Opdycke) now approaching us in quick-step like a wall of steel. A salvo from these into the tangled mass of our troops was enough to make us, those still able to, seek the protection of the trench in front of the breastwork. During our advance we had Guibor's Missouri Battery under Lieutenant Kennard with us; this had sent a rapid and deadly fire toward the front line (Conrad and Lane) of the enemy. Later, that battery made use of that enemy barricade for cover until night put an end to the bloodbath. The cries and groans of the dying and wounded, which weren't heard until dark, were limitless, for the enemy renewed firing at the slightest movement, and many of our wounded were killed after night fell. So far Captain Boyce's writing about the Southern Army.

The Battle after Dark

We have described the battle from the viewpoint of the Southerners, when the enemy made repeated death-defying attacks on our defense line. Now we would like to turn our interest to the equally brave Union defenders and especially to the critical points in the wooded area with the locust trees where our soldiers had retreated from the front line and held fast to the quickly erected second barricade.

We remember that the main line crossed the Columbia highway and after running straight west for about 50 yards, then made a bend to the northwest, following the curve of a hill and then sank at the foot of the hill into a low area. A considerable number of the enemy now held fast to the outside of the first barricade there and filled the trench west of the bend, which provided the rebels with protection from our crossfire from the cotton-gin. Their position was somewhat lower than east of the road and the flat area to the east. The enemy now was completely disorganized and could only attack in an unorganized pile, made up of all the remnants of annihilated brigades. The center of our side too, wasn't much better. Those of the enemy that could be reached by our flanking and crossfire were swept away, but the pile in the trench just in front of the barricade could not be reached by our people from the inside of the earth-wall and therefore had better protection than those that tried to retreat over the open battlefield to get out of our line of fire. The enemy in the trench still able to load the guns handed the freshly reloaded weapons to their comrades that had a sure hold on the facing of the barricade. In this way, they could keep up a steady fire at our Union line.

With the flanking and cross-fire from the cotton-gin as protection, General Cox wanted Strickland to take possession of the front line again. In order to carry that out, the 112th Illinois Regiment from Stiles' left flank was moved to Strickland's center. First Lieutenant Bond in command of the 112th Illinois, along with Inspector-Major General Dow of the 23rd Army Corps, led the regiment to Strickland's right flank, where Captain Sexton (later Chicago's Postmaster) was in command of the 72nd Illinois

Regiment. (The Colonel, Lieut.-Colonel, Major and a few Captains from this regiment had already been killed, so Sexton became the commander.) Together with the 112th he led his regiment forward. They tried to reach Moore's flank, but the night was so dark that it was almost impossible to know exactly where the enemy was positioned, or even to see where Moore's flank was. Sexton, who had inspected the field before sundown, found it less difficult to find his way and in order to help Col. Bond find his way better, sent Captain Carter of the 72nd Illinois Regiment as guide. So they went forward on hands and knees into the doubly dark night, for besides the darkness, there was also the cloud of gun smoke, which mournfully lay over the bloody field and made it impossible to see anything. The only light with which to make out the barricade was from the flashes of gunfire. The 112th Illinois Regiment crossed over the second barricade in Sexton's line and creeping forward they had to stay low in order to keep out of the enemy line of fire. They soon reached the front barricade this way, but when they tried to get up to take possession of it, they were so close to enemy fire that Colonel Bond's face was burned by powder.

But those troops that had advanced weren't the only ones exposed to enemy fire in darkness. In spite of orders to our troops on the left and right in Strickland's brigade to hold fire, the noise of the battle made it almost impossible to understand the order correctly, and it was difficult to hold back on the crossfire in front of our line, because the flashes from the enemy guns showed that the enemy was still in complete control of the south side of the barricade. Sexton's 72nd Illinois Regiment advanced left of Col. Bond's 112th Illinois, and both lay flat on the ground, waiting for the end of the firing. Bond said that they were so close to the enemy line that the latter couldn't aim low enough in order to reach them. Colonel Bond was slightly wounded twice and once had the heel of this boot blown off during this maneuver. When he realized that the two regiments would not be able to hold our front line because of our own cross-fire, they retreated. The 112th Illinois Regiment turned west, passed through the locust grove and in this way reached the west end of the second barricade, which in Bond's opinion was 50 yards from the smoke house, without coming in contact with Moore's line, which ended at the downward slope of Carter Hill, as Moore's report also informs us. The regiment from then and throughout the night served as a back-up for Strickland's brigade, and waited for an opportunity to advance in order to retake the first barricade. The officers reported that the two lines were about 40 feet from each other here.

In order to clear the front of Strickland's line of the enemy, General Reilly was ordered to send a portion of his brigade over the barricade by the cotton-gin and to increase flanking fire on the enemy in the trench in front of Strickland. As soon as the enemy saw this movement, those Southerners that had found protection in the trench until then, shouted that they would surrender, but their shouting wasn't heard by our men right away because of the terrible noise.

Richard Heuchon, the flag bearer of the 57th Indiana Regiment, who now lives in Commerce, Missouri, described the situation in the trench as follows: Our regiment, he said, belonged to Lane's brigade. We were in the first line to the right of the Columbia Pike and had just started shoveling out dirt to make ourselves a trench, when the magnificent war-panorama unfolded before our eyes. With flags flying and music playing, the Southerners advanced toward us from all sides. There was a low area about 150 yards in front of our line in which the enemy found some protection so it could get closer to us. At the first sight of them advancing out of the low area we sent well-aimed fire toward the enemy which caused them to pause but didn't stop them; he actually attacked with new freshness. Surrounded on all sides, we had to retreat to the main line. But on the way there, the enemy was mixed up with us. When we reached the trench, I fell exhausted into it with my flag. Our people behind the breastwork now opened with rapid fire and I am convinced that many of our comrades were also hit. Naturally, I protected myself as much as possible. Many of the enemy tried to climb over the barricade and were shot by our men and fell back with a last sigh into the trench dead. So I pulled several of these bodies nearer in order to get some protection from our own bullets. I spent five full hours in this terrible situation.

Not far from me was Col. Stafford, a Southern commander. On my right was General Stahl, also in command of the rebels toward the pike. Both tried to encourage their people and gave orders to hold the barricade and not to give in. Finally one didn't hear their voices any more, a sure sign that they had been hit by a bullet. But with their deaths, the fight didn't stop until finally the crossfire from people in the trench on our flank near the cotton-gin started. Then the Southerners shouted, "Enough, enough, we surrender!" Now many of them handed their guns butt first to our people on the other side of the breastwork and others threw them in a pile in the trench and climbed over the barricade. The trench was then cleared of everything that could still crawl. I myself, he said, went with my flag into our line, and in this way saved my life. Looking the next morning, I saw that my flag had holes from nine bullets. Col. Stafford was found upright but dead between his dear comrades, as if he still commanded this gruesome company. Since our people didn't have time to collect the weapons thrown away by the enemy, they ended up back in their hands. Comrade Heuchon tells further of the anguished cries of the dying and wounded and said that the five hours that he spent with them in the trench were certainly the most terrible hours that a person could ever witness. While they lay there, they clearly heard the sounds of the wipers of the artillery of a nearby Union battery getting ready to reload, which always made a sound resembling "Who is next?", and then the guns were fired again, one after the other. The flashes and thunder and the screams in the trenches still gives me shivers when I think of it.

This climb over the barricade increased the number of prisoners and enemy flags in our hands. It was now almost 9 o'clock at night and General Edward Johnson's division from Hood's regiment made its attack and was repulsed by our troops. The rebels now moved out of the low area in front of our line and pulled back to the first ridge where the barricades of Conrad's and Lane's brigades had been originally. Those that were still in the trench or lightly wounded, moved under cover of darkness into the low area where they were somewhat more protected. Heavy and continuous fire was still given us by the enemy, but from a greater distance and no longer from the face of the breastwork.

Captain William C. Cunningham of the 41 Tennessee (Southern) from Strahl's brigade was himself wounded and was one of the last who moved from the dangerous position in the trench in the locust woods and found protection in the low area. He describes for us the position and experiences very clearly and exactly. He said that the few survivors of Stahl's brigade held their position on the south side of the breastwork in sheer desperation. To retreat over the open plain in front of the breastwork was certain death. The same if one stayed at the barricade. For a long time the troops kept up the fire without officers and with great stubbornness...and with no light, just the flashes of the enemy artillery guns which also blinded us. But he said, they held the barricade despite all attempts by the enemy to recapture it, until the advance of the Yankees on our right flank made it impossible for us to hold on to our position.

The locust grove was mowed down by cannon balls as if it had been cut down by a machine. The plain was plowed up by the low angle of the artillery. Shortly after nine o'clock, the heavy fire gradually gave way until it ended with a kind of sharpshooter fire. Those that didn't want to surrender moved on hands and knees in great danger back to our line.

Sergeant-Major Cunningham, a relative of the captain above, also relates a true picture of the disastrous and deadly fight, when he says: There was hardly a single soldier between us and the Columbia Pike that was still fit enough to reload a weapon and hand it to his comrades on the barricade. It has been proven that we couldn't hold out much longer, but none of us believed that we would get out of this alive. When General Strahl was asked what we should do, he answered, "Keep on firing and don't give up." At the same time a comrade on my right was shot and fell dead against me with a loud cry. At the same time, General Strahl was shot and fell on his face. We thought he was dead. I said a few words to my dying comrades, asking where they had been wounded. Then our general, who wasn't dead yet, thought the words were meant for him and answered that he had been wounded in the head and asked that Col. Stafford be notified to take command of the brigade. He worked his way over the dead in the trench, now three men high. Col. Stafford was about 20 feet away.

Strahl's staff officers wanted to carry him there, but a second and a third bullet hit him and he was instantly dead. Captain Wm. E. Cunningham lost an eye, and as he sat in the trench during these long hours waiting for daylight in this terrible night, he told his faithful comrades about his suffering. Sergeant Cunningham wanted to get help, since there weren't enough still alive to be of help, and they also knew that the superior commanders didn't understand the situation at the breastwork. He looked for General Brown, but Major Hampton from Brown's staff, said that Brown had been carried off the battlefield severely wounded, and Strahl was next in command, but Strahl was dead, so Stafford was now next in command. But Stafford was also dead, as well as all staff-officers in Brown's division. Herewith had Captain Cunningham become the commander and highest ranking officer in Brown's division when the battle ended at about ten o'clock, and he had already lost an eye.

Sergeant Cunningham told further that he had tried to find General Cheatham, but after he was unsuccessful and saw that the fire was ending, he lay down exhausted and fell asleep. His shoulder had turned black and blue from the recoil of his rifle and his strength was completely gone. These are personal memories of people who had taken part, and because it was dark night, it was not possible to report on anything more than what they themselves had experienced. But he said further, it wasn't long before the reserves went into position and last shot of the battle was fired and the quiet of the night announced the end of the terrible battle.

Hood's reserves consisted of Clayton's and Stevenson's Divisions from General Stephen D. Lee's Corps and Johnson's Division, which were ordered to attack, but as already mentioned, were repulsed. General Stovall, who commanded the advance brigade of Clayton's division, said that he had captured the first enemy breastwork (which the enemy identified as Conrad's and Lane's position) and that behind him in the low area, the rest of Lee's Corps stayed, in order to get ready for another attack by the whole army at dawn the next morning. In this center, the survivors of Cheatham's and Steward's army corps all gathered, to which Johnson's division and the handful of Brown's division had retreated after escaping complete annihilation, as both Cunningham's had so clearly reported.

The lines of both sides were now protected by outposts and the Southerners didn't attempt another attack. But attack alarms were given repeatedly until about 11 o'clock, and were accompanied by rifle and occasional artillery fire. These occurred mainly on the right or west side of the Columbia turnpike in Strickland's front line. Such demonstrations were usually made by the enemy in order to find out if our line was still occupied.

We have now followed the enemy from the beginning of the battle until he pulled back in defeat and tried to bring his devastated divisions into the protection of Lee's corps, which had not been involved in the battle, in order to reorganize. Because of darkness, we no longer could evaluate what was going on, other than through what our outposts were doing, but once in a while a salvo of fire would roll along Hood's reserve's entire line. Our outposts then ran back and sought protection in our trench and fire was returned. After a short time then, all was peaceful and still again and the outposts were pushed ahead again until a single shot would cause the whole thing to be repeated. After this was repeated a few times, the commanders were convinced that the enemy no longer planned to attack and that we had convinced the rebels that we would protect our position during the night.

General Schofield had issued orders that, should Hood's army not attack us before night, the army should retreat over to the north side of the Harpeth River as soon as it got dark. This order was issued to Wagner when he was still on Winstead Hill, to the effect that he was to function as rear guard for the retreat. Under those circumstances, the south side of the river would have been completely cleared by six in the evening and Wagner's divisions would have been the last to cross the river. But Hood's attack changed all that.

General Schofield had a better view from his position at Fort Granger on Figure's Hill than if he had experienced everything in the noise and gun-smoke of the front line. In order to stay informed of individual details of the battle, he had the help of his staff, whose members were constantly coming and going. Between him at Fort Granger and General Cox's headquarters in

Carter House there was constant traffic. During the heat of the battle he had ordered Wood's division of the 4th Army Corps to be ready to cover the bridges and crossings over the river in case the enemy should be successful in breaking through our line. The preparations were carefully carried out and General Wood led a brigade under General Beatty east of Fort Granger between Wilson's cavalry and the bridges. The 40th Missouri Infantry Regiment, mostly made up of men from St. Louis, belonged to this brigade. This move prevented Hood's army from crossing the Harpeth River on our left flank. But before Wood could carry out this order, Hood's attack on our center was already underway, which made clear what the enemy's intentions were. General Wood now made preparations to cover the retreat. Beatty's brigade stayed somewhat nearer Fort Granger, north of the city, from where he could cover the railroad line. General Steight's brigade was posted directly across from the town on the north side of the Harpeth River. Colonel Post's brigade from Wood's division was positioned on the river below the town.

General Schofield, who had constantly been in contact by telegraph with General Thomas in Nashville, when informed by Schofield that Hood would cross the Harpeth River on his left above the city, Thomas ordered that the wagon train, now stopped in Brentwood, should be sent back to Nashville, to be followed by Schofield's army as soon as possible. But the excitement and noise of the battle happened so quickly that a retreat was impossible. Naturally, the order to begin the march around 6 o'clock was cancelled, for by sundown the battle was in full force. But the defenders of the line were already convinced that Hood's attack had been defeated and that our troops were completely capable of holding the line.

Colonel Wherry, chief of staff for General Schofield delivered Cox's letter of trust to General Schofield, who now issued new orders that the army shouldn't retreat until midnight, when the battle would most likely be over. The order directed that line from the right and from the left of the center at Carter House should both retreat simultaneously, the left crossing the river over the railroad bridge and the right passing over the foot bridge further north. Then they were to march north along the Nashville

Pike until they reached Brentwood. The outposts of the entire line were to stay at their posts until the read guard had crossed the bridge and then be pulled back at the same time. General Wood would cover the crossing (for which he was prepared) and then protect the retreat to Brentwood.

This order was issued between 6 and 7 o'clock. When General Cox received the order, he was afraid that Schofield didn't know that he had complete faith in the ability of his troops to hold the line against anything that could come. He sent his adjutant-general, Captain Theodor Cox, to Schofield's headquarters and promised Schofield his personal responsibility for holding the line fast, and to end the fight to our advantage without withdrawing. But the wagon train was already several hours toward Nashville as General Thomas had ordered. With very friendly greetings and congratulations, General Schofield sent General Cox a message that it was necessary to carry out the order to retreat.

At the same time that General Cox's staff officer was at General Schofield's headquarters, General Stanley, the commander of the 4th Army Corps, had gone there too, after having his wound bandaged by Dr. Hill. Shortly after this meeting, Major Dow, General Inspector of the 23rd Corps and Colonel Hartsuff were ordered to come to the headquarters (Hartsuff was General Schofield's General-Inspector) in order to arrange the details of the retreat and to bring the outposts in together around midnight.

Colonel Rousseau of the 12th Kentucky Regiment said in his report that after the line had been reestablished in Reilly's brigade, he had led his regiment into the reserve. He said further, that it wasn't necessary for our army to retreat from Franklin, and were fully capable of completely destroying the enemy should he have attacked us again the next morning. Col. Casement and General Reilly both voiced that same opinion. Their lines were not in serious danger from the enemy after sundown. In Opdycke's front, the line had, as it was getting dark, been reinforced with reserves and was reestablished in good military order, for there wasn't enough room in the front line for all of them. The people from Conrad's and Lane's brigades that had remained in the front line, now pulled back to the river in order to march under their own banner, which is where General Wagner had already gone in early evening and had been busy reorganizing his division.

Wilson's Cavalry Skirmish on our left

Before we talk about the midnight retreat, now would be the place to relate what part the cavalry played under Wilson. So that story can be understood, we have until now touched on the active participation of the cavalry as little as possible. We will now go back to their position in early morning as well as reporting in detail about their actions in the lively skirmish during the afternoon.

During the night of 29 November, the main part of the cavalry under Wilson was rounded up at the crossing of the Triune and Franklin Road, about 2½ miles east of Franklin. General Wilson's headquarters was at the Mathew's House, and his outposts were in possession of the fords over the Harpeth River several miles upriver from the city. The single significant unit was Hammond's brigade, which had been sent to Triune, in order to find out if Forrest was intending to carry out a flanking movement, which is what Wilson was expecting. Hammond's cavalry stood under direct orders of the cavalry commander, General Wilson, himself. The rest of the cavalry was divided into two divisions, one under General Johnson and the other under General Hatch. Wilson was the superior of all of them. Johnson's division consisted of brigades under Croxton and Capron; the latter being provisionally under the command of Colonel Thomas J. Harrison. General Hatch's division consisted of Coon's and Stewart's brigades.

Shortly after daybreak on the 30th, Wilson, following orders from General Schofield, sent General Croxton's brigade south over the Harpeth River and then south on the Lewiston Turnpike toward Douglas Church. Here Croxton was to cover the flank of our infantry, which was marching from Springhill to Franklin on the Columbia Pike, and he stationed his men at Winstead Hills to the left of Wagner's divisions facing south. Wagner, as mentioned before, had halted at Winstead Hills and formed a front line, hereby causing Hood's army to hold back. After similar orders from headquarters, General Wilson sent a message to Hammond's brigade not to stay in Triune unless the enemy showed itself with great forces, but to withdraw by way of Petersburg to Wilson's Mill. This was a spot on the Brentwood Turnpike, northeast of the important position at Matthew's Corner, which would in this way cover our connection to Nashville from the east and our rear. General Hammond had not seen or heard of any enemy at Triune and in the course of the morning had taken his post in the designated place.

In order to cover the right wing of our army, quite far to the west, and at the same time to connect with General Cooper who was in command of two brigades under Centreville at the Duck River...now in retreat toward Franklin, the 5th Iowa Cavalry Regiment from Harrison's brigade was sent downriver to the crossing of the Hillsboro Turnpike which went to Nashville, to keep an eye on things. The placement of all the forces in General Schofield's army was in this way completely carried out according to his orders. With the exception of the misfortune that our position crossed a river which was forced on us by our situation, the preparations in expectation of the enemy were very satisfying, i.e. the placement of the cavalry in connection with the other parts of the army.

General Hood, who most likely was aware that Cooper's division (of our army) was somewhere to the west of him and could at any moment attack his left flank, let Forrest split his cavalry into two parts and let Chalmers' division and a small portion of another division proceed forward toward the Carter Creek Turnpike, in order to keep watch over the movements of Cooper's division and to protect his left flank during their march forward. Forrest himself, with Buford's and Jackson's divisions marched in front of the Southern army and with flanking attacks, tried to break into our retreating line and to destroy our wagon train.

When General Wagner halted at Winstead Hills and thereby caused the Southerners to pause, Croxton's cavalry-brigade, as we saw, was on his left. Forrest waited for Stewart's corps to move up, and let that officer deal with moving forward on the highway, while he and his riders marched straight across the field and through a wooded area in order to get around the flank of Opdycke's brigade on the hill. Croxton was pushed back to

Franklin by this move. This was followed by Wagner's retreat to his fateful position between the two armies. But Forrest with his superior forces wasn't in any great hurry in his attack on Croxton. He waited until Hood's army had been organized and was moving forward, intending to attack at the same time Hood did. He ordered Buford's entire division to dismount and to form up alongside Loring's infantry, so that when Stewart gave the order to attack, they would attack with him. The horses of his riders were left behind in protection of a tree-covered low area, in which he and his troops also were organizing to attack. He was also protected here from the artillery fire of our rifled cannons near Fort Granger, north of the Harpeth River.

    Jackson's division of Forrest's cavalry did not dismount at the same time as Buford's troops, but were ordered to keep watch of the area around Hughe's Ford, which was in a straight line with the enemy's right flank as it passed the Winstead Hills. The road from this ford led directly northward to Wilson's position beyond the Mathew's place. If the army attacked us, Jackson was ordered to cross the river and attack the hill that Fort Granger was on and where the 15th Indiana Battery and Battery D, 1st Ohio Artillery were posted and wipe them out. But these batteries opened fire on Forrest's men as soon as they could be reached and held them back.

    Croxton reported that it was about two o'clock when he was charged by the enemy cavalry and he had repulsed them. They then moved to Hughe's Ford and the infantry had taken their place. But the reports of the enemy cavalry are very clear and tell us that Duford's dismounted riders held the field between the Lewisburg Turnpike and the river, while Jackson's move was toward the ford. There is no doubt that Croxton mistakenly considered the dismounted riders to be infantry, as often was the case when the horses or their attendants couldn't be seen. We saw the same mistake in Kimball's report, in which he reported Chalmers' actions in our right flank as being of the infantry. And we will see it again in Forrest's reports, when he describes his actions on our left against Wilson later in the day. Within the boundaries of the battle-line, there were two fords over the Harpeth River: Hughe's Ford already mentioned, was about three miles upriver from Franklin and about the same distance from the Columbia Turnpike, where it crosses Winstead Hills. McGavock's Ford was one and a half miles from the center of the town and not far from the Lewisburg Pike which followed the river for quite a stretch.

When Croxton saw Hood's army move forward in battle formation, he pulled his brigade on the south side of the Harpeth River back and crossed the river at McGavock's Ford, leaving one regiment (the 2nd Michigan Cavalry) on the south side however. They immediately exchanged shots with Buford's riders as soon as these could be reached.

At about 3 o'clock, and just as Hood's infantry attacked our line, Wilson received a report that couldn't be doubted, that Forrest was crossing the river at Hughe's Ford. Wilson was ready to confront the enemy movement. The first reports from the outposts indicated that, as Jackson's division got closer to the river, cavalry as well as infantry were on their way to the ford and were threatening to cross the river. When General Schofield received this report, he ordered General Wood to send a brigade of infantry to this ford to support the cavalry, as was mentioned earlier. But the desperate attack of Stewart's and Cheatham's corps, which was now taking place, caused Schofield to retract his order until he could see if the reserves were needed more in the center than on the flank against the riders. It turned out that Jackson's cavalry was not supported by any infantry and that his was the only cavalry that crossed the river. Wilson was fully capable of dealing with these. He ordered Hatch's division to advance from Mathew's House and to attack the enemy from the front and Croxton to march through McGavock's Ford in order to come at Forrest from the flank. Harrison's brigade stayed in reserve on Wilson's left and rear. The enemy cavalry which moved forward through Hughe's Ford pushed our outposts and their reserves back. Ross's riders, who under Forrest's eye where in the lead, carried out some brilliant attacks, which were however just as stubbornly repulsed by Wilson's riders, often by single regiments, even before General Hatch could move ahead with his division.

The Southerners had reached the tops of several hills from which peaks they could look straight down into a little valley between them and our advancing cavalry and see every movement. The enemy line spread out considerably on Hatch's left. The latter had his riders dismount and now moved his line toward the bottom of the hill and ordered an attack. The order was immediately carried out and the brave warriors reached the peak of the hill. After a little pause, so his men could catch their breath, Hatch again ordered an attack. This second advance was too much for the enemy, which now retreated in a disorganized pile and fled. Jackson's troops now also pulled back over the river and our outposts were sent to guard the ford again. From then on there was no action between both cavalries at this flank of our defense line.

  At the time that Croxton received the order to support Hatch's attack on Jackson, he pulled his regiment back from the south of the river at McGavock's Ford, but was held back from quickly marching forward by the false report that the enemy infantry had crossed the river between him and the city. He left two regiments in place here in order to keep an eye on the enemy movements, and with the other part of his brigade, hurried to help Hatch. As soon as it became apparent that the report of the river crossing was false, the two regiments followed him and Croxton was still able to provide valuable assistance on Hatch's left against Jackson. Together they chased Jackson in wild flight across the river. At about 5 o'clock, Wilson was able to report to the commanding general, that the enemy in front of his line had been defeated. Wilson's staff-officer reached General Schofield with this report about a half hour later, at the same as the enemy had been repulsed by our infantry on the left. This gave Schofield the confidence that we were completely capable of holding our position in every part of the battle field against repeated attacks of the enemy.

  Wilson followed his adjutant to Schofield's headquarters, in answer to an invitation that he had received before the battle started, and early in the evening the two generals had a conversation in which Wilson was fully instructed about his duties during the coming withdrawal toward Nashville. The cavalry was to hold its position until daybreak, and the outposts were to stay at their posts at the fords and then be pulled back on the Wilson Turnpike to Brentwood. Hammond's brigade was to join them on the way, and wherever possible, the riders were to follow Wood's division, which was to leave the river at the same time and move toward Brentwood on the Nashville Turnpike; it was there that the next confrontation with Hood was to take place. On the Southern side, Forrest led Buford's division back to where the horses were being held. Jackson's division remained at Hughe's Ford as observers and to cover the right flank of the southern infantry. One hour had resulted in a significant change in their future prospects; this was recognized too, by the leaders of the rebel cavalry. When the attack had been first organized, Forrest was very impatient and rode between Stewart's infantry brigades, encouraging them to speed it up and attack, to force the Yankees to take stand so they couldn't retreat. But around midnight, it required all his courage and spirit to strengthen the belief of the few remnants of the Southern Army, that Hood's actions in Tennessee had not been a total failure and that their career as an army was at an end.

That General Forrest rode with Stewart's troops was reported to us after the war by a staff-officer in French's division. "From the position of our battery, we had a wonderful view; first the brave advance of the infantry on our right, then the brilliant passage of arms by the cavalries on our right under Wilson and Forrest; the two best cavalry officers of the North and South. The sight of both fights was magnificent and solemn, for it was the end and doom of the Southern effort to form a slave republic on American soil. For the southern ruler to hold fast to this idea was pure desperation and insanity."

The Work in the Field Hospital

With the preparations for the withdrawal of our line around midnight, the removal of the wounded from the battlefield and out of the field hospitals was a very important task, and one should understand the basics about the organization of the hospital units in battle campaigns. For that reason, we would like to describe that here.

Our surgeons did not perform their field and battle services without significant obstacles. With the collection of patients during the last week, the ambulance train had reached Franklin pretty much filled up with wounded from the battles at Columbia and Spring Hill. Along with that were the sick, for the first winter weather produced the usual results, and made more work for the hospital than usual. The ambulances therefore had to be gotten in order again to be ready for the new work.

As soon as General Cox became the provisional commander of the 23rd Corps, Doctor Frink, the chief wound doctor of the 23rd division was entrusted with the management of the corps hospital system. He went right to work and got ready for active duty. The setting up and furnishing of the hospitals was excellent and the natural result of experience in various other campaigns. The main wound doctor of the army, also called Medical Director, was responsible for overseeing the whole system.

Under him was the division-organization of field hospitals, the main unit of an independent administration in the field. The medical provisions train was independent and contained all the furnishings for a field hospital; tents, wares, medicines, instruments and bandages. A wound doctor was chosen by the "Chief Surgeon", who acted as the chief of the hospital and was then told where to provide service from headquarters. The medical civil servants were responsible for choosing the location of the field hospital, as well as the erection of the tents, operating tables, and general administration, so that everything in the hospital would be carried out smoothly and quickly. The hospital and ambulance train was under orders of a line-lieutenant who was chosen for his special abilities for this job. The teamsters and stretcher-bearers stood under this lieutenant's military command, just as he received his orders from the staff wound doctor. The stretcher-bearers were permanently attached to this service and were trained in their duties so that they could best carry them out. The hospital train consisted of 36 ambulances and six provisions wagons for each division. The Medical Director was supported by an "Operations Board" consisting of three surgeons and as many helper surgeons as the bloody operations required. These were chosen from out of the regiment doctors by the Medical Director.

Every operation of significant importance was carried out under the personal oversight of an "Operations Board". Surgeon Frink and his team and the doctors Callamore, Rodgers and McMillen, made up this board. Surgeon Sparks was Chief of the hospital and Lieutenant Beighle was in command of the ambulance train. These officers had all worked together in the campaigns of the last two years, and the harmony and discipline of the system and their professional experience was of great and wonderful advantage for this unit.

In order to complete the description of the practical organization of the field-surgery-department, it is necessary to add, that in a battle, a brigade-depot for the wounded is usually placed very close to the line of fire; as close as safety allows. It is here that the wounded receive their first care, and from here an ambulance takes him back to the hospital in the rear. These collection points are served by the regiment's surgeons and their helpers which have not been ordered into the hospital service. The division's chief surgeon divides up the work according to the situation. The entire medical corps works here with such energy and devotion to duty that the comrades on the line should never forget that this branch of the army does its full duty and obligation.

When the ambulance train from Columbia reached Franklin in the morning, it was Doctor Frink's first duty to unload all the wounded and sick and accommodate them so the ambulances could be gotten ready for further service. By a stroke of luck, he found a train of freight cars filled with fodder on the north side of the river that was just ready to go to Nashville. The doctor talked the engineer of the train into waiting a few minutes. He galloped to General Schofield's headquarters and received the personal order to unload as many cars as necessary in order to transport his sick and wounded comfortably and to have them sent to Nashville. The ambulances with their loads couldn't get to the north side of the river safely because the banks on both sides of the ford were rough and steep; these having been made even rougher by trying to get the artillery, munitions and provision wagons through, which often had gotten stuck in the muck and had required three or four extra teams to get them out.

So they had to wait until the repairs on the county bridge had been finished, which then opened up the street to the north side of the river. It was quite late in the day when the unloading of the ambulances was completed and the train with the wounded and sick could move off to Nashville.

During this time, Doctor Sparks of the 23rd Army looked around for a suitable location for a field hospital and decided on a stretch north of the bridge on the Nashville Turnpike, where he soon had tents and tables ready for the bloody work of the coming battle. Hood's delay had barely given him enough time to get everything organized for receiving the wounded.

In the 4th Army Corps, the hospital organization was similar to what I described for the 23rd. The field-hospital was set up on the west side of the Nashville Turnpike near the location where our battery had crossed the river early in the morning. It was under the supervision of Doctor R.J. Hill, then of Kimball's division, under whom Doctor J. T. Heard served as Medical Director of the 4th Army Corps. The staff surgeons of both corps worked hand in hand in best harmony and the description of the methods applies to both.

The failure of the enemy attack on our wing and the early let-up of fighting in our flanks made it significantly easier for the system to work in those areas. After the first hour of battle, the ambulances could easily reach the brigade depots and wounded were taken without delays to the field hospital on the north side of the river.

But in the center, the situation was very different and there were serious difficulties. The highway ran downhill from the city, so that it could be reached by enemy fire from the barricade all the way to the river. This lasted until late in the evening and the ambulances could not reach the front line on this road but had to try to get as close to the wounded as they could through the low areas on each side of the road, from which they could be reached by the brave stretcher bearers.

Those that fell during Conrad's and Lane's retreat, lay outside the main line, mixed together with enemy dead and wounded and could not be reached. Others were lying between the two lines of Opdycke's and Strickland's brigades. When the battle gradually tapered off, these were carried in and taken to the hospital in the rear. But during the night, the battlefield couldn't be seen by the officers, and many wounded worked their way and hands and knees to the buildings nearby while the battle was still going on, only thinking of having immediate protection and not considering that they might be overlooked in the retreat and could fall into enemy hands.

Others that weren't wounded, but were so exhausted from several days of marching and battles that they fell asleep on the spot and didn't wake up until their comrades had marched away. They were taken prisoner, for the order to fall in line was given very quietly. Those lagging behind tried to find safety and peace in various places in the village, protected through the night by darkness but could only be found in the morning by the provost guard. That was the reason that many ended up in enemy hands that wouldn't have been taken had the battle and retreat taken place during the day.

The late hour also hampered the doctors in the division hospitals on the north side from doing more than putting a provisional bandage on the wound and all that could be transported were sent on to the hospital in Nashville. The ambulance train couldn't handle everyone however, and many had to remain in the field hospital. For these, regular units of surgeons were left behind, along with the necessary medicines and other hospital necessities. When we returned two weeks later after the battle of Nashville, most of the wounded came back into our hands, as well as another 4000 seriously wounded rebels, who were not in good enough condition to survive transportation, and which most likely were never fit for service later, for the raw December weather was no balsam for the severe wounds of the Southerners. The official reports and the various lectures at meetings and reunions of those who had taken part, give us a true picture of the gruesomeness of war, which the field surgeons experienced during a battle.

  Dr. Stephen C. Ayers told his friend General Cox an interesting story. He served on the staff of the field surgeons at Cumberland hospital in Nashville shortly before the Battle of Nashville, but is now professor for eye diseases in the Cincinnati College for Medicine and Wound Healing. He said that among the wounded that had been brought there from the hospital in Franklin, was a young soldier that had barely reached the age of a youth and was completely unconscious from a head wound. The long trip from the battle field had completely exhausted him, but Dr. Ayers noticed that he was still alive and tried to relieve some of his pain. He had been wounded in the brain by a ricocheting musket ball and his skull had been quite pushed in and torn up as a result. After the doctor washed the wound and had cut off the hair in the area, he tried to lift the pushed in bone with forceps in order to relieve the pressure on the brain. The young man immediately opened his eyes and looked in the doctor's face with full comprehension. He took the opportunity to ask the boy's name and where he had come from. He answered clearly, gave his name, company, regiment and residence. But hardly a minute later, the force of the bleeding put so much pressure on the boy's brain that he became unconscious again. Before any permanent help could be given him, the poor youth was a corpse. Those few minutes of consciousness saved him from the "Grave of the Unknown" and gave the family the consolation and peace of knowing what a glorious end the veteran and hero had won on the battlefield, and the ability to identify the body and get it to his final resting place in northern earth.

The Retreat to Nashville

The methods by which the troops were pulled back from the battlefield where carried out in the usual way under similar circumstances.

The outpost lines were under the command of the corps and division general-inspectors and the commanding officers of the day for each brigade joined a unit of staff-officers. (Colonel Hartsuff was the Corps General-Inspector and Major Dow took care of this service for the 3rd Division of the 23rd Army Corps.) The general-inspectors of each division got together at headquarters already in the early evening in order to discuss the details of the retreat, so that everything could be carried out smoothly and quickly according to plan, for the most insignificant mistake by one of the subordinates, with the river behind us, could cause a catastrophe as long as the army was still on the south side of the river.

With the order to retreat, the command of the defense in the main line ended for General Cox and his command was then limited first to the 23rd Corps, and as soon as Nashville was reached, to just the 3rd Division, while Schofield, on reaching Nashville, once again became the corps commander, and General Wood, the division-commander of the 4th Corps became the main commander of the 4th Army-Corps, since General Stanley was now unfit for battle because of his wounds.

The inspector of 23rd Corps went right to work and instructed the day-officers of the corps about their duties and carefully and quietly readied the entire outpost line so that they could carry out the order with attention and intelligence. Major Dow was ordered to gather the outposts and, after the last troops had left the battlefield and had marched over the bridges, to lead them over the river. The withdrawal of the artillery wasn't as easy as the infantry because many batteries had lost a large portion of their teams and organizing new horses and getting them harnessed was necessary and required time.

Colonel George W. Schofield, the artillery chief of the Army of Ohio, had several talks with Captain Bridges, the chief of the 4th Corps Battery. Both had their headquarters at Carter House.

Since it was his intention to get the batteries over the river before infantry had left the barricades, Captain Bridges was commanded to withdraw the batteries, two at a time, as quickly as possible and with as little disturbance as was possible. He was to start with the batteries that were positioned in the outermost flanks, since these had been used least during the battle.

Captain Scovill's Ohio battery, which was still in reserve, and the regular battery under Lieutenant Canby withdrew already at 8 o'clock. Ziegler's Pennsylvania and Baldwin's Ohio batteries followed soon after. Between 9 and 10 o'clock, the 20th Ohio Battery that had been in the battle at Carter House, the focal point of the worst fighting, was pulled back. Lieutenant Burdick, the commander of the battery, had been badly wounded in the last attack of the enemy, just minutes before the battery was ordered to withdraw. Since all the other officers had been incapacitated earlier, the Gunner-Sergeant Horn was in charge of the battery. The losses of officers, men and horses was so great that Captain Bridges asked General Opdycke for a unit of infantry to pull the guns away from the barricade to the highway by hand. Captain Marshall's Ohio Battery followed next, but the Kentucky Battery and Captain Bridges' own Illinois Battery under Lieutenant White, stationed in Strickland's line in the center, had to remain in place to support the line. It was almost midnight before the last of the guns headed toward the bridge.

The movements and withdrawal of the infantry from the barricades and over the river were so quiet and still that they weren't noticed by the enemy. The details show however, how errors could happen in orders that weren't correctly understood. The orders of General Schofield only gave the general outline of the withdrawal. The exact details of how this was to be carried out depended on how the corps commanders of the 23rd and 4th Army Corps understood them. The center at the Columbia Turnpike was the dividing line of the army for the withdrawal. The northern portion, or the troops on the right, was to cross the river on the foot bridge, and those on the left were ordered to march across on the railroad bridge. The artillery hadn't received specific instructions, but the artillery chiefs had already made arrangements to get the batteries over the river before the infantry.

We want to refresh our memories of where the troops were positioned in the front line. To the right of the Columbia Pike was Opdycke's brigade from Wagner's division, as well as Ruger's and Kimball's divisions. On the left was General Cox's 3rd Division under the command of General Reilly. The two brigades under Conrad and Lanes had regrouped under Wagner near the bridge, somewhat left of the Columbia Pike or the Main Street of the village, near the foot- or County bridge. It was here that Wagner, under Cox's orders, had set up guard.

An earlier order from headquarters of the 4th Corps to Wagner before the battle, when we were still of the opinion that there wouldn't be a confrontation here, was that Wagner's division should withdraw over the railroad bridge and Kimball's over the foot bridge. The order to pull back after midnight came from headquarters of the 4th Corps as a transcription of Schofield's order, wherein special requirements were included that Kimball should pull back from his right flank. Then Wagner was to follow him. This order brought three divisions to the county bridge (a grave error on the part of the commander of the 4th Army Corps, which could really have resulted in tragic consequences if the enemy had been able to break through our line. Later in the evening, Wagner was informed, and we can see this in the diary of Adjutant-General Fullerton, that Wagner was ordered to cross the river with his division ahead of the others. At 12:30, he wrote further, that the troops of the 4th Army Corps started to pull back from the battle-front south of Franklin; Wagner's division first and then Kimball's should cross the river by the foot bridge.

Kimball had not been informed of this change and when he arrived at the bridge with his division, it was occupied by Wagner's troops. In his official report, Kimball said, "At midnight I, according to orders, pulled my troops back from the battle-line, left my outposts in their place in front of the line, and marched to the bridge in order to get them over the river here as I had been ordered, in order to march immediately toward Brentwood where we would be stationed until the rest of the army could arrive there. But to my surprise, I found the road occupied by other troops who had left their position before the designated time. So I was not able to cross the bridge then and had to wait and was in the way of the others who had been ordered to march across behind me."

But when we hear Wagner's side of it, it was Kimball who was in the wrong. In his public report he recalls the situation and says: "About midnight I found troops which were supposed to follow me, already on the bridge and were in the process of marching over the river. I ordered my brigade commanders to prepare to march forward and to cross the bridge immediately and then to continue marching on the Nashville Pike." He had two brigades, as he said. These must have been Conrad's and Lane's, because Opdycke's had not yet been given orders to leave his position, as we will see later. Kimball's expectation was most likely that Wagner's whole division was stationed in the center where Opdycke's brigade was still stationed. If this had been the case, as is very well possible, then naturally Kimball would have been surprised if he found troops already at the bridge that were considered to the be the keystone of the defense line, and should have been holding the enemy back, even before his division, which had to protect the outermost flank. The reader, if he has followed the story carefully, will immediately see that such a major error had not been made.

Wagner's two reorganized brigades in the reserves were first in place to cross the bridge; but Opdycke's brigade from the same division was still in position at the front line in the center, between the divisions of the 23rd Army Corps and were still stubbornly holding the line which they had so bravely reestablished during the late afternoon, and there they remained until everything from the right part of the line had withdrawn. Then they marched together with a portion of Ruger's division to the bridge. In his report, Opdycke said, "I pulled my brigade back under orders from General Cox, and this was accomplished as ordered and without the least disruption."

The entire action was carried out without any action from the enemy, which didn't notice anything in the least. The 3rd Division (Reilly's) moved with the left flank and crossed the river over the railroad bridge. The 2nd Division marched through the city with Opdycke's brigade and crossed the wagon bridge, about a third mile downriver from the railroad bridge. General Cox remained at headquarters and oversaw the movements of the various divisions as described above. We were not certain that Hood wouldn't make a surprise attack on our troops, as soon as he learned that we were pulling back. It was an absolute necessary duty not to leave the center exposed until the outer flanks were already on their way and that both bridges were available for the use of the last troops.

As already mentioned, the bridges and the ford were closest to our left flank. Reilly's division alone, if it had pulled back through the city would have been all the two bridges could handle. This division was therefore kept in the line until all the other troops had marched off. Then the left flank moved to the railroad behind the breastwork and toward the crossing of the river. According to the plan of the retreat, General Cox and his staff were the last at the rear of the column, except for the outpost pickets, who crossed the river later.

Late in the evening, something happened that was unforgettable to everyone that saw it. A building was set on fire by some of the enemy residents of the city and the dark night was brightly lit by the flames. Against the brightness of the flames, every man stood out like a silhouette and could be seen better than during the daylight. Naturally, one couldn't think about pulling out as long as the building was burning. So the fire had to be put out first. General Wood sent some staff-officers over from the north side of the river and with the help of some soldiers and citizens and an old fire-squirt, they soon mastered the flames and the night became as dark as it was before. Naturally, the troops had to be held at the line so that the enemy wouldn't see them. It was a great relief for the officers as it became evident that the fire wasn't going to spread and that now the retreat could no longer be delayed.

Since there wasn't the least disturbance of the retreat by the enemy, it is certain that none of the enemy troops had remained near the barricade except the dead and severely wounded. But there is other evidence that the enemy wasn't near, for Major Dow, our Inspector-General told us what he had seen after the troops had pulled out. He said, "When the army marched away from our barricades at midnight, I stayed with the outposts in front of barricade for another hour, as I had been ordered to. I went on foot over the works and walked quite a stretch toward the enemy line. I didn't notice any enemy except the wounded and dead, and the calls for help from those hurt was heart-breaking. At that time I did not see any troops to the east or to the west sides of the turnpike. During the night, several sharp salvos had been fired off, but that had also stopped and during the time that our troops pulled out, not a shot had been fired, not during the time that I stayed, and not during the time in which I pulled the outposts back. We marched without the least disturbance and reached our unit after dawn."

General Schofield let the troops halt after they reached the north side of the river until the outposts were also over. Then he marched, with General Cox's division in the lead, toward Brentwood, halfway between Franklin and Nashville. According to orders, the 16th Army Corps under General A. J. Smith was to come to help us there. We halted and got ourselves ready to take our position, for the chain of hills with a southern front were ideally chosen for defending ourselves against an enemy attack.

But Smith's troops, after they were unloaded from the transports, didn't have any vehicles with which to make the move. Steadman's troops, which had been transported from Chattanooga, were also delayed, so that General Thomas decided to pull the whole army back to Nashville, in order to give General Wilson a chance to greatly strengthen his forces. For that reason, the march toward Nashville was continued. The first troops reached the place during the morning; the other parts arrived during the afternoon of 1 December in good order. As soon as every unit reached its appointed position in the line, the soldiers, exhausted almost beyond human endurance, lay down to rest and before evening on 2 December there was little disturbance or movement in camp, for their bodies, after seven days of superhuman exertion, finally demanded rest.

Since I have given a general history of the course of the battle, the reader will excuse me if I now finally add a few comments about our own battery. As already mentioned, our position had been at the outer left flank of our line. General Beatty's brigade from Wood's division, 4th Army Corps, served as our cover. When it got dark, the firing of the two batteries on the north side of the river ended (15th Indiana and Battery D from the 1st Ohio Artillery Regiment). We remained battle-ready however, with guns not connected to the caissons, and could see from our elevated position an awesome view of the entire battlefield. From the right and left, the roar of the guns continued uninterrupted until 9 o'clock, accompanied by the rattle of rifle fire. Then there started to be a series of quiet pauses. It was then that talk went around among the officers that we would be pulling back to Brentwood and that the provisions stored in the fort would now have to be destroyed. (The fort was on a hill, similar in form to a star-shaped fort, and had several heavy cannons, under which were Columbiads and howitzers, which were mainly for the protection of the bridge.) Inside the fort under its upper deck were several chambers for provisions for the quarter-master commissariat and ammunitions that would last a small unit stationed there a long time. Hardly had this news reached the artillery before a unit was sent there to "organize" their portion of the loot, which consisted of beautiful new red blankets for the horses and mules. There were also horse harnesses and gear of every kind available, and at the next inspection, not a single curry comb or brush was missing, at least in our battery. Foodstuffs were also divided up. The Infantry received their part too, and around midnight, with the exception of the gunpowder magazine, the provision chambers were empty. About this time, we hitched up and moved out toward the Columbia and Nashville highway and started marching toward Brentwood. The various divisions moved past us wordlessly and quietly. While we waited there for them, a young officer approached us and asked whether we could take a corpse along on one of our artillery caissons or wagons for several miles, until we would meet one the ambulances that were coming to meet us from Nashville. It was an officer of his regiment that had been in battle for the first time and the young man was the adjutant of the regiment and the nephew of Major Anderson from Fort Sumter (1861). He told us later, that the officer had been severely wounded. His men had carried him over the river on a stretcher, but he died on the way. They didn't want to leave him in the enemy's hands and for that reason asked for transportation, which we willingly offered him.

When all of the troops from south of the river had passed, our battery moved in behind them. We were followed by Wood's division from the 4th Army Corps as the rear guard. Just before we reached Brentwood, the fort was blown up into the air. In the meantime, Hood had his entire artillery move up for the morning attack and they now started firing on our front line, but the barricades had been empty for a good three hours already by then. When we reached Brentwood, Wood's division was sent into battle-formation. Our guns too, were driven up into the line and we could now see the enemy advancing. About 9 o'clock, shooting from Wilson's and Forrest's cavalries toward our line indicated that Hood' army was approaching. But the enemy wasn't serious about attacking, but just observed us in our new position. Since the reserve troops under General A. J. Smith couldn't reach us because of lack of transportation, the army under Schofield, following Thomas' orders, was led on to Nashville, as mentioned above. On the way there, many exhausted infantry men sat down in the ditches. We set as many as we could on our gun carriages and let the exhausted comrades ride the horses or on the gun carriages. In this way we saved many of our brave people that were completely unable to march and would have ended up in enemy hands. After arriving in Nashville, we were immediately positioned on a hill west of Fort Negley and as quickly as possible, horses and men were allowed to get the rest that they hadn't gotten for eight days. Other than for feeding and watering men and animals, no one was disturbed until the evening of 2 December. Just as the enemy showed up on a hill south of us, all units received orders to fill out reports of losses during the last days. To the right of our battery was Strickland's brigade from the 2nd Division and to the left was Reilly's brigade from the 3rd Division of the 23rd Army Corps. The drums called to "fall-in" and the horn signal was given to line up, and soon the artilleries and infantries were standing in formation to answer the corporal going through the list. In our battery, this was over quickly, so we turned our attention to the infantry. To the right of us were the 183 Ohio and 44 Missouri, left were the 104th and 16th Kentucky, all regiments that had suffered the most losses. As the names were read, the answer was given as to what had happened to those missing....dead...severely wounded and back in the hospital...head wound...right shoulder shot up...lost his right leg...received a shot in the chest...etc., the same answers in all the regiments mentioned. During the reading, many of the veteran's voices trembled as they reported what had happened to their missing comrades. Others answered in a loud voice, which showed that they were fresh and ready for the next fight again. General Reilly stepped forward after the roll-call and gave a very moving speech in which he mainly emphasized that war had made it necessary for us to fight against our fellowman, although we have no gripe against him personally.

We turned then to the 44th Missouri Regiment, where First Lieutenant Barr made comments with similar results. His regiment had suffered the most losses and Colonel Bradshaw had been wounded by seven musket balls. The regiment had more dead than any other in our army.

On the afternoon of the 3rd, as we were all lounging in camp, a young man rode up and greeted me friendly and asked if I remembered him. When I had to answer no, he told me his name. He was the son of a very well-respected German family in our village and he told me that his three older brothers were all in the service. Two had been wounded and sent home, and he, as the fourth, wanted to serve but his mother hadn't allowed it. Then he went to Cincinnati and joined the 175th Ohio Regiment. They didn't have to wait long until they were ordered to march to Tennessee. Here they first were on duty guarding bridges, but then were pulled back to Franklin, where his Colonel requested permission to remain on the south side of the river, which was granted and so it was that he had taken part in the bloody battle. In answer to my question, how he had liked it, he said, "If I had known that, I would have stayed with my mother." all the while with tears rolling like pearls down his young unwashed cheeks.

The Horror of War

Hood's stubborn intentions were not allowed to bend because of the terrible defeat and the lessons of those days. At midnight he issued orders to renew the battle at daybreak. He had his artillery drive up so that it could open concentrated fire in early morning focused on the center of our front line, and had his infantry form up to be ready at a signal to begin the charge with bayonets mounted.

It is likely doubtful that his troops would have been ready again to attempt an attack, had we stayed in our front line, for the murderous character of the battle had given the rebels such a sense of defeat, that every report of the battle is full of it. The daily journal of Cheatham's army corps contains a short, but meaningful statement. It said on 1 December: "The present day was spent burying the dead, taking care of the wounded, and getting our army-corps, as many as had survived, reorganized." Brigadier-General James A. Smith, who arrived on the field after the battle and became Cleburne's successor, reported heavy losses, especially of officers. Major-General Clayton reported the terrible setback that his brave comrades had borne and survived, as had been mentioned earlier, and that came from someone whose unit had not even been active in the battle. It was evident that he was convinced how worthless another attack would be, even if fate and dark night had saved him and his troops from the same fate that befell Cleburne. When we read this, we are convinced that Hood's subordinates would have issued a protest against a renewed attack, since they and everyone else could see how little hope there was of a victory. Had Hood however insisted on the attack, we would have been fully capable of repulsing him more easily the following day than we had been the first day.

It should not be forgotten, that had we stayed behind our barricades it would not have been pointless. We had strengthened our earthworks and the reserve troops from Nashville, as had been part of the plan originally, would have joined us. Gen. A. J. Smith's corps would have come during the night and taken their position where our 15th Indiana Battery and the 1st Ohio Battery where situated opposing Hood's right flank. Alongside them, the many guns of the reserve artilleries would have sent crossfire down on Hood's line. Kimball's and Wood's divisions had hardly been involved in the fight on the first day and at the first sign that the enemy was weakening or hesitating, our fresh troops would have been ready for a decisive flanking movement. And we, who were still in the front line, would have joined this successful movement which most likely would have led to the same victory then that completely annihilated the Southern army at Nashville, but two weeks later.

Hood certainly wouldn't have had any reasons to believe that he could have driven us out of our position with superior artillery fire early the next morning. For such work he would have had the best chance of success at Columbia several days earlier, where General Cox's division alone held him back, in spite of Hood's artillery surrounding and able to look down on us, while we held out on the low tongue of land in the river bend. Since we too, were aware that preparations had been made to withdraw and that reserve forces of every type were on their way doesn't mean that we were any less involved or less steadfast than we had been on the Duck River at Columbia. But the decisive battle was not supposed to take place here, and we now know that the Southern officers and their men breathed more easily when it became apparent at daybreak that our lines had moved.

Since Hood had become more cautious as a result of his experiences, he didn't follow us on the straight highway to Nashville. Most likely he thought that Schofield would try to attack him as soon as the rebels had crossed the Harpeth River. Hood sent Forrest ahead to Brentwood with his cavalry over the Wilson's Pike and followed with Lee's and Stewart's corps until the road to Nashville split and the enemy could use both roads. One of Hood's division commanders sarcastically reminded the Southern leader that the same flanking movement could have been carried out the day before; they could then certainly have avoided the loss of blood and life by which their army had been made incapable of further attack. The skirmish between Forrest and Wilson was the only disruption that made the march to Nashville somewhat lively and after a few days, Hood brought his army into a curve around the capital city of Nashville, but only...as we have reason to believe...so that the world would think that he had been victorious at Franklin. Had he followed sensible military strategy, he would certainly have pulled his forces back over the Tennessee River before Thomas could completely annihilate him at Nashville. For the heart of his army had been broken and Beauregard was certainly correct when he said it was his opinion that after the great loss of life at Franklin their army was no longer capable of making a successful attack at Nashville. Military principals were sacrificed to the pride of the commanding general and only resulted in greater disasters; the first sign of the complete collapse of the already sinking Confederate States.

The personal experiences of the Carter family were certainly nothing to be envied. They give us a picture of the terrible situation into which a private person can get during a war. Our story would not be complete if we did not follow with their own story. The head of the family was J. B. Carter, an elderly man. Living with him in the house were four daughters, one married, and a daughter-in-law. Of his two sons, one was Captain Frederic Carter, on the staff of General Thomas B. Smith in Hood's army, who stood in the center of Bate's division as it advanced over his father's plantation to attack our line somewhat west of the residence.

The other son, Colonel M. B. Carter, was a Confederate prisoner on parole at home. He had been taken prisoner in a previous battle. Three families with not yet grown-up grandchildren were also living in the house and along with these were several female servants (previously slaves), which brought the total to 17 persons. To these we must also add a five-person neighbor family which had sought shelter in Carter's solidly built brick house before the enemy attacked us. When the storm let loose, there were three men, 19 women and children in the house not taking part in the bloody battle.

Still very early in the day, Mr. J. B. Carter had nervously asked the commanding General of our line, if it wouldn't be better if he would get his family to safety and leave the house to its fate. Without knowing how large the family actually was, General Cox had in answer given his opinion that it would be better for him not to leave the house unless it was certain that there would be a battle, for as long as the tents and flags of the 23rd Army Corps were in the yard of the residence, there was no danger that he or his house would be bothered by the troops. But if the house was vacant, it would be impossible to be responsible for the house or its contents. Should a battle take place however, then it would not be a place for women or children, for the focal point of the battle would be right there in the center of the defense line. General Cox continued that he had no idea that Hood would attack our front line, for the extensive and comprehensive preparations on our side in order to defend ourselves against such an attack, was the reason we believed that the enemy would not charge us. Therefore it seemed best that the family should stay until they saw that an attack would be made, and then retreat to the village as quickly as possible.

Shortly after noon the tents at headquarters were taken down and loaded onto wagons and sent over the river. From this time on, General Cox and his staff were in the saddle and didn't have time to give the Carter family any further attention. The Carter son, the paroled prisoner, held himself the whole time more in the dark in order not to be questioned, because of his own status, by General Cox or his men. But when the danger suddenly burst over the family, he took charge of the helpless group, now frightened to death. We will follow his story. He said: While preparations were being carried out for the coming battle, the members of the family were by no means idle onlookers. In earlier battles they had been witnesses to the actions of the roving enemy raiders against the Union outposts, who had often been posted on the plantation, in which the dead from both sides often were left on the battle field. The skirmish itself would take place in the trees around the buildings. Through this they had become somewhat familiar with the excitement of the war and blood-letting was no longer so new. But they could only watch with ominous pain the strength of the army which was now rapidly destroying buildings to build breastworks and barricades for the defenders. The sight now presented to them was so much more immense and extensive in scale then what they had ever seen and caused them a feeling of great apprehension. Should they leave their home and what little they could still call their own, after three years of war in which the rest had already been lost, in order to gain their personal safety by fleeing? This question was not an encouraging one for any of them.

Leaving the home would mean that it would be exposed to certain looting and black ruins would likely be all that would remain when they returned. With all in agreement, they decided to stay. Perhaps their presence would be respected and the house saved from ruin. They would rely on God, who would certainly protect them from all harm.

Although Hood had the reputation for impulsive action, it was hardly expected that he would follow his impulse in view of the extensive preparations in earth-works and barricades that we had made for him. But in case the attack would be made after all, clothing and bedding was tied into bundles and assigned to each according to how much he or she could carry, so that should all be lost that they could save as much as possible and it could serve at the same time as partial protection during a retreat, should they be forced to leave the house. Should that become necessary, the instructions were that each should throw his bundle on his back and follow the leader wherever he should lead them.

In short time, doubt about Hood's intentions was lifted. The solid lines advancing in quick-step from left, right and center, showed clear and plain that the attack of our line would happen almost instantly. Although the house had withstood several battles in earlier years, those were children's play in comparison to the coming battle. The cellar was the safest place for the inhabitants and the family had barely reached it when the attack on our line began and the noise of the battle caused them the most terrible terror. In the darkness of the cellar the deathly frightened children grabbed onto the knees of grownups and their parents, while musket balls like hail hit the building. Cannon balls crashed through the house from one end to the other. All were in anxious expectation of what would come next but no one made a sound of fright.

As soon as the first attack was over and no one had been injured, several took courage and hope. But for others, the pause only caused greater anxiety and increased the worry over unknown dangers still ahead of them. In this state of hope and fright they spent many hours until the last shot was fired and relief from this horrible situation seemed possible. They had hardly congratulated each other when a southern soldier announced that Captain Theodor Carter, the son and brother, lay severely wounded on the battlefield. The older brother, who had been comforting his family until now, went out right away in order to search for him, but because he had been given the wrong directions, he went to a different part of the field. But in the meantime, General Thomas B. Smith, in whose staff the young Carter served, went to the Carter House and reported that the young officer had a life-threatening wound. He led the father, three sisters and a sister-in-law to the place where the brave son and brother had fallen. They carried him carefully back to the house that he had not seen in more than two years. He had fallen, almost in fulfillment of his heart's wish, just a few hundred paces from the home of his loved ones.

As day dawned, it was discovered that wounded and skulks had taken over the main portions of the Carter house. Many of the wounded had hidden themselves here in the dark, and since they were in the house and were lying down, they were overlooked by the ambulance-corps whose job it was to carry all the wounded back our line on the other side of the river. Others had been put down on the ground in orderly rows, waiting for the overfilled ambulances to return, but many of these ended up in enemy hands. The movement back from our positions after midnight had taken place so quietly that many veterans that served in the line, but had been overtaken by sleep, didn't awaken soon enough to march off with their comrades. These were shaken awake by the outpost pickets and sent after the column. Among these was a comrade from Lane's brigade that had joined Strickland's line of fire. He was a simple soldier from the 26th Ohio Regiment, who in later years became a professor at a university. He wrote very humbly about his own experiences in this battle. Gist, was his name, was one of those who was overcome from lack of sleep, and we can get a true picture from his story of the condition and mood of an army that had spent several days in battle and marching.

He said that after the firing stopped, we were apprehensive for a while what would come next and we thought the battle would be renewed any minute, but had gotten so apathetic from the marching, the terrible scenes of the last two days and the powder smoke that he was overcome by exhaustion that he stretched out with his head against the breastwork and fell asleep. It must have been almost midnight when he awoke and was surprised to find that the battle line had already withdrawn and only the outpost skirmishers were still at their stations. I thought, he said, that one of these must have awakened me; at least he took hold of me and said I should see to it that I got to the river, because all the troops had already marched off. Without any question and not losing a minute, I followed his advice. As I passed the back of our line, I saw a terrible sight; a whole row of severely wounded lying side by side. Their moaning and screams were heart-breaking. They of course did not know that the troops had already marched away and that they would soon fall into enemy hands.

When I reached the highway, I doubled my pace and was soon on the north side of the Harpeth River. The road to Nashville was overfilled with soldiers and vehicles. It didn't seem as if anything was organized. As soon as I crossed the river, I met a comrade from my company and I have him to thank for my escape. I was so exhausted, he continued, beyond anything I had ever experienced before, and so hungry that I could not march more than a quarter mile without resting. As soon as I sat down, I was overcome by sleep. After a few minutes, my comrade would wake me and talk me into marching further. Even today I believe that was repeated a hundred times. There are limits to the endurance of every human, beyond which one cannot go. Excessive bodily and mental exertion is just as disabling for service as are wounds or collapse because of illness. For exhaustion too, will reach a point at which the brain, as well as the body, fails and is no longer reliable. Normal motivations lose their force. Hope and even sense of duty and obligation have no driving strength left. Under these conditions, the body and spirit require rest, whatever the cost. The weaker and those carrying the heaviest loads usually are the first to show signs of lost strength and stragglers are the first result of exhaustion. Strict discipline can probably postpone the ruinous results of this, but it can't be avoided indefinitely, even with strict orders. It is very difficult to create an exact table of how long a man or horse can hold out and it is not uncommon for historians to get the notion that an army can march and fight continuously.

This description of his suffering and dangers would be similar to those of many others. It was repeatedly told that many people on this retreat fell asleep while marching and it wasn't until they hit an uneven spot and lost their balance that they woke up again. Repeated exertion during consecutive days and nights brought a large portion of Schofield's little army to the end of their endurance and this was the real reason why the troops should have stayed in their positions in the line so that they would at least have had one night of rest after a week full of continuous fighting and marching, in spite of the prospect of another battle in the morning. One should consider whether it hadn't been better to move the support troops to Franklin from Nashville and then to continue the battle the next morning with victory certain, than to burden the men, already exhausted beyond measure, with a night march. What could have been decided to our advantage in a few hours in Franklin the next morning (1 December), ended up taking two days in winter weather two weeks later in Nashville.

The story of this battle would not be complete without mentioning Cooper's brigade from Ruger's division again. We left them in the neighborhood of Centerville on the Duck River, about 30 miles below Columbia. In doubt whether the messenger on horseback sent by General Ruger would reach Cooper with the order to march in a straight line to Franklin, General Schofield asked General Thomas to send an order with the same contents to Cooper. Consequently, in the early afternoon of 29 November to General Thomas sent a telegram to Col. Thompson, who was commander of the post at Johnsonville on the Tennessee River, and ordered him to send a mounted courier to Cooper with the expressed order that Cooper should march on the Nashville Turnpike until he crossed the Harpeth River at Widow Demos' Plantation and from there he should contact Schofield in Franklin.

Ruger's message reached Cooper at Beard's Ferry in the early morning of the 30th, at the time that Schofield's army was gathering at Franklin. Cooper sent the portion of his brigade that was with him to Killough's Plantation, five miles north on the Duck River, and sent orders to the rest of his brigade still in position at Centerville, to join him as soon as possible. On the map, the distance between Centerville and Beard's Ford was about four or five miles, but Cooper had found that the shortest distance was really 14 or 15 miles and since the ford was closer to Columbia, Cooper was right when he set up headquarters at the ford, for from there he would have a close connection to Ruger and Schofield. It wasn't until 1 December that he was able to get his whole commando together, when our little army had already reached Nashville.

At two o'clock Cooper received Thomas's order, which had underway for two days. He now marched at full speed to Nashville and crossed the Harpeth at evening of 2 December at the appointed spot. During the day he learned from some rebel deserters that our army had marched from Franklin to Nashville and his own path there was now most likely already in the possession of Hood's army.

On the 30th when Schofield was still in Franklin, he learned from Thomas, what orders the latter had sent to Cooper. Schofield sent a mounted courier to follow the Harpeth with orders for Cooper to proceed with his brigade without delay to Nashville. But at this time Cooper was still at Centerville and the courier was chased by enemy riders back to Nashville. After this incident, Thomas telegraphed Lieut. Colonel Sellon, who commanded the post at Kingston Springs, a village on the railroad which ran to Johnsonville, to order General Cooper to march to Clarksville, a place on the Cumberland River, 40 miles below Nashville, which was now the collection point for all such troops that had been cut off from Nashville by Hood's army.

This message did not reach Cooper, who now set forth on his march and reached the Harpeth on 2 December, as we already have seen. He now marched cautiously on the Hardin Turnpike toward Nashville until he reached a high hill about 8 miles south of the city. From here he could overlook the camp fires of the enemy which blazed below him on both sides of the road.

He directed his march overland to his left and behind until he reached the Charlotte Turnpike which followed the westward run of the Cumberland River and marched without pause the whole night and crossed the Harpeth River again in daylight. His own good judgment showed him that Clarksville had to be the goal of his movement. He continued marching in that direction without pause and reached the place on the evening of the 5th and joined Colonel Thompson's commando from the Johnsonville garrison. After two days of rest, he continued on to Nashville where he joined up with the 23rd Army Corps and on the evening of the 8th, reported to General Schofield for further orders. But instead of 55 miles, as he had expected, he had to make a round-about journey from Centerville to Nashville of two hundred and ten miles. So we have seen how close his whole brigade had come to being taken prisoners. His cool-headedness as well as his quietly considered decision made it possible for him to escape being taken prisoner and to avoid the dangers that surrounded him. Good discipline and the great trust that his veterans placed in him were in part also to be thanked that he was able to get his commando without losses back into the safety of the main army. General Cooper's brigade played a most laudable part in the attack of the battle of 15 and 16 December in Nashville.

In spite of the great superiority that Hood had during this campaign, the success of his actions was way below expectations. Even after he reached Schofield's lines, he still let him march past at Spring Hill, and at Franklin, Hood suffered a severe setback. The resulting defeatism of his army did not leave much expectation of great results in his northern campaigns. The hopes that Mr. Davis (Confed. president) had prophetically expressed in Palmetto, had all turned to water.

On the Union side, General Sherman with his army of 65,000 men swept through from northern Georgia to Savannah, in contrast to which the Southern army, from which so much had been expected, was close to total collapse. Opposing Hood's army now, an army had gathered that, as we will see, he could not withstand.

Results, Lessons and Comparisons

It isn't so easy to determine the number of troops that stood on the battlefield at Franklin in both Schofield and Hoods armies, or the number of dead and wounded. The Southern leaders and commanders always made the greatest efforts to report their forces and losses as small as possible and their reports were never dependable, especially so in these battles. The results of these battles awakened the greatest astonishment and mourning among the Southern states. The result was generally considered a disastrous blow to their hopes for independence.

On the Union side, the army under Schofield had no permanent organization, but was to some extent just thrown-together out of such units in the Mississippi Division under General Thomas that were available to him with which he could oppose General Hood's advance. Examining the official records of the strength of the army which have now been published, we can eliminate the errors and give an estimate that would come close to the actual numbers.

The official reports of Hood's army, on which we totally depend, are from 6 November and 10 December. No other reports between these dates seem to have come in. Since there were a few insignificant skirmishes on the way north of the Tennessee River toward Columbia with rapid advances at Duck River and Spring-Hill, there naturally were losses in Hood's army to report before the battle at Franklin, but these were more than sufficiently replaced by new recruits that hurried to join them. One of the expectations that Hood counted on, was that a stream of volunteers would flow to his flag from the residents of the state. Should that not be the case, replacements were to be gotten by way of the harsh Confederate conscription laws. There is evidence that up until the battle of Franklin, very many Southern deserters reported to their units again and that many new recruits were pulled into the army through their laws. Hood had been considerably strengthened in this way. We can then with certainty state that Hood led as many troops into the battle at Franklin as Hood had led across the Tennessee River, and the losses of his army, as were determined by Schofield and Thomas after our return through Franklin, have not been understated.

On 6 November, Hood indicated that his infantry had 32,861 men fit for active service. Jackson's cavalry division with him numbered 2801 men on horseback, ready for battle, but Forrest's cavalry corps consisted of three divisions. Their officers were Jackson, Buford and Chalmers, and there is no doubt that Buford's division was significantly stronger than Jackson's. It is therefore quite possible that each division was made up of about 3000 men, so that altogether, the cavalry under Forrest made a corps of 9000 battle-ready mounted men. In his report of 6 November, Hood stated that Forrest had not reported the number of his troops. Later he stated that throughout the whole campaign there had been no report available from the cavalries. We therefore will have to rely on the reports that we had collected from prisoners and deserters and compare them with other reports. General Schofield stated in his official report, that the number of a 10,000 man cavalry under Forrest was not an exaggeration and came close to the truth. The total strength of Hood's forces would therefore certainly stand at between 42,000 and 43,000 men for all types of units.

It is easier to determine General Schofield's army, for the three monthly reports, as well as the daily reports give us everything as exactly as one could expect. Of the infantry and artillery, the reports are mostly exact. The units which were serving elsewhere, such as those under Cooper who marched with his brigade from Centerville on 30 November and two other regiments that had been newly assigned to him from the 23rd Army Corps, since Cooper hadn't reported to his corps until he reached Nashville several days later, cannot be counted as troops that had taken part in the battle at Franklin. From the cavalry that served Schofield's army under Wilson, there are no special reports until the morning of the 30th, and since the organization of this body of troops was only provisional, it is difficult to separate them from the riders in Nashville and elsewhere. It is of no significance if we cannot give the exact number of cavalry on both sides since the Battle of Franklin was essentially a battle between artilleries and infantries.

On the morning of 20 November, the number of infantry and artillery in the 4th Army Corps ready for battle was 13,119 men and the 23rd Army Corps was 9823, a total on the morning of the battle of 22,942. On 30 November, the 4th Army Corps was 15,207 men and the 23rd Army Corps was 10,527. Two regiments from the Tennessee Army and the 44th Missouri and 72nd Illinois were provisionally added to the latter corps at that time. Both these troop units were about 1000 men strong and outnumbered older regiments. The whole, which increased the number of the corps by 2792 men, consisted mainly of new regiments and recruits who reached Schofield at Columbia, but the absence of Cooper's brigade reduced the 23rd Army Corps by about 3000. So, Schofield's artillery and infantry counted 23,734 men at the beginning of the battle.

The Union cavalry under Wilson must be counted as part of Schofield's army. General Hatch reported his division as counting 2638. General Johnson reported his division as having 2286 riders in the battle under his command. General Hammond did not leave behind a report of the strength of his brigade, but the whole cavalry didn't add up to more than 5500 men and when the battle started, Schofield's army was made up of 29,234 battle-ready men in all weapon categories.

Since we are at it, for a military overview we can give the strengths of the troops on both sides, which participated in the charge and in the defense. Of Hood's divisions, two divisions under Stephen D. Lee's corps were kept in reserve and didn't take part in the fight, and one brigade of Stewart's corps (Ector's) was absent, as guards for a pontoon train. Only two batteries of Hood's artillery were under fire. The numbers of Hood's army, which made the attack and came into our line of fire, were 23,700 men from infantry and artillery. The charge was made on our "entrenchment" between the Harpeth River upriver from the city on our left and the Carter Creek Turnpike on our right. As we saw, Kimball's division of the 4th Army Corps served really more as reserves for our right flank, as well as for the defense of our spread-out breastwork, and with the exception of their left brigade, this division had only limited confrontation with Chalmers' division of the enemy cavalry.

These, as well as the cavalry on the other side of the river, we can completely leave out of our calculations concerning the results of the enemy attacks and charges. However, for historical reasons it is necessary to count them too. In order to determine the end results for the whole, we would first like to list the losses of the enemy in detail.

After we again took possession of Franklin on 18 December, we had the unusual opportunity to expand and enrich our knowledge about enemy losses. Their overfilled hospitals and field medical stations, as well as the field surgeons and their teams, fell into our hands. Our own severely wounded and their doctors that we had to leave behind on 1 December also came into our hands again. Through this recapture, General Schofield was given the opportunity to determine exactly what Hood's losses where in the Battle of Franklin. It turned out that 1750 brave Southerners had been buried on the McGavock Plantation. 3800 severely wounded that could not yet tolerate transportation, lay in the hospital and medical stations in Franklin, and we had already taken 702 prisoners with us to Nashville on 1 December, which comes to a total of 6252 men unfit for battle. To these must be added the lightly wounded and the dead, whose families had gotten them home for burial. The enemy losses of generals were particularly heavy. Six died on the battlefield, six were severely wounded and one was taken prisoner by us. Hood's own report to the rebel government in Richmond gives us the best information about the number of lightly wounded.

On 5 December, Hood tried to downplay the terrible defeat that he suffered through the loss of his generals in a telegram to the southern war-minister in Richmond. He said, "Our loss of generals is extraordinarily large in comparison to that of the troops. The Chief-Surgeon reported a large number of lightly wounded." If we make a comparison based on our own experience of the ratio in military terms between dead and wounded, then we can believe that to the above listed severely wounded, approximately another 4000 lightly wounded would have to be added that were being treated in their quarters or had been released from the hospital and were back in the ranks when Hood issued his next report on 10 December. We can therefore claim with certainty that Hood's losses at Franklin amounted to 10,000 and that this number is conservative.

In order to support the above claim, it is very interesting to compare the public report that Hood issued on 10 December with the one he made on 6 November, which we mentioned above. In his December reports, he states the strength of his battle-fit infantry and artillery at 24,074 men. To these must the added the four brigades which were absent before, which in comparison with other divisions would add up approximately to another 2387 men, so that Hood's army would have reached a strength of 26,641 men. The difference between this number and the report of 32,861 on 6 November is 6400, which number would confirm the losses of infantry and artillery. To these we must add losses of the cavalry, which based on the 6 November report, would add up to 269 men, which brings the total loss, not counting the lightly wounded, to 6669 men. A comparison of this number to that of Schofield's report from that time gives it, by its similarity, the stamp of truth.

It would have been desirable to have full reports of the losses in the Southern armies in order to avoid the comparisons that we had to make, but there were no reports at all from Cleburne's and Brown's divisions from Cheatham's corps, which had the most losses, or these reports have been lost, had they ever actually been written. For that reason we have to rely on the evidence and comparisons given above. What astonishes the world most is the unusually large number of generals that were listed among the dead or wounded. Hood sent the list in his telegram to the rebel government on 3 December with great indifference. "We regret", he said, "having to report the loss of many brave and good officers."

Major-General Cleburne, Brigadier-General John Adams, Gist, Strahl, Granbury and Stafford are all dead. The Generals Brown, Carter, Manigault, Quarles, Cockrell and Scott are severely wounded. He didn't even mention Walthall and Jordan, who had also been wounded. The last two were taken prisoner. But this list was only a small portion of the report attached to his orders to his corps-commanders right after the battle. In this order he asked that exact reports of dead and wounded division's, brigade's and regiment's officers be made immediately, including those that had become incapacitated for further service on the evening before. This complete list is an "honor list" which covers three pages of the public reports. Altogether were 6 generals dead, 6 severely wounded and one taken prisoner; 6 colonels dead, 15 wounded, 2 missing; 2 lieutenant-generals dead, 9 wounded; 3 majors dead, 5 wounded and 2 missing; 2 captains dead, 3 wounded and 4 missing. The whole number is 65. But we shouldn't forget that none of these commanded less than a regiment; every captain took over the command of a colonel or a regiment commander, since he had advanced to fill the position which the fate of war had opened for him. The other field and line officers are included in the list of the thousands of dead and wounded that shed their blood in this terrible battle. As peace descended on the battlefield, there was more than one brigade in which a captain had become the commander. This was the case in Quarles' brigade, in Walthall's division and Gist's brigade from Cheatham's corps.

Results and Comparisons with European Battles – The End of the Battle of Franklin

The losses on the Union side are much easier to determine than those on the Southern side, since we can get the truth from the official reports that are now available to us from the various divisions of the 4th and 23rd Army Corps that were sent to Schofield then. Reports for the cavalry were made for the entire campaign, including the battle of Nashville, so that General Wilson's specific losses in his commando at Franklin are not available, but it is probably understood that the losses were not significant. General Schofield lists losses in his army as follows:

1st Division, 4th Army Corps (Kimball's): 5 dead, 35 wounded, 18 missing...total 58.

2nd Division, 4th Army Corps (Wagner): 25 dead, 519 wounded, 670 missing...total 1214.

2nd Division, 23rd Army Corps (Ruger's): 74 dead, 241 wounded, 313 missing...total 628.

3rd Division, 23rd Army Corps (Reilly): 48 dead, 185 wounded, 97 missing...total 330.

Close examination of this list of total losses points out some important things that we can learn from. First is that half of the losses are among the missing. Although it is true that a portion of the missing were deaths of men that fell outside the breastworks during Conrad's and Lane's retreats, and some were stragglers and runaways from the battlefield, which couldn't reach their flags again, so it is likely that the largest number of these missing were either wounded or not wounded but taken prisoner. In his telegram on 3 December, Hood claimed that he had taken a thousand Union soldiers prisoner. This statement is confirmed by the number of 1104 missing from our side.

Secondly, almost all the missing are found in Wagner's and Ruger's divisions, and two thirds of these are again from Wagner's division alone. If we look further into the details of these divisions, we see that the number of missing in Moore's brigade of Ruger's division is insignificant. The same is the case in Casement's and Stiles' brigades in Reilly's division. As far as the 23rd Army Corps is concerned, almost all are from Reilly's and Strickland's brigades, the two that were positioned to the left and right of the Columbia Turnpike, and in Strickland's were three times as many as in Reilly's brigade. Wagner's division had 70 missing in Opdycke's brigade and 600 more in Lane's and Conrad's brigades. The number in Opdycke's brigade was the same as Reilly's losses.

These numbers point out that where the line had stood fast, and among the troops that held tight to the barricades, losses were very small. Even where the line had been broken through but had been restored quickly, such as in Reilly's and Opdycke's, the losses from prisoners were insignificant in number. But where the line was not reestablished for a longer time and the enemy had possession of the line, as in Strickland's line, the losses were heavy. And where the enemy streamed in together with our troops, as when our people were driven back almost a half mile from their front, the number of wounded and missing was naturally much greater, as could be expected. Thirdly, the list shows a similar correlation to the number of dead, which were insignificant in number except in the center of the Union side. In spite of that, losses on the Southern side were just as high in front of the left wing of our line under Stiles and Casement as on any other portion of the battlefield. The character of the fight in front of the Strickland's line is evident when we find that the number of dead were 53 men, while Conrad's and Lane's brigades only had 36 dead and Opdycke's had 16 dead, which together make 52 for Wagner's division and 74 in Ruger's division. This doesn't only show that Strickland's regiments stood together and offered stiff resistance, but also that the provisionally erected barricade offered significantly less protection than the first barricade in the main line. We can see from this that every list of losses confirms what we have described in the previous chapters.

The improvements that have been made in repeater or self-loading rifles since the Boer War and the usual calculation of actual distance and velocity of fire have received much adjustment as the result of our experiences at the Battle of Franklin. We also saw that small changes in elevation in the battle field could not be perceived from our parapet. They were however, always deep enough to provide Hood's advancing infantry with such good protection that they had already passed Wagner's two brigades before they could be reached by our infantry fire. The enemy got within 600 yards of our line before he was within our line of fire. Seldom have we found a battlefield during this war that was as open and free as at Franklin, and it is doubtful whether our weapons would have been able to reach the enemy sooner, or our fire had caused more damage to the enemy, if the plain had been any larger. A musket shot beyond 600 paces distance is quite uncertain.

The rapid fire that the enemy accused us of is likely unjustified. The few repeater rifles with which several companies had been armed, don't account for much in comparison to the number of troops in the line. The enemy gave these weapons much importance and overestimated the number of the repeater rifles that our troops had available, and claimed that their heavy losses on this battlefield were due to them.

But in truth, it was the advance to the barricade with second and reserve lines which made their weapons into rapid-fire weapons with a firing line of men three or four rows deep. Those standing behind served those in front with loaded rifles so quickly that it is doubtful a normal front line with repeater rifles could keep up such a rapid fire as what we observed them delivering here and represented a front line three or four times what was normal. When it got dark, the front line looked like a living line of fire which poured through the opening between the head-logs and the earthwork without a break. It would have been difficult for someone on our side, who had taken part in the battle, not to have remarked that our entire barricade offered a continuous flame until the end of the battle and that this was a phenomenon of the battle. With the improved rifles of today, one could achieve a similar result with just two rows. This fight also throws significant light on the question which is often asked, how much endurance, and the loss thereof, do well-trained and disciplined troops have before they reach the breaking point beyond which they can go no further?

No one capable of critical thinking will dispute that the combination of courage and intelligence in the material of the Union and Southern armies in the year 1864 could not have been surpassed. Discipline in battle was also apparent in both armies to a high degree. Some 24,000 such men under the Southern flag stormed our line behind a barricade between the Harpeth River and the Carter Creek Turnpike, about a mile long, which was held by about 10,000 Union troops under Reilly and Ruger, along with artillery. Another approximately 5000 from Wagner's division were in this battle, although as already mentioned, more to the disadvantage than advantage for the Union army.

This stroke of luck did much to strengthen the confidence of the Southerners. It raised their hopes and their courage far above normal. Their combined losses including the lightly wounded must have been well over a third of the forces that they sent into battle until they finally resigned themselves to the unavoidable and put an end to further attacks. It would be very difficult to find better evidence of what bravery, discipline and heroism can accomplish.

One cannot go beyond the impossible, least of all on the battlefield, and to try to do so can neither count as bravery nor eagerness to do one's duty. It is much more being at the border of insanity. The troops that stood behind the barricade and replaced the line after it had been broken, can also say that they have proved what courage and perseverance can accomplish in turning the threat of danger into victory.

Among the booty from the battle, General Schofield could report 33 battle-flags; 20 of these were captured from the top of Reilly's breastwork, 10 were won by Opdycke's troops and three were from other locations. Many were captured during hand-to-hand fighting, and others were found lying on the field where no one survived the devastation that could have raised them again. Hood claimed to have captured some flags from Wagner's people during their flight, before they could reunited with the main line. Many other flags than those mentioned were kept by their captors. For example, Mr. Merrifield has two flags in his possession today that he himself captured. Mr. Heuchon from Commerce, Missouri has the flag of an Alabama regiment from a trench in which he had taken shelter, took it over the breastwork and still has it today.

The effectiveness of the artillery that played a part here can be shown; of the 1750 dead Southern soldiers, 225 were unrecognizable. If we now look at the lists of the dead by states, we see that Alabama 149, Arkansas 124, Florida 24, Georgia 89, Kentucky 26, Louisiana 48, Mississippi 450, Missouri 150, North Carolina 22, South Carolina 76, Tennessee 255, Texas 109 and "unknown" 225 were buried on the battlefield. If we want to make a comparison with other world-famous battles, Wellington's battle at Waterloo is the only one to compare with. Out of 43,000 men that he led into battle against Rey at Quatre Bras from 16 June 1815 until Waterloo on 18 June, he reported 1756 dead.

The Battle at Gettysburg lasted from 1-3 July 1863. Here General Lee lost 2600 men out of 76,000 in a campaign of 30 days. Gen. Mead lost 2800 out of 90,000 men in the same period. At Gettysburg, the attack under Picket, Wilcox and Pettigrew was made with 18,000 men; at Franklin the attackers numbered 23,700 men. At Gettysburg the Southerners reported four generals killed; at Franklin, six Southern Generals fell on the battlefield. If we compare the list of the dead with that of the Franco-Prussian War, we find that the Germans led eight army corps into the battle at Gravelotte but only had a loss of 15,000 of dead and wounded.

At Königgratz on 3 July 1866, the Prussians had three armies of 220,000 men with only 1100 deaths. The lists of the grand Napoleon at Borodino on 7 September 1812, near Moscow proved that losses in that great battle only amounted to eight percent, while Hood, as mentioned, had 10,000 dead, severely and lightly wounded to mourn out of 23,700 men at Franklin.

Although everyone who took part in this battle demonstrated great courage and deserved all the fame and honor that a grateful folk was willing to hand out, the "Fortuna" of war has justly chosen four persons on which to shine its light above all others. These are General Schofield, who commanded the army, General Cox, who commanded the defense line, General Opdycke, who like Blücher at Waterloo joined the battle at the right moment and General Wilson of the cavalry, who covered our rear and drove Forrest's cavalry away.

Why General Thomas did not take command of the battle himself at Columbia, since he knew that Hood was not a dreamer, and from Nashville he could have reached the battlefield at Columbia in two hours, is something that none of his friends have been willing to answer. General Stanley, next in command after Schofield, did not arrive with his corps at the battlefield until the battle had started, and shortly after arriving he was painfully wounded and had to go to the field-hospital and retire from the battle. He wasn't at the battle more than 20 minutes, but in that time he lost his horse and was wounded. General Cox directed the fate of the battle until the end.

General Opdycke had led his brigade into the reserves behind the main line against the will of General Wagner, who on that day was suffering from an excess of heroism and courage, and was fortunately in the right place to be able, not to undo Wagner's grave error, but to repair the damage, and General Wilson held Forrest off our backs in guarding our left flank. We may discuss later why General Thomas did not get his troops together right away at Columbia as soon as Hood moved into Tennessee. Also, why Sherman didn't let Thomas have another army corps, the 14th, with 15,000 men, since he could have reached Savannah just as well with 50,000 men as he carried this out with 65,000. Had Thomas or Schofield had another 15,000 more troops at Columbia or Franklin, they would never have allowed Hood to reach Nashville and would have saved General Grant and the nation much anxiety.

We have now pretty well come to the end of our story of this battle and have truthfully and in detail represented its bloody character. I can assure the reader that I have embellished nothing, but that I left very, very much out. This story shows how Americans by birth or by immigration, will support and defend an idea that he feels is just. The South lost almost half of the men that they sent into battle here, while the great battles in Europe rarely show losses of more than seven percent; those battles that are considered to be the bloodiest in Europe only show losses of five to eight percent. For that reason, Franklin remains the bloodiest battle fought since the invention of gunpowder.

Wagner's Conduct during the Battle

Since the army corps is made of departments and armies, a corps spirit had naturally developed among them and many prominent officers of the 4th Corps, especially those from Wagner's division, have challenged the justness of the criticism that has poured out over his handling of his troops during the battle. However, the written orders that Wagner received from his superiors, which he evidently correctly understood as shown in his own reports, provide enough evidence that the responsibility for the mistake of remaining in the forward line can't rest on his superiors or his subordinates, but on him alone. There have often been remarks and accusations made against General Schofield and the 23rd Corps that they were unfriendly against Wagner in their testimony at General Thomas's investigation, which took place in Nashville right after the army arrived there. This rests only on conjecture, for after everything ended well and enemy had been hindered in its intentions, no one harbored a more comradely and well-wishing feeling for Wagner than the generals Cox and Schofield. Both had done all they could to present Conrad and Lane's holding steady, as well as their collapse, in the best light. For that reason Wagner met with Cox as soon as they arrived in Nashville to discuss with him the report that he was to write. He seemed defeated and depressed. Cox promised that everything would be done that could be to present his situation in the best possible light, but one cannot fight the powers of fate, and misfortune travels fast. Although General Conrad had had no rest for three days, as soon as he arrived at camp in Nashville and could get to his desk, he made his report of what had happened at Franklin, which had the appearance of an accusation against Wagner. On 5 and 7 December, Col. Lane and Opdycke also wrote their reports and both expressed themselves very critically of Wagner's orders and conduct in the Battle of Franklin. General Thomas immediately had the whole thing investigated and after thorough consideration, he decided to relieve Wagner of the command of his division and to give him command of a brigade. So the good will of Schofield and Cox was no help. After Wagner had handed in his own report on 3 December, the testimony of his brigade commanders was in opposition.

Already on 3 December, Colonel Fullerton wrote in the daily record of the 4th Army Corps: "Brigadier-General Elliot has been given command of the Second Division of this corps and takes command of it today, and General Wagner will continue to command his earlier brigade. (The 2nd Brigade of the 2nd Division.) This was the brigade that Lane had commanded during the battle of Franklin.

That General Wagner was outraged at this demotion is easier to understand than to describe, and it moved him to voluntarily renounce any command in the Cumberland Army. For that reason a paragraph appeared in the daily orders of the army that reads somewhat as: Brigadier-General George W. Wagner is, by his own wish and will, relieved from further service with the Cumberland Army and will return to Indianapolis, Indiana, from where he will offer his services for further duty by letter to the Adjutant-General of the United States in Washington.

Further investigation shows that General Wagner's report, in which he states that he gave his brigade commanders timely orders to retreat, did not represent the facts, so Generals Schofield's and Cox's good will were of no help. We should remember that the order Wagner issued to his subordinates just before the attack, was in agreement with orders from the commanding general of the 4th Army Corps, but the time was too short in which to correct the wrong that had been made. General Thomas was therefore convinced that Wagner could not command a division and the responsibility was too great for him; that is, that his brigade commanders had lost their trust in him.

General L.P. Bradley, who permanently commanded the brigade which Conrad led at Franklin after Bradley had been severely wounded at Spring Hill, told us that General Wagner as division commander had already ordered him at Columbia, where he (Bradley) and his men were also on an outpost picket line, to resist Hood's entire army. Therefore, he had no doubts that Wagner was solely responsible for the catastrophic situation that Conrad and Lane found themselves in at Franklin. Wagner ordered both brigades to stay in their positions after Conrad's staff officer had informed him that Hood's army was already marching to attack. Opdycke held the same difference of opinion with Wagner, whether a picket line dare engage in a fight with an advancing front line, and took responsibility for leading his troops into the reserves regardless of his orders. Bradley had told Wagner before he was wounded, that he would do the same if the enemy was marching forward to attack. When Conrad became Bradley's successor as commander of the brigade, he shared that opinion with his predecessor, for his report leaves us in no doubt about this. Lane's report, which was made after Wagner's demotion, agrees with Conrad in the main point. These statements delivered the evidence which formed the basis of Thomas's dissatisfaction and the reason he lost trust in Wagner.

Another cause for further discussions on both sides was the question, whether the main line to the right (west) of the highway at Carter House had been reached by our troops again during the battle. General Opdycke, whose brigade had moved to the barricade (after Conrad's and Lane's brigades fled over the breastworks and through the drive-through on the highway), claimed that they had reached the front line. But when at sundown, General Cox inspected the positions of the various units to the right of the highway under Strickland and Moore and found that it was still in the possession of the enemy, and it wasn't until he sent the 112th Illinois under Colonel Bond, and the 72nd Illinois and 101 Illinois that belonged to Kimball's division forward, and with help from cross-fire from Reilly's division from the cotton-gin, had Strickland's line been cleared of the enemy. The buildings of the Carter Plantation as well as the powder smoke, restricted a clear view, and so it couldn't be determined from the highway, whether the line was in our hands again. Strickland's assurances had led Cox to believe that the former was in possession of the front line again and this was in part correct, for his right, the 72nd Illinois Regiment, touched Moore's brigade which was still in the front line, but the distance between the two lines was very small in relationship to its length. After the battle in Nashville in December, when we marched through the area again, we had the opportunity to look at the battlefield again and we could hardly tell where the second line had been because the fence posts and rails that had provided the structure for the breastworks had been used by the troops as firewood, but the barricade of the 44th Missouri Regiment, which had formed a large part of the second line, was still there. If we compare our opinion with information from Mr. Carter, the owner of the plantation who carried away the barricade, we get to the truth. In spite of that, there are still many intelligent officers and soldiers who insist that through the actions in the center and on the right, the front line of the barricade had been reached again, just as had been the case to the left.

General Opdycke, as were the others, thought this too, also the officers of the 183rd Ohio Regiment, which made up part of Strickland's brigade, couldn't remember a second line and still thought that the line that Strickland's brigade had established, and which they held fast to until midnight, was the only line between them and the enemy. It is not possible to find better evidence. In spite of this, the statements that the enemy held the trench and the outside of the barricade near the locust grove sound so true that we, in order to solve the problem, have to rely on more truthful witnesses. The claims of Col. Opdycke can certainly be explained. His reserves were in a low area more than 200 yards behind the Carter House. Because of the buildings, the hill and the trees, he couldn't see the barricades that our people had possession of. and so, as he led his brigade forward and drove the enemy back that had taken the barricade, he was completely convinced that this was the first barricade that we had built for our protection. This retrenchment stood in a straight line with the buildings of the Carter Plantation, and to the west of these were the enclosures for six guns of the 20th Ohio Battery, and further west were the barricades of the 44th Missouri Regiment. These houses and lines were in possession of the enemy, which from here sent heavy fire until Opdycke's forces advanced on both sides of the Carter House. One couldn't see anything of the barricades from the highway, even if the weather had been clear and the air clean. As a result, the second line had the appearance of being the first and only line. Opdycke mentions in his report, the recapture of the battery, which he believed to be in the first line. The continuously repeated attacks didn't give him any opportunity to investigate further, for the continuation of the heavy fighting until deep in the night in trying to hold on to the earth-works prevented him from making any further observations. The trace of bullets still found on the outside of the buildings is evidence that they came from the outside of the line. The statements of the officers of the 183rd Ohio Regiment that advanced from the reserves and then were involved in the hardest fighting of all are based on not being able to see the line through the powder smoke. When they were informed of the front line later, they had been very surprised, but there is never a battle where differences of opinion aren't common. In the chaos of the battle very little notice is taken of things, even of those that take place in front of their eyes. But Captain Bates, who belonged to Opdycke's brigade, told us that he was ordered to strengthen the second barricade and this is corroborated on the map made by General Schofield's chief engineer, Major Twining. The presence of a second line cannot be denied.

Another topic that is often discussed in gatherings of former officers and soldiers is the question, where Wagner's two brigades went during the battle after they were forced back. The flight back has been described earlier, how they arrived at the city along the highway, and that many stayed at the defense line until the fighting ended. Most likely this question would never have come up if Wagner hadn't claimed in his report that both brigades and he himself were in the line until the end and until the brigades under Reilly and Strickland, which had been pushed back, had recovered their position. It was natural that Wagner would want to put his error in as positive a light as possible, but putting the blame on his comrades for the collapse was unjust. Had Wagner's troops been pulled back early enough, as Opdycke's had been, no one in Reilly's as well as in Strickland's brigades would have been pushed back. The claim that Wagner himself, as well as his brigade commanders, stayed in the line during the battle has not been proven and wouldn't have been necessary anyway after the brigades had retreated. No one disputes or doubts that Opdycke's brigade was in the line and in the right place, and that Wagner should have been in place with Opdycke, Conrad with Reilly and Lane with Strickland, but nowhere do we find evidence that they were there, and all three should have turned to Stanley for further orders as long as he was in the line, since he was Corps commander and had reached the battlefield right after the two brigades had fled through the front line. The number of Wagner's men, not counting Opdycke's, that stayed in the front line is uncertain, but even the liberal observers said that it was not over 800 men. Among these were several line officers, but field officers had not been seen. But we have been told that those from Conrad's and Lane's brigades were among the most courageous of the brave that fought with the others in the front line. That the brigades reorganized near the river has not been reported, is however the truth. That not all stayed in the line cannot be held against either Wagner, or Conrad or Lane.

The battle was hardly over when "honor-hacking" started, and the main storm was aimed at Schofield. In the front line the attack was made at General Cox for claiming in his report to be the commander of the battle line. Stanley disputed this and said he would have had to be relieved first before Cox would have had sole command of the line. But General Stanley was in conference with Schofield on the north side of the Harpeth river when the battle began and hurried as fast as he could, but was hardly at the line more than 20 minutes when he was wounded and his horse shot dead and Cox was again the highest in command. General Schofield had often been criticized for his retreat and hair-breadth escape at Springhill, and this still happens, perhaps because certain circles would rather have the victory at Franklin attributed to the 4th Army Corps and General Thomas, who wasn't even there. But General Grant and Sherman have given Cox and Schofield full justice in the Battle of Franklin and their verdict cannot be disputed.

The Battle of Nashville under the Personal Command of General Thomas against Hood.

Gathering the Troops

Schofield's army reached Nashville after marching 20 miles without any significant delay on the morning of 1 December. The last (Wood's) division of the 4th Army didn't move into their assigned positions until late in the afternoon. Now the troops that Schofield had until then commanded became part of the army that General Thomas had gathered in Nashville. General A. J. Smith reached Nashville with his unit of the 16th Army Corps after many misfortunes and unexpected delays. It was made up of three divisions with about 12,000 men. Of these, about 9,000 arrived in Nashville on the morning of 30 November and the rest on the next morning and evening, 1 December.

Since the position of our army at Franklin was not the choice of Schofield or of General Thomas, and General Hood wasn't thinking of an attack until he noticed the great advantages for himself there (for no general would choose a battlefield with a deep river behind his back). It was intended that Schofield's army would pull back to Brentwood and for all the reserve troops under General Smith and Steadman to be moved forward to that point. After further consideration however, Thomas decided to unite the forces at Nashville. The cause was likely the report from Schofield and Wilson about the actions of Forrest's cavalry, which were moving eastward. Because Schofield hadn't seen our cavalry since crossing the Duck River at Columbia, he knew little about the movement of these troops under Wilson. For Wilson was too far away from Schofield and Forrest tried very hard to keep them that way. Wilson kept Schofield informed however, of every movement of the enemy, as well as was possible under the circumstances.

General Thomas sent commands to General Steadman in Chattanooga to leave a garrison there and to withdraw with the rest of his troops to Cowan, a railroad station near the Elk River on the Chattanooga & Nashville Railroad Line. On the morning of 30 November, Steadman arrived at the place and put his troops into position. But when Thomas heard about the attack on Schofield at Franklin in the evening of that day, he ordered Steadman to move his troops to Nashville as soon as possible. Steadman's troops were put on the train right away and most of the trains reached Nashville on the evening of 1 December. One train was held up by derailment. The troops on that train were attacked by Forrest with superior forces about 5 miles from Nashville, but the unit fought its way through and reached Nashville on the evening of 2 December. The abandoned train was taken by the enemy and burned. Of the 8,000 troops that Steadman had in Chattanooga, he brought 5,200 along with him to Nashville. Among these were two "colored" brigades and one unit of Sherman's troops that arrived in Chattanooga too late to join his great army and its own regiments on the march.

The majority of troops under General Granger in northern Alabama and under Milroy in Tullahoma were ordered to gather in Murfreesboro. About 8,000 men, all under Rousseau, were left in Murfreesboro as occupation forces until Hood's defeat on 15 and 16 December. The blockhouse garrison at the important Chattanooga Railroad bridge over the Elk River between Murfreesboro and Stevenson was the only important unit remaining on the railroad line. In Nashville, besides Smith's corps of 6,000 infantry and artillery and 3,000 dismounted cavalry, Thomas also received the new regiments which now streamed there in mass, and all were fitted into the old divisions, plus an uncountable number of recovered wounded, which for the most part came from Sherman's army. These were formed into a division of 5,000 men under General Crust, which were also available to Thomas.

In a short time, the commanding officer had almost 30,000 more troops in Nashville than Schofield in Franklin, and why at least a third of those forces weren't sent to help Schofield on the 30th must have its reason...that it was no Blücher or Moltke or Sheridan that was in command in Nashville. The distance from Nashville to Franklin is no further than from Franklin to Nashville, which we, exhausted after annihilating Hood at Franklin, had to march.

Col. Donaldson, the chief of the Quartermaster Department, organized his workers, also a defensive division, which served as occupation forces during battles in various forts and communication trenches. Although these workers didn't show any particular wish to take part in a battle, they were familiar enough with a weapon to be of use.

As General Schofield said, his meeting with General Thomas in Nashville was not the friendliest. Schofield of course greeted Thomas as soon as they met. Thomas congratulated Schofield on his success at holding Hood back. Schofield behaved rather coolly however, and as soon as his division commanders had been assigned their positions, he withdrew to a hotel in the city and lay down to rest and wasn't completely refreshed until the evening of 2 December.

That Schofield wasn't in the best of moods can be understood, for the danger that he was exposed to was too great. Had the battle not gone well, he alone would have had to carry the blame because the army was under his personal command and not General Thomas's. Schofield wasn't supported as best he should have been. We saw that in the missing pontoon-bridge at Franklin. It was only through his tactful, personal intervention, that the campaign was a success. But General Thomas acknowledged Schofield's valuable services in full measure, for in his endorsement of Schofield's report about the Battle of Franklin, he expressed himself with much praise and gratitude. The troops that could have come to our aid in Columbia or Franklin were those under Steadman and Rousseau. But Thomas kept Steadman on the Nashville & Chattanooga Railroad, in order to better keep an eye on Breckenridge's in-roads into East Tennessee; somewhat longer than expected but necessary. Thomas also expected that Hood would march past our army, in order to get to Louisville without having to fight a battle. But because Hood had a much larger force, he attacked us and the result was..."The Battle of Franklin"

On 1 December, as soon as all the troops were assembled in Nashville, General A. J. Smith received command of the right wing of our line, from the Hardin Pike to the Cumberland River.

The 4th Army Corps had the center, from Granny White Pike to Smith's left wing. Schofield's corps reached from the Nolensville Pike to the Granny White Pike. The cavalry covered our left wing to the river above the city. Steadman's Negro Corps were sent forward about a mile on our left flank to Montgomery Hill. Steadman's corps didn't reach Nashville until the evening of 2 December. A few days later, Wilson's cavalry was moved to the north side of the river at Edgefield. On the morning of 3 December, Hood's troops showed up on the Franklin Pike and moved forward to within 600 paces of our front line. If we are to believe Hood's own reports, he was leading about 44,000 men in all weapon categories to Nashville. His intelligence service furnished him with complete details of the gathering of all troops under General Thomas in Nashville. What moved him to come to Nashville is worth looking into further.

General Beauregard said in his provisional report to the Southern War Department: "It is perfectly clear to me, that after the terrible loss of life in the battle of Franklin, the army under Hood was no longer capable of making a successful attack on Nashville." Hood's own testimony would perhaps have carried more weight if his later writings hadn't shown clear evident of an attempt to make an excuse in order to cover up his mistakes. He said he wanted to hunker down at Nashville until the expected reserve troops from Texas would reach him, and he had hoped to defend himself until Taylor's troops from the Gulf States were with him. And it wouldn't have been impossible to have defeated Thomas if Thomas had attacked him. But waiting for help from Texas was all for nothing, since an organized troop of Southerners had not crossed the Mississippi for quite a long time. On the other hand we learn that Hood completely depended on enlisting new recruits in Tennessee and since Governor Harris had come back with him, he tried to get the conscription laws of the Southern States passed in Tennessee. This and the stocking of foodstuffs give us reasonable evidence that Hood wanted to cover as much terrain as possible. At the same time he wanted to show the world that he had not been defeated in Franklin but was still capable of making an advance. Perhaps he also believed that, even if his veterans were forced to retreat, that in the next fights he wouldn't be beaten and annihilated.

But he underestimated how discouraged his troops were, which was now fermenting in them after the terrible lesson they had received at Franklin. Also they now knew how hopeless the dreams of victory were, with which their leaders had tried to enthuse them when they crossed the Tennessee River. Hood also said that he had learned that Schofield's army had retreated in complete disorder and panic, but never was he in greater error than there. Schofield's officers from the line at Franklin reported that they were completely capable of holding the line, until the reserve troops from Nashville could reach us, and that the withdrawal over the Harpeth River had been made because it was expected that Forrest and his cavalry would advance toward Nashville behind us to disrupt our connection there.

The truth was that Hood's situation was dangerous, marching forward and well as backwards. For that reason he followed his natural instinct, which was always to advance, and so he followed Schofield's army to Nashville. Having arrived there, he positioned Lee's corps in the center over the Franklin Turnpike; these had suffered least in the last battles and were now his strongest corps. Cheatham's corps was set up to the right and Stewart's got the left end of the line, while Forrest's cavalry took charge of the area from Steward to the river below Nashville. Hood made efforts to get the railroad from Corinth to Decatur into working condition again and then over Pulaski to his line. Hood said the he had a few locomotives and cars which he wanted to use for transporting supplies. But he wasn't given enough time to make much valuable use of them because his railroad corps wasn't nearly as well-organized as Sherman's. The Southerners didn't have enough means with which to keep the railroad in working order. General Wilson and his cavalry already had a strong position at Thompson's Chapel on the Nolensville Turnpike, with which he covered the stretch between Schofield's left and the Cumberland River.

General Hood still had great superiority in his cavalry which he, as General Thomas thought, would make use of to separate the Union army from the North. In order to prevent that,

Gen. Hammond's brigade of Wilson's cavalry was sent to Gallatin on the 2nd of the month, in order to cover the river to Carthage. On the next day, the other three regiments were taken over the river to Edgefield and General Steadman's commando was pulled back to cover Thomas's left wing to the river.

When we arrived in Nashville, our division was put in the battle-line on the Franklin Turnpike. Our battery found a place alongside a blockhouse. The usual breastworks hadn't been built yet, and as already mentioned, men and animals rested here from the terrible toils of the last three weeks. At about 10 o'clock in the evening, a provost guard appeared with a pile of people of all classes along with tools, a number of black women and men among them, to start working on the barricades.

A comrade told me how he had gathered the colorful company together. He said: "We belonged to Sherman's army and were on vacation. However, since Sherman was already long gone, we were held back in Nashville and had to serve as provost guards. On the evening after the battle at Franklin, when Schofield's army reached Nashville, I was sent out with a unit to round up workers for the breastwork. I made my way to "Smoky Lane", a quarter of the city where the blacks like to go. Here there was one dive after the other where whites were the owners who liked to rob the blacks that worked on the levee of their money in the evening. A banjo and a fiddle provided the gruesome dance music; buxom lasses, as black as ebony with their dark lovers, jumped around doing the hop-waltz or stamped around wildly, faces full of sweat. In other shacks there was gambling and all tables were occupied. I was supposed to look for workers to throw up the breastworks. Here, he said, I found what I was looking for. Naturally, my appearance made some cautious and many, suspecting nothing good, tried to slip away in order not to have to provide information where they had come from. I told them what I wanted and it was impossible to get away, and without allowing any resistance I had them all line up and brought the whole group to the line near the blockhouse. Here all of them, black and white, had to work on the barricade until dawn." None of the "freedmen" of both sexes had expected to be led from the dancehall to working on the barricades.

The enemy arrived in Nashville on 3 December and made their appearance immediately apparent by forcing back our outpost pickets and establishing their own line for defense or attack. By the next morning, Hood already had a fairly good earth-work established with a 10 foot deep trench and a wall almost 20 feet thick. In front of the trench were felled trees in a tangle somewhat resembling an abatis, so that an attack on the hill would already have been quite difficult. Hood's line spread to a hill southeast of Brown's Creek about 600 yards from our front line and reached then from the Nolensville Pike, over the Franklin and Granny White Pike, then in a south-westerly direction toward Richland Creek and along the creek to the Hillsboro Pike. On the right; from Nolensville Road to the river above the city, and on the left, from the Hillsboro Road to the river below the city, his cavalry was deployed. Paying no attention to our artillery fire aimed at him from various batteries in our line, he strengthened his line but didn't return fire. It was very necessary to him to be sparing with his ammunition, it being very difficult for him to be resupplied with further provisions from his base at Corinth.

General George H. Thomas, supreme commander of the Federal Army during the Battle of Nashville. 15 -16 December, 1864

Defending the Railroad

Although Hood remained quiet at Nashville, he was quite active in the area of Murfreesboro. He sent Bate's division of Cheatham's corps to capture Murfreesboro and to destroy the railroad and especially to burn down the blockhouses. His attack completely failed. Milroy attacked him with three regiments of infantry, four companies of cavalry and two artillery guns and Bate was driven back. During the 5th, 6th and 7th of December, Bate received support troops and advanced on Fort Rosecrans near Murfreesboro which had been occupied by 8,000 of our troops under General Rousseau. Since the enemy didn't want to attack, Milroy attacked him on the 8th with seven regiments of infantry. Milroy took 207 prisoners, captured two artillery guns, but lost 30 dead and 175 wounded. On the same day, Buford's enemy cavalry galloped into Murfreesboro, but was chased out again right away. After that, Murfreesboro was no longer attacked by the enemy. In spite of that, the government kept a strong garrison there which wasn't disbanded until the complete collapse of the rebels. Bate and Forrest now moved downriver along the Cumberland River. The former still tried to destroy the railroad and the blockhouses and Forrest tried to cross the Cumberland in order to reach the Louisville & Nashville Railroad.

Sherman's army in 1864 was the only large army during the Civil War that completely depended for its support on the railroad. They had provision warehouses and depots along the tracks and their battles were centered at those points of the railroad that were controlled by the enemy. These were points which had become important through the building of the railroads, and brought a complete change to the mode of transportation that had been used since the Napoleonic wars. Students in the war colleges had always studied those reports but now it was the job of the commanders to change all that. It hadn't been possible for any other army to move through enemy territory and to transport and protect their provisions in this modern way. But if the water level in the Cumberland and Tennessee Rivers permitted it, these waterways were also used.

South of Nashville, the only means of connection was the railroad. When the army camped at Chattanooga, they had to rely on a single track to Nashville which was 151 miles long. When the three armies, Ohio, Cumberland and Tennessee, advanced on Atlanta, the iron "ribbon" to Louisville extended 473 miles (about as far from Paris to Hannover). Almost the entire length of which was through enemy territory. The success of the campaigns depended entirely on guarding and maintaining the railroad. The destruction of a single bridge by a cavalry charge or by angry residents in the district could have disastrous consequences for the Union efforts on the front and the destruction of several bridges could mean that a retreat would be necessary. It was of utmost importance that the railroad be held under all circumstances, and a defense system that only required a few people at any spot was established, otherwise the advancing army would soon have been reduced so significantly that it wouldn't have been strong enough to attack.

During the long periods of inactivity of the army under Rosecrans at Murfreesboro, a distance of 30 miles from Nashville, stockades in the form of Greek crosses were built for the defense of seven bridges. These stockades were blockhouses in every way except that they had no roofs. During the advance of the army from Tullahoma to Chattanooga, a unit of men was stationed at every bridge, but this couldn't be considered systematic cover. The army was too overburdened to hold their positions east of the Cumberland Mountains. One didn't want to spend time continuously guarding the already captured stretches, for when the army under Rosecrans reached Chattanooga, it was already necessary to guard the 600 mile long stretch of the East-Tennessee Railroad to Knoxville, every foot of which was in enemy territory and subject to the dangers of war, not just from regular roving raiders but also from bands of guerillas or even from pro-enemy citizens.

Usually the bridges were built in places where the river banks were very steep on both sides, which made it very difficult to build the blockhouses to protect the bridges. To be safe here, protection for their heads had to be very strong. The natural result was that the garrisons were made as small as possible, although large enough to guard the bridge. The strong stockades that had been built until '64 were now replaced by blockhouses. There were three classes of these; the rectangular, octagonal and artillery-blockhouses, the first two were built with towers and the artillery blockhouse was provided with an upper story.

Most of the small bridges just had one blockhouse and the larger ones had two, one on each side of the river. Occasionally there were four and at Bridgeport even two blockhouses for artillery were built. The building of these blockhouses became the task of the Michigan Engineers, who designed and built them to their honor. The plan and idea for an artillery blockhouse was first copied by our engineers from a half-finished fort that our enemy had built around Strawberry Plains in East Tennessee upriver from Knoxville in the winter of '63 – '64. An artillery blockhouse is expensive and difficult to build and hence can only be justified in exceptional cases. Bridgeport, Ala. was evidently suited for that sort of defensive structure.

Since the survival of the army depended on both bridges over the Tennessee River, artillery was required on the island as well as on the mainland and the guns could only hold their positions if they had cover. The enemy quickly noticed that our blockhouses were safe from normal attacks and little units left the defenders in peace. But damage to the tracks could also be quickly repaired if that took place. The only significant disturbances of blockhouses were as follows:

In August of 1864, then Rebel General Wheeler marched northward with a cavalry division to Knoxville, then west to Nashville and southwest to northern Alabama. Throughout that raid, he swept over a large portion of the railroad from Atlanta to Chattanooga, tearing the tracks up in several places, but not destroying any bridges and also not attacking any blockhouses. He reached the Nashville & Chattanooga Line between Nashville and Murfreesboro and stormed Blockhouse No. 5. Lieutenant John S. Orr of the 115th Ohio was in command. The enemy artillery wounded about a third of the garrison (of about 30 men). But the brave lieutenant didn't surrender and the bridge was not destroyed or damaged. A smaller blockhouse in the area was defended by a sergeant who lost his head after a little bit of resistance and surrendered. His bridge was burned, but otherwise no other bridge on the line was destroyed and also none on the railroad to Decatur.

In October 1864, Hood marched north of Atlanta and Sherman followed him. All blockhouses south of Dalton were abandoned and burned on Sherman's orders, only the one at Altoona was captured by the enemy. After Hood had captured Dalton, he wanted to march west through the Buzzard Roost Gap, but in that "gap" at the bridge crossing Mill Creek, there was a blockhouse with a 30-man garrison. This blockhouse guarded the road through the gap and no wagon or artillery could get through here unless the blockhouse was captured.

Bate's infantry division with three artillery batteries from Hood's army were ordered to take the little fortress. The infantry fired away uselessly and the artillery, after they were driven away from several positions, limited their fire to one corner. The weight of the shots made holes in the blockhouse but the garrison didn't surrender. During the night, an enemy column was organized to storm the blockhouse and covered the gun openings. They then climbed on the roof and from there tried to fire down on the defenders. At daybreak, an attack column also went at it. But in order to prevent further bloodshed, the commanding officer of the attackers called down to the defenders to surrender. A white handkerchief was the answer and the garrison surrendered. Half of the garrison was either dead or wounded and General Bate was full of praise for these brave "defenders of the fatherland". Hood himself said that he and the rest of his army would have had to march another 20 miles to get around them.

This is the place to point out that blockhouses and their garrisons are not intended to defend themselves against complete columns, only against cavalry raiders which rarely have any artillery with them. The most important destruction of blockhouses happened probably in September 1864 through Forrest on the railroad line from Nashville to Decatur. This indefatigable cavalry general gives the following report:

The first blockhouse that I attacked, he said, was not quite finished and stood on the south side of that railroad. The first ball crashed through the place and wounded many of the defenders. They surrendered and the house was burned. At the next, he pointed out the prisoners from the first one, which convinced the defenders that blockhouses could be captured. In this way he convinced many to surrender and was able to destroy the bridges without loss of life. But he said, a German captain in one of the blockhouses refused to surrender. Forrest had several bottles of "Greek fire" along and some of his men approached the bridge behind the railroad bed and smashed the bottles on the wooden timbers of the bridge and set it on fire. The bridge burned down but the German captain held his blockhouse and didn't surrender. Forrest destroyed eleven blockhouses on this raid.

When Hood's army advanced to Nashville, the blockhouses were unwisely abandoned and destroyed by our troops because the Nashville-Decatur Railroad wasn't our main line and the loss of the bridges was unimportant. From the time that blockhouses were first built, to the end of the war, only six bridges were burned down. These six were near Nashville, and two were destroyed during General Wheeler's time and were rebuilt. The 7th blockhouse at Overalls Creek was held and the garrison consisted of 30 men under Lieutenant Glosser of the 115th Ohio Infantry Regiment.

Bate's enemy infantry division maneuvered here for more than a week, as he said, against his advice and will, for he already had that bitter experience at Buzzard's Roost, that there was little that could be done against a well-defended blockhouse. Bate's artillery fired 73 shots at the Overall blockhouse from 12 pounder cannons without breaking in. A sortie from Murfreesboro brought the garrison food and ammunition. The blockhouse was not captured and the bridge wasn't burned down.

The Atlanta campaign would have been completely impossible without the blockhouses, for usage of the railroad from Louisville to Nashville (185 miles), from Nashville to Chattanooga (151 miles), Chattanooga to Atlanta (137 miles)...the whole stretch a single track...was so minimal that one man would have been able to loosen a rail in one minute. But every train usually had the tools and materials along with which to repair such breaks. A strong guard had to watch every bridge, because rebuilding them took time, but a small infantry unit was sufficient for adequate protection. As my son Albert reported, after his return from

Manila where he served in the regular artillery for 14 months (1898 – 1899), that the Spaniards in 1896 or earlier had surrounded Manila with 16 blockhouses, not to protect bridges, but to defend themselves from the insurgents. When the United States took possession of Manila, they armed the blockhouses with Gatling cannons and Colt rapid-fire guns. So, we see that the Europeans have found our blockhouses to be worthy of copying and using in defense-lines.

The Army under Thomas

After Atlanta was captured, those officers that were politicians, such as General Logan, General Blair and General Benj. Harrison, were sent north on vacation to work on their political campaigns. The campaign of 1864 didn't show much success for the Union side until Atlanta was taken. After Atlanta came the astonishing victories under Sheridan at Winchester. But like lightning out of a clear sky, Hood's army was standing at Nashville. Acknowledging the Union victory in Franklin and then retreating; such a thing couldn't be and the people couldn't accept it. At the same time, General Thomas requested 30-day troops from the governors of Illinois, Indiana and Ohio. General Grant ordered Thomas to attack Hood immediately and drive him out of the state. But large bodies move slowly and Thomas was one of those who move slowly but surely.

Among those that belonged to Sherman's army but weren't in place soon enough, was General Benjamin Harrison, who later became president. He received command of half a brigade, and according to his report, it must have been a pretty company. But we can get an impression of how anxious the Northerners were about the steadfastness of our army, if they sent such inexperienced troops into the field, as he describes them to be. We follow with Harrison's report: He said, his brigade was made up of three battalions, each of which was part of a similar division of the 20th Army Corps. A significant, large portion of this brigade wasn't even fit for duty; many still suffered from wounds that they had received in the Atlanta Campaign, others had just gotten out of the hospital and were still recovering from grave illnesses, while the largest portion was made up of new recruits that didn't have the least training in weapons or service on the battlefield and weren't at all used to the strains of war. The recruits also represented almost every European nation and most of them couldn't speak a word of English and so couldn't understand our language at all. (So far Harrison.)

With white troops one could manage, but what could be done with the blacks that had been gathered here in Nashville, and here served as substitutes for the citizens of Indiana and Illinois that had been drafted through the conscription laws? One doesn't wonder that General Thomas hesitated to attack with such forces, and waited until he had enough white troops to ensure a victory.

Since the newly organized black regiments were being led into battle for the first time, on the 5th General Steedman asked permission to lead them on his left flank into battle. Our battery was ordered to support them from our position. At about 2 p.m. the brigade under the command of Colonel T. J. Morgan then also advanced. A white regiment, the 68th Indiana and the 6th Indiana Cavalry, also white, accompanied the "Freedmen" to discover the enemy positions. The enemy naturally pulled back behind its barricades and our troops, after they had reached them, did the same. The same action was repeated again on the 7th. The 14th Negro Regiment was under the command of Col. Corbin; later the Adjutant-General of the United States Army. The 17th Negro Regiment was commanded by Col. Schafter; later a Major General of the U.S. Army, who commanded our army at Santiago in Cuba and defeated the Spanish and forced them to surrender. The Negro brigades suffered losses of several dead and wounded at Nashville, and their perseverance under fire was considered satisfactory. Our, the 15th Indiana Battery, was pulled back from the front line on the 8th and took quarters near the stone walls of Fort Morton. Our horses, which had suffered much during the campaign, were handed over to the quarter-master and in their place we received brand new teams of excellent, heavy artillery horses, which also meant the prospect of further battlefield service in the near future. Right away we received orders to have them shod with sharp shoes by the regimental blacksmith. The government had brought a large number of northern farriers to Nashville and the 110 horses were quickly shod, so we were soon ready to go on commando again. The men were given the opportunity to visit the city in groups, where they, like most soldiers, likely amused themselves with gambling. The same took place in camp; and with an energy that should rather have been spent on something more worthwhile. One of our men, Gunner S......., came one evening into camp depressed. When asked what was wrong, he said had lost all his money and what angered him most was that a black man had taken it from him in "Chuck Luck". Every veteran most likely knows what "Chuck Luck" is, so it is unnecessary to describe it.

Naturally the loss was painful for S.... and he quietly planned revenge. He came up with a plan and with that went back to his opponent, who was still playing. At first the black didn't want to have anything to do with the new plan, but he finally tried it. Our dear S..... won his own loss back and more besides. Just how S.....talked the black into playing this game doesn't appear in the diary that I got this story from, but the honest face of S.... had much to do with it. In 15 minutes the black was a poorer but wiser man.

In Nashville plays were given in the theaters, whereby the actors were mostly members of the army. One of our gunners wanted get in with a free pass. At home he had been a print-setter or newspaper man. "I", said B...., "belong to the press and am writing a report." But the ticket taker hadn't heard about the value of the press yet, and with a soft voice but serious demeanor told our newspaper man to get out now and buy himself a ticket. But since he decided to insist on it, the doorman (also a soldier) took him by the collar and made room for others. There wasn't anything else for him to do than to buy a ticket, but he didn't think it was worth his money, for it was only a "Negro-show". Another group of our men often visited the State Capitol, where Governor Johnson, the newly elected vice-president and later president, governed. The city and the hotel were overfilled with contractors of all kinds, as well as masses of buyers for cotton, horse-dealers and spies. The number of Tennesseans that were pro-Union "for the way it used to be" was quite large and usually they were from the better class of citizens, which however, still believed that the South would win. (It was very difficult, even after Gen. Johnson's surrender in North Carolina, to convince the Southern citizens that their cause had been lost.) Among the strangers that made Nashville dangerous then, were a number of recruiters which looked for substitutes for mostly wealthy businessmen in the north, since with the retreat to Nashville, a mass of slaves had gathered there. Usually a recruiter paid about 100 Dollars to the "Freedman" for which he received 1000 or 1500 Dollars from the buyer of the substitute if the draftee was freed. However, since the provost-marshal often sent patrols out to round up workers for the breastworks, the non-combatants would disappear as soon as possible

General Grant was very dissatisfied that Thomas hadn't sent any reserve troops to Franklin, which he should have done in order to end the fight there. Now that the army was at Nashville, General Grant was even more uneasy and the telegraph line between City Point and Nashville was in use by him daily in order to move Thomas into action while the weather was still good, hoping at the same time to prevent Hood from any further movement toward Kentucky. On the 9th, a portion of Forrest's cavalry under Lyon had already crossed over the Cumberland River above Clarksville intending to break up the Louisville-Nashville Railroad. But Thomas wouldn't be pushed. Wilson's cavalry got new horses and his forces were greatly strengthened. Lieutenant-Commander Fitch patrolled the Cumberland above and below the city with cannon-boats. With the freshly arrived horses and mules, the transportation for every army corps was quickly completely restored. While this all took place, the Union people in the north were getting extremely anxious and the "Copperheads", the last supporters of the rebels, rejoiced loudly over our sad situation in Nashville. From spies spread throughout the north, the rebels were well informed about any sympathy. General Grant was so outraged by Thomas' slow progress, that he convinced the president to issue the order that General Thomas be relieved and supreme command be given to General Schofield. General Thomas couldn't resist this order but General Schofield supported Thomas and after the first petition the order was repealed for a few days. Although the order to relieve Thomas still hung over his head and the prospect that his whole life's work would be for nothing, he still didn't stop for a minute in continuing his preparations.

Not for an hour was he idle by day or night. No one, not even his most trusted officers on his staff, knew the contents of the telegraphed dispatches from General Grant and from Washington. But outwardly it showed that something was bothering him terribly. While the weather stormed and ice and snow covered the roads and fields, he would often sit for hours at the window without saying a word, and gazed fixedly out as if he was trying to calm the storm. But during these dark days, his time was taken up by other things that weren't exactly military; so we were told by his officers. First he was visited by a delegation from the city, to ask him about municipal business; then from a citizen whose horse had been taken for the cavalry; then a committee of citizens begging for wood for poor families that were freezing; and in the evening Governor Johnson, the newly elected vice-president, visited him somewhat excited, who wanted to tell him of his opinions about secession, rebellion and reconstruction. He often impressed Governor Johnson with his knowledge about constitutional questions, but through all of this it was General Grant's dissatisfaction that was always on his mind, and that he could only regain his trust through a victorious battle.

During the rest in the last week, several changes were made in the 23rd Corps. Shortly after arriving in Nashville, General Ruger, who was unfit for service due to illness and wounds, but mostly from anger at Franklin, asked for vacation. In his place, General Darius Couch from the Eastern Army was sent to us. Couch was a very educated West Point graduate and although he had been suggested as successor to Hoofer in 1863 to command the Potomac Army, and in 1862 had served in the high position as Corps Commander, he was not accepted in a friendly way by our officers and men. The good man tried very hard to make himself liked, but it didn't work. He was the commander of the 2nd Division of the 23rd Army Corps. Everything "spit and polished" had long ago disappeared from this division through all the battles it had been in and we were no longer "parade" soldiers. The raw, intense earnestness of the western soldier to oppose the enemy near and far soon shone from our faces, in order to decide the question "Union" or "Not Union". Since the 3rd Division of our corps had two rifle-batteries and the 2nd none of such guns, we, the 15th Indiana Battery was transferred now to the 2nd Division. In our place, the 3rd received a smooth battery, the 23rd Indiana. A short time after our transfer, we were inspected by Couch's Inspector-General, which went smoothly, except that our teamsters didn't have any sabers and the gunners no revolvers; the whole company didn't have any side-arms, whereat we indicated that we ourselves never carried a saber except in parade. He thought that wasn't very military. Finally we convinced him that if our men had been carrying side-arms at Franklin, they probably would have abandoned the guns and fought with pistols.

During the battle on the 15th and 16th, General Couch became more familiar with the western character of the army and was then full of praise for us. But he never managed to get the affection and trust of his division, for the troops and the officers, after four years of fighting experience, could not be convinced that an officer from the east which had served in the Potomac Army, should ever fill a position in the Western Army, especially after so many good and experienced officers of high rank among us had proved that they could lead a division. Couch remained commander of the division until we captured Wilmington, North Carolina, and was then relieved of service at his own request.

Since General Stanley had been wounded at Franklin, on arrival in Nashville he was put on leave and General Wood, the senior division commander, became the commander of the 4th Army Corps in his place.

General Wagner was ordered to resume command of his former brigade on 3 December, which had been commanded by Lane at Franklin, and General Elliot, who was cavalry chief on General Thomas's staff during the Atlanta campaign, took over the command of Wagner's division. The demotion of Wagner caused him to depart and separate himself from the Cumberland Army, which was granted him. He was ordered to return to Indianapolis and from there to report to the Adjutant-General of the army in Washington for further duties. Wagner had gone through very hard battles from 1861 to Franklin and beneath his rough exterior beat a faithful soldier heart. Had all gone well at Franklin one could have forgiven his conduct there, namely that the main headquarters was more to blame than Wagner himself, which probably, had General Schofield remained in command in Nashville, would have brought him before a war-tribunal, which certainly would have determined the guilt.

General Thomas had intended to attack Hood on the 7th, but Wilson wasn't ready to attack with his cavalry yet. On the 9th he could report that 12,000 of his men were mounted. Wilson immediately was ordered to bring this commando to the south side of the Cumberland River in order to participate in the well-planned skirmish the next day from the Hillsboro and Harding Pike. But ice and snow came when everything was ready and made any move at the time impossible, for neither man nor beast could stand or walk with the whole region covered in several inches of slippery ice. The horses had a terrible time because there wasn't the least shelter against the storm and snow. The men of the battery had no tents but the covers of the guns and caissons offered splendid protection against the weather. By fabricating temporary shelters with open fronts where usually a fire was kept burning, the men of the battery made it bearable for themselves. While some rested, the others stoked the fires, for there was plenty of firewood. For the old veterans it was quite comfortable but for the new recruits and the laborers rounded up by the quarter-master-department under General Donaldson that now had to spend the nights at the barricades, it was a bitter experience. These only had a choice between two things: to stay in their camp sites day and night under their blankets to keep warm (which most of them did), or to gather around an often weak fire, the smoke and ashes of which the wind blew into their eyes. So many men crowded around such a fire that many couldn't even feel the warmth. In the crush of people shivering from the frost, the fire and the people usually gave up.

  The only comfort that we had in this unhappy state was that the enemy didn't have it any better. According to their reports, they had to bear much more. It was reported by General Bate that on the day the bad weather started, a full quarter of his men were barefoot and suffered from a terrible lack of clothing. A southern soldier, who at that time served in Stewart's corps and now is a respected citizen of St. Louis told us a short time ago, that after the battle of Franklin, they had pulled off the footwear and overcoats of the fallen Yankees and divided them up amongst themselves, so that their whole army looked like Union soldiers. They had enough food but there was very little firewood, for earlier campaigns of the army in the area had used all the fences, as well as the trees, as fuel. There was very little available now.

  Forrest's appearance with his cavalry below Lyon on the Louisville & Nashville Railroad in the first half of December caused General Grant great anxiety concerning General Thomas's slowness to action and he even expected the same enemy movements as those against Buell in 1862.

Finally on the 11th, a great war-counsel was held at headquarters and the corps commanders were informed of the plan of attack. Grant too was informed that Thomas was ready to attack. But since the ice still didn't allow any movement and even on the 12th nothing happened, General Logan, who was in Washington at the time, was ordered on the 13th to go to Nashville to replace Thomas. General Grant, still impatient, left City Point on the morning of the 15th to go to Nashville personally, but on the 14th the harsh weather finally ended. During the three days, the corps commanders had used the time to study their appointed duties in the coming battle and to discover any possible errors, which then made several changes necessary. At 3 o'clock on the afternoon of the 14th, the corps commanders were again ordered to come to headquarters and the following plan for the next day was determined: Major-General A. J. Smith, who commanded a portion of the 16th Army Corps, after getting his men into a battle line on or near the Harding Pike in front of his present position, would strongly attack the left flank of the enemy across from him. General Wilson, in command of a cavalry corps of three divisions of battle-ready riders, would support General Smith's right flank and try to help him as much as possible to storm the enemy's left, and to pursue them if the opportunity presented itself. General Wilson was also to send a division of cavalry toward the Charlotte Turnpike, to clear that highway of the enemy in order to protect our right flank, and if the enemy line was pushed back, to reunite with the rest of his cavalry. Brigadier-General Wood, the commander of the 4th Army Corps, after establishing a strong picket line from Laurence Hill to his right wing, would advance on the Hillsboro Pike on General Smith's left flank in order to attack the enemy position on Montgomery Hill. General Schofield in command of the 23rd Corps would replace Kimball's division of the 4th Corps at the barricades and with the rest of his corps would support Wood's actions and protect his left flank. General Steedman, in command from the Etowah-District, would take the inner line of his present station, which extended from the reservoir on the Cumberland River to Fort Negley, and hold the rest of his men at the ready in case they would be needed. General Miller, who commanded the Nashville Garrison, would man the inner line from Battery Hill No. 210 to the ford on Hyde Ferry Road.

The troops under General Donaldson were entrusted with the defense of the city as long as the actions against the enemy were taking place. Should the weather allow it, the movement would start at 6 a.m. But a suggestion from General Schofield caused a change in the plan, that Gen. Steedman would make a strong fake attack on the left flank, and that the 23rd corps should first serve as the reserves for Smith's corps. As soon as there was enough room to the right of Smith, Schofield was to strongly attack the left wing of the enemy. We see here again, that Schofield was the leading spirit behind this attack, for Thomas accepted this suggestion and had it carried out. At 4 o'clock a.m. on the 15th, the army was armed to attack the enemy.

First Day of Battle

Brilliant Cavalry charge by Wilson, in which a company of "Plat-Deutscher" boys were covered with laurels by storming a redoubt and turning the captured guns on the enemy. Their cheers were: "Boys, hold fast" and "Boys, let thunder!"

On the evening of 14 December, after the corps commanders were let go, General Halleck was informed through Thomas that the ice was melting and that he should attack the enemy in his position at 5 o'clock early in the morning. Thomas felt somewhat relieved and for the first time in two weeks, his visage was again that of a self-confident man. His movements were quicker and with satisfaction in his eyes he took care of miscellaneous things that a commanding officer usually has to take care of before a battle. He signed several orders, signed various letters, issued his last instructions to his staff officers and then went to bed in order to be in the saddle exactly at 5 o'clock. But it was high time that the weather changed, for when he notified Halleck of his intended action, General Logan was already underway from Washington to Nashville with orders written by General Grant himself to relieve him of duty. Whether Schofield or Logan would have taken command was not determined.

But since Grant had already arrived in Washington from City Point in order to go to Nashville himself, Schofield would have remained in command of all the troops, after he so bravely defended himself from the superior forces of Hood at Columbia, Spring Hill and Franklin. As already mentioned, the official reports show that Grant had telegraphed Thomas, either he attacked or the command would be given to Schofield. The feeling of the Cumberland Army (4th Corps and Steedman's corps) was not friendly toward Schofield. Schofield was still young and only had the rank in the regular army of an artillery-captain and didn't even belong to the Cumberland department, since he commanded not only the 23rd Army Corps but still had to take care of the Department of Ohio. It is certainly because of Schofield's loyalty to him that Thomas wasn't fired, for the responsibility that Schofield bore at Columbia, Springhill and Franklin actually rested on Thomas, and Thomas himself should have been there. But hardly was the victory of the Union troops certain, that they wanted to rob Schofield, Cox and Opdycke of the honor and give it to him who wasn't there. Thomas himself wasn't guilty of that, but his staff officers aren't to be excused.

Early in the morning of the 15 December, the Union Army was up and at 6 o'clock every division and every corps was moving to their assigned positions and stations. The movement was hidden by a dense fog and the ice had been turned by the thaw into foot-deep mush which made movement, as in all winter campaigns, very sluggish. Following the revised plan according to Schofield's idea, Steedman's division, consisting of the black-brigade under Col. Morgan and the white brigade under Lieutenant-Col. Grosvenor, was sent ahead to make a strong demonstration against the right wing of the enemy. General Wood in command of the 4th and General Smith with the 16th Corps, were brought into position pretty much in a straight line from east to west starting at the Hillsboro Pike. To the right of General Smith was the left flank of General Wilson's cavalry corps.

At the same time, the reserve lines from Fort Negley to the Lebanon Turnpike were occupied by the troops under General Miller and protected the city against an attack from the Murfreesboro side. General Crust moved his division forward of the barricades that the 4th and 23rd Corps had just vacated. These troops stretched from Acklin Place to Fort Negley. General Donaldson took over the line from Crust's right wing to the Cumberland River behind General Wilson with the workers in the Quartermaster Department. Schofield's 23rd served first as reserves for Smith's 16th and Wood's 4th corps. The idea was to have both wings of the army advance to the left and right, while Wood's corps would function as the axle of the movement.

If we would take a position on the Acklin Plantation in Wood's line, from where we could overlook the whole Nashville area, we would find our left flank toward the east in the valley of Brown's Creek which flows northeast into the Cumberland River. The source of this little creek is the Brentwood Hills which in our view ends about four miles south. On our right, or a little further, is Richland Creek which also starts in the Brentwood Hills but flows in a northwesterly direction into the Cumberland River. Both creeks have their origin close to each other, but get further apart as they flow northward until they join the Cumberland River about seven miles from each other. Between both creeks, lies the city of Nashville. The Granny White Pike follows the banks of the creek. Southeast of this and about a mile away, running 30 degrees south-east, is the Franklin Pike and in similar distance further east is the Nolensville and Murfreesboro Pike. All go outward from the city. If we turn toward the west at our standpoint, we see the Hillsboro, Hardin and Charlotte Pikes, all leaving the city in the order given. The region is hilly. The hills, reaching an elevation of about 200 feet above the plain, are mostly free standing and not forested.

The enemy line started on the other side of Brown's Creek at the elevation of the Nolensville Pike and the Chattanooga Railroad line and from there to the Franklin Turnpike; it then it crossed the creek, climbed a hill west of it and reached the Hillsboro Pike, where it connected with a stone wall along the turnpike. The isolated earthworks that we will mention later were west of Richland Creek and the line and crowned the hills as independent little forts. The stations of the various enemy troops were the same as mentioned earlier. The main line of the enemy on the left was about a mile away from Wood's line but the enemy sharpshooters were further forward, until they ended in a strong outpost position on Montgomery Hill, which was furnished with very good earthworks for protection.

Somewhat before 9 o'clock, before the sun drove off the fog, Steedman's black division under Morgan and Grosvenor's white division (from our left) made a strong attack against the outer right wing of Hood's forces between the turnpike and the railroad. It was more than just a feint, for the thunder of the cannons and the rattle of rifle-fire didn't only get the attention of the enemy, but also announced to the rest of our army that the decisive battle had begun. The distance that Smith's troops, on our right, had to cover was greater and took longer than expected. It was almost 10 o'clock before an opening was large enough for

Wilson's cavalry to march through. The majority of the riders moved on the Hardin Pike, but Johnson's division moved forward on the Charlotte Pike with the intention of disarming the enemy battery at Bell's Landing on the Cumberland River. Croxton's brigade was between the pikes and Watson's division completed the line connection to Smith's infantry line. Smith moved Garrard's division to his left to connect with the 4th Corps and McArthur's division on his right. At first, Moore's division was in the reserves. On the enemy side, the alert cavalry general Chalmers tried everything he could to oppose Smith and Wilson, but he was overpowered and was driven back step by step.

A half mile southeast of the Hardin Road was the first earthwork of the enemy on a little hill and armed with four guns. Two batteries from McArthur's and another two from Hatch's division opened the fire. After a short period of bombardment, the brigades under McMillen and Hubbard from McArthur's division and Coon's cavalry brigade charged. That resulted in the capture of the first redoubt with four guns and 200 prisoners. Coleman's enemy brigade, which had been supporting Chalmers from the stone wall, was now pulled back by Stewart, and Walthall led these troops to the left of his division on a hill which overlooked the Granny White Pike. This action left the other redoubts to their fate, for Chalmers couldn't hold back Wilson's cavalry. After that swing and the capture of the first redoubt, the 7th Illinois Cavalry Regiment, which belonged to Coon's brigade, stormed the second redoubt, which also had four guns. Company M of this regiment, made up of Low-German speaking boys (from the Illinois Horse Prairie near Red Bud, Illinois) covered themselves with laurels here. As these brave dragoons moved up to the fort, the enemy guns were thundering and flashing against them; but in no time, the Westphalian sons were in the midst of them and the cheer, "Boys hold fast" became fact. After a brief hand-to-hand fight, the guns were in their hands and now these heroes shouted out with ringing voices, "Boys, let thunder!" The captured guns were quickly turned around and they thundered down on the fleeing enemy. But Sergeant Hartman, the flag-bearer, forfeited his life here. As he planted the standard on the breastwork, an enemy ball killed him.

The enemy now fled, but the brave sons of Germany weren't satisfied with the capture of the enemy guns and the fort, but got in the saddle again and pursued the enemy. After a chase of several miles, in which stone walls and fences didn't seem to make a difference, these sons of Hermann the Cherusker and Wittekind were in the midst of the rebels. Now Chalmers' headquarters and personal belongings, along with many prisoners, was their booty. In the chase these riders bypassed a little fort with two guns untouched. Colonel Hill's brigade of McArthur's division of Smith's corps stormed this fort. But this attack, although successful, cost Hill his life. Smith's entire corps now moved to the left and stormed Walthall's outer flank, which was still in possession of portions of the stone wall along the pike.

Let us turn back again to early morning, and we will see how Steedman and his division stormed the enemy on our outer left flank from the Murfreesboro Pike to Riddle's Hill and drove them back and then stormed his earthworks near the Nashville & Chattanooga Railroad. In this attack, the performance of the troops was excellent but they were exposed to such ferocious crossfire that they couldn't defeat them, for the enemy sent reinforcements as quickly as possible. Our troops, after they had carried out the feint-attack well, were pulled back, but around 11 o'clock the attack was renewed somewhat more to the left near the buildings of Rain's Plantation. The troops in this attack were successful and from the protection of the buildings, kept up a steady fire against the enemy until it vacated the field in the dark of night.

Col. Morgan, in his report, rebuked the commander of his regiment, Lieut.-Col. Corbin, for not making a successful attack and had him put before the war tribunal. The court found him innocent and even praised his caution. Col. Grosvenor, who commanded the white brigade in Steedman's division, called his men cowards, because they hadn't taken the enemy position. These troops however were old veterans who were the survivors of many battles that had been thrown together from many melted-down regiments. The fieldworks of the enemy were actually just as strong as those as those at Düppel in Schleswig-Holstein, where the Prussian had to build communication trenches for protection in order to get near the Danes. But here, where our opponents were certainly as courageous as the Danes, they were supposed to storm the works head-on without stopping for the pointed planks that served as an "abatis". Although Gen. Morgan and Gen. Grosvenor commanded brigades here, they proved to be better politicians later, while Corbin, that they put before the war-court, proved to be the best of the three as a soldier, and later became the Adjutant-General with the rank of a Major-General in the American Army.

General Wood, in command of the 4th Corps, moved then to the right of Steedman with Elliott's division (formerly Wagner's) on his right, Kimball's in the center and Beatty on his left, touching Steedman's right wing.

When the fog lifted, the position of the Union Army was a surprise for General Hood. He knew Thomas personally, as he had served under him as adjutant in Texas, and probably knew how difficult it was to push him into action until he was completely prepared and victory was certain.

It wasn't until 1 o'clock that Wood's corps moved forward and got in position. Post's brigade of Beatty's division of the 4th Corps was held at ready to make a charge on Montgomery Hill. That hill was the outermost station of the enemy near our line. Several batteries were moved forward and a fast, effective fire from the artillery preceded Post's charge. This was bravely and brilliantly carried out and a general attack was now being made by the entire line. The artillery, of which Thomas had plenty, where moved to every available advantageous position and they weren't sparing with the ammunition. The Southern Army was in the shape of a right angle across from us. Kimball rushed straight at the enemy. Elliot of Wood's corps and Garrard of Smith's corps followed Kimball to the right and left and in the attack captured several enemy guns and took many prisoners. When Post received the order to take Montgomery Hill, he doubted he would be successful, but good cover from the artillery made it possible for him without great losses.

Hood now moved his line to the right and further back and strengthened his left flank with Bate's division which had just arrived on the battlefield from Murfreesboro. Since Smith's corps didn't reach far enough to the right now, Schofield was ordered to move his corps forward and to join the fight.

Smith now moved Moore's division from his corps to the right to fill in the gap in his line. To this division belonged the 40th Missouri Regiment and Capt. Henry Troll's battery A of the 2nd Missouri, then under the command of Lieutenant Zepp, but the division wasn't large enough to reach to the outermost left wing of the enemy. As Wood's 4th corps advanced, it moved to the left and Smith followed with the 16th, giving Schofield a chance to bring his forces into position to the right of Smith and go around Hood's left, which stood west of Richland Creek near the Hillsboro Turnpike. During the few hours, the sun had pretty much driven the ice off the surface of the ground, but in its place now was a kind of liquid muck several inches deep. Since we had moved all morning like snails on side-roads like flies crawling through molasses because of repeated accidents, we finally reached the Hillsboro Pike and solid ground around 2 o'clock in the afternoon.

Cooper's brigade from our division was ahead of us. Wilson's cavalry was to the right in front of us. To the left of the Hillsboro Pike was a low valley through which Richland Creek flowed toward the Cumberland River. Just east of this creek were several hills 100' to 250' high, here and there covered with some trees, but unusable for agriculture because of the rocky soil. On these hills Smith's corps was involved with the enemy in heavy fighting and Moore's division had hard work advancing. Cooper's brigade of Couch's division and Schofield's corps were ordered to attack and to drive the enemy from last western hill. Cooper's sharpshooters swarmed ahead really splendidly then. This brigade charged down the Hillsboro Pike Hill and crossed the valley and the Richland Creek. The other brigades of the division had hardly reached their stations, when we were also pulled into it and on command the guns raced half to the left to get into position in the line. This move by an artillery battery looks to an observer, who doesn't understand artillery maneuvers, as if all the guns and caissons were running into each other and looks like a knot that couldn't be opened. But when the command "in battery" or "action front!" is given, six guns with six caissons are standing ready, a gunner at each place and either one after the other, or all six together, start firing over the heads of their infantry which is already advancing but is waiting for support. As soon as the first loading has been fired off, the infantry charges with a "hurrah". Other batteries on the left and right joined the fight in a similar fashion and in a short time a terrible noise came from both sides, certain evidence that war isn't anything but, as Sherman said, "hell gone wild". If the artillerist watched the valiant infantry men advancing, we saw the skirmishers about 14 yards from each other with their officers standing, cheering them on. They fired, sought cover now and running, many fell together like sacks of flour. But as soon as the artillery had covered the brigade or division's infantry, they advanced in double step and stormed the enemy position which, after strong resistance, had to give up. But before the success of our troops, the rebels brought two batteries, each with four guns, and for a long time fired at us until, just before sundown, one of their ammunition cases exploded.

At the same time, they were attacked by Gen. Smith's 16th Corps on their flank and Cox's 3rd division of the 23rd Corps marched to the right past us on the Hillsboro Pike, trying if possible before the end of the battle, to attack the enemy's outer left flank from behind. But the sun was already gone and darkness put an end to the first day of fighting. Generals Schofield and Cox and their staff had taken position to the right of our battery and observed the magnificent attack in close ranks of Cooper's brigade. To the left of our guns, the new division commander, Gen. Couch, held his breath in astonishment, when he saw that same brigade climb the hill, and thought it was risking too much to attempt to capture the peak. But the valiant troops that stormed the hill here were certain of victory, since they were fighting **for noble human rights and God, who let iron grow and didn't want slaves.**

Besides the splendid advance of the batteries, as these were galloped into position and opened fire, Cox's division that was sent forward in a staggered line on our right and Wilson's dark cavalry columns even further to the right, made an unforgettable impression. It is perhaps possible to reenact everything, but the sight of a division moving into fire can't be reproduced with paint and brush, and hardly with a pen.

Smith's corps had received similar orders to march forward on the Granny White Pike. Schofield's corps was supposed to follow south on the Hillsboro Pike but night made further advance impossible. Thomas now informed General Grant and the government in Washington of his actions and its results; that he had attacked Hood in all parts of the battle field and during the day had pushed him back two miles, with the results that he had captured 16 guns and taken 1200 prisoners, while his own losses were insignificant. But the work was not yet finished: should the enemy stay in this position however, the prospect for us on the next day were very advantageous for us.

Hood was now being taught a lesson by the mistake that his great self-confidence had gotten him into. But even larger was his mistake of letting Forrest separate himself and his cavalry so far from him that there wasn't enough time for him to be called back to the battlefield.

Lewis's enemy brigade was brought back to the line from Murfreesboro, but two other infantry brigades were still on the Duck River. The enemy commander now got to work to correct these mistakes with all earnestness. The cavalry was too far away in order to be back again in 24 hours' time, but he sent orders to Forrest right away to return and made preparations to hold his line for 24 hours. His right flank now rested east of the Franklin Pike on Overton Hill and his left flank on Shy's Hill, with a connection to the left and south with the Brentwood Hills. By the movement of our division, our battery was led down the hill and into position again in a woodlot near the plantation home. Here, with the help of a dark lantern and a compass, we opened fire in the darkness parallel to Richland Creek in order to bother the enemy's left flank. At 9 o'clock, we stopped firing and tried, as best we could, to get some rest between the rows of dead and wounded, friend and foe, which were laid out on the long veranda of the plantation home.

After General Schofield had received his orders for the next day, he rode over to Granny White Pike to meet Thomas, who he expected to find there. But when he reached the spot, Thomas had already ridden back to his quarters in Nashville. Schofield followed him and in their conversation, it became apparent that Thomas was totally convinced that Hood was in retreat and already far away. Schofield however, informed Thomas that he likely knew Hood better than Thomas did and was certain that they would find Hood in his position at Brentwood Hills again the next morning. After further discussion the orders were changed; that the enemy was expected to be in his present position and would be attacked there.

The Battle of Nashville under General Thomas

The army moves into formation on the second day at the Brentwood Hills line. Gunner Swain gets three years imprisonment for his refusal to fall in at midnight to measure gun enclosures.

    The whole army spent the night in the position they were at in the evening, except Wilson's cavalry, who had Knipe's division move forward on Hatch's rider's right side, and Hammond on Hatch's left to an area near Richland Creek and the Granny White Pike behind the enemy. Johnson's division moved further west of Cumberland in order to oppose actions of Chalmers' riders in that region. General Croxton of Wilson's cavalry corps on Johnson's left had ridden further forward and had cleared the enemy from that region. Croxton's brigade extended to Six-Miles Post on the Charlotte Pike and another brigade of dismounted riders covered the backs of Hammond and Hatch on the Hillsboro Pike in case there might be some action by the enemy cavalry on that road.
    In spite of the impatience of the government and the people, the army had not lost its full confidence of a victory in the coming battle, and now that the enemy had been pushed back from every part of the field, the troops were certain of victory on the next day. The officials in Washington and the public had been so anxious because of Thomas sitting still while making preparations for a brilliant victory that now had made such a good beginning. Now they had full sympathy for the troops, in the grips of a battle in winter during bad weather that would totally annihilate a large main army which the rebels still depended on.
    General Grant had been so impatient that he was on his way from City Point to personally look at what was going on in Nashville. But on the evening of the 15th, he was informed in Washington of the victorious advance of the army and didn't go any further. Logan was already in Louisville when he heard of Thomas' victory and received word from Washington that his presence in Nashville was no longer necessary. Now congratulations were being sent from all sides to Thomas. Grant,

the government and the public were full of praise. Never in history did the swing from mistrust to trust take place in such a short time as here on the first day for Thomas. The public recognized the significance. Had Thomas been defeated at Nashville, the chances of saving the Union would have been nil. It wasn't that there was a lack of troops in order to continue the war, but gold was at its highest price and Sherman's army at Savannah was too far away to give help while Hood was marching to the Ohio River. The Union man in the north filled with doubt now regained solid confidence and the "Knights of the Golden Circle", the "Sons of Liberty" and all the other "Copperhead" societies fell apart because the government now laid a heavy hand on the leaders of these groups and many of their members were pulled into the army by conscription.

During the few hours that we had been in battle, we had pretty much emptied the ammunition cases on the guns and caissons of our battery, and after these were filled again, man and animal took a rest where they stood, without unhitching horse or guns. Just at midnight a staff officer visited us with the order to immediately send a unit of gunners up the hill to measure the embrasure that had been thrown up for the guns. The sergeant from the second gun reported that gunner Swain had refused to follow the order. I had Swain come forward and asked him why he didn't want to obey. He said he was sick. The sergeant now led him to the doctor, who reported that nothing was wrong with him. The next day, Swain was always in the thickest fighting and carried out his duties very well. But fourteen days later, when we had some days of rest, he was put in front of the war court and got three years of hard labor on rip-raps for the Hampton Road and was disgracefully hauled off. Swain was a good soldier; as far as cleanliness, he was an example for all of us. He had served five years in Texas before the war in the regular army under the later rebel General Hardee, who he knew very well. I have always regretted this case but his own words to the sergeant, before coming to me, were his undoing. Since it was disobedience before the enemy, the war court didn't want to treat it lightly. The officers of the battery had bedded down, as I had, on the long porch of the plantation house among the dying and wounded and until 2 o'clock in the morning, a terrible headache gave me no rest. At 4 o'clock we were already awakened to get the battery into position on a hill lying in front of us. This position brought us to within 350 yards of the peak, now known as Shy's Hill, which became the core of the enemy line. Six horses were required to get the guns up. The caissons and wagons remained below and behind the hill for cover. It had snowed a little bit during the night. Before daybreak we were already told not to be sparing with ammunition. Wilson's 19th Ohio Battery was brought behind us as reserves before daylight. With the first rays of light, we saw that the enemy was in position on the hill opposite us, Shy's Hill, and we brought the ammunition from the caisson chests to the guns. Before we could open fire on the enemy, he had sent his sharpshooters armed with English Whitworth guns into position. These opened well-aimed fire at us as soon as they saw us and if we hadn't had the cover of the barricade that had been thrown up during the night; we wouldn't have been able to hold our position, for both lines were very close together here. Our gun embrasures had been covered with branches until the battle started and no one from either side let themselves be seen, for the sharp eyes of the sharpshooters could pick out even the least movement, which then immediately resulted in a hail of bullets.

The length of the enemy line from Overton Hill to Shy's Hill could have been about two miles. From Shy's Hill, Hood's line made an angle toward Brentwood Hills, where it was protected by Chalmers' cavalry. Schofield had to bring Cox's division from his corps in this same angle, which sent his right flank into the clear. To provide cover he asked Moore's division of Smith's 16th Corps to be reserves and the hook of his flank. Moore's division, to which the 40th Missouri and Troll's Missouri Battery belonged, was then also moved forward on the Hillsboro Road during the night and into position.

Schofield, who was personally well acquainted with Hood, was worried that he would try to carry out a flanking movement such as Jackson had at Chancellorsville and Hood made through Hardee at Atlanta, which Hood admitted to later. He had wanted to do it, but Forrest's cavalry was too far away and for that reason, he had wanted to hold us back for another 24 hours and would then have carried out the flanking movement by which Hood hoped to win the battle. Hood's artillery had been gathered in his line in places where there was protection and could do us harm. His troops were kept busy all night trying to make themselves shelter. Even in darkest night we could make out approximately where his line was from our position, because over the whole stretch, every three or four hundred feet, fires had been made large enough to act as torches and to show the engineers the way. The night was completely dark and without definite markers it would have been impossible to establish a line.

    The enemy line, as mentioned, rested between two hills, Overton's and Shy's. Between them the ground was lower, but wavy and was cut through by Brown's Creek which ran straight north and crossed Hood's position at the right angle. Overton Hill was wide and round and the earthworks ran in a curve toward the hill but had no angle where it could be weakened. Shy's Hill, although higher, was not so large and Bate's and Loring's lines here formed a right angle. Bate complained about the position, but Hood's engineers had laid the line out and Cheatham didn't feel justified in changing it. It couldn't have been done well either unless the entire army had pulled back more. Coleman was driven back at sundown by Schofield on Shy's Hill and had enough to do, just to hold his position.

    The extension of the line of 23rd corps east of Richland Creek left one hill south of Shy's Hill unoccupied, and it was there that Thomas's right flank could expect resistance. The Union picketers were so close to the enemy line that they had to dig out a trench on the inside of the barricade in order to have at least some cover for the men. The earthwork nearest us, as mentioned, was not over 350 yards away and had to be built under fire; it was weak and didn't provide good protection. Further southwest were the hills that Cheatham and Schofield had occupied, and those in the enemy line were significantly higher and well covered with trees at the top. A strong earthwork was established on top in the enemy line, held together with wood timbers, and embrasures for artillery and a parapet high enough to protect the inner line. Our sharpshooters prevented them from building an abatis however. The Union lines were moved forward into position during the night and early morning and were readied for a prompt attack. In Schofield's corps, as Couch's division moved to connect with Smith's corps on our left flank, a space resulted between his and Cox's division. Although the two brigades of Cox were spread out east of Richland Creek and only in a single line, there still remained an opening of about 300 paces between them and Couch's right. This was covered with five regimentals and a battery of artillery. At the same time, the 4th army under General Wood moved on the Franklin Pike and Steedman's "Black Corps" on the Nolensville Pike and over the vacated enemy earthworks until they could see the new enemy positions. Here both corps swung half to the right and again in line. Steedman connected to Wood's left flank and Wood's right connected with Smith's left. Beatty's division of Wood's corps was east of the Franklin Pike, while Kimball's division of the same corps was positioned west of the road and Elliott's (earlier Wagner's) division made up the reserves. But when the corps was in formation, there still was a large empty place in the center of the line. So Elliott's division was taken out of reserve and moved into the center on Kimball's right in the main line. The left of the 4th Corps remained east of the Franklin Pike across from Overton Hill, where Hood's line curved right toward the south.

The Union line, which on the previous day had turned southeast half left facing the enemy and bypassing him on his left, here was directly parallel to him from east to west, not extending past in any place, with the exception of the moment when Wilson's cavalry on Schofield's flank tried to go around the enemy.

Around noon, when everything was ready for the battle, Wood was ordered to take over command of Steedman's corps too. The sharpshooters on the entire line were now moved closer to the enemy.

On many places now, reconnaissance was made to determine whether a successful attack could be made. General Thomas did not issue any orders to attack, but left that up to the good judgment of his corps commanders. General Wood pulled the artillery from Steedman together with those of his own corps, almost 100 guns, and opened a concentrated fire on Overton Hill. Gen. Smith's and Gen. Schofield's batteries carried out terrible and fast crossfire toward Shy's Hill and lively returned fire from any other batteries in the enemy line.

Already in early morning, as soon as the troops were in position, General Thomas made an inspection tour of the entire line in order to see how strong the enemy defenses were in the various parts of the line. Shortly after he reached our post and rode on to Schofield's headquarters, we were instructed to open fire on the enemy. The vines and branches that had covered our embrasures were quickly moved to the side by the artillery corporals and after the first salvo we were no longer bothered by the sharpshooters hidden in the trees on the enemy hills, since they left their stations and sought shelter. Our fire was so exact (we weren't more than 300 yards away), that we rolled the enemy's head-log back into their communications trench and no enemy could show himself on the top of the hill.

Schofield had Stiles' brigade from Cox's division, which was in reserve, march in good time further south and east with orders to spread out in a line on a wooded hill in back of the enemy and to join Wilson's cavalry attack and to attack at the same time as the main line. The enemy's left under Cheatham ended in an earthwork on a hill on which four guns were stationed, and four more guns were stationed halfway in the line on another hill, which connected with Shy's Hill. But the rifle batteries of the 23rd Corps on both sides of Richland Creek were capable of reaching the enemy earthworks and the southern artillerists were forced to pull back their guns with ropes by hand, reload them and then shove them back and fire again. Besides all of that, their powder was bad and even with best of intentions; they couldn't reach our line with their smooth-bore cannons, while the Union artillery proved its superiority with every shot. When Thomas looked over his army from Schofield's position, he wanted to extend his line to the right of Schofield with another division and sent order to Smith, to send one of his divisions forward. But when Smith told Thomas about the situation in his line, the order was rescinded.

Wilson made good progress on Schofield's right with his cavalry. Johnson's division didn't have enough forces with which to attack Chalmers at Bell's Landing. But with Chalmers' cavalry pulled together during the night, Wilson was able to pull Johnson back on the morning of the 16th. Wilson now had his three divisions together and under his complete control. Hammond's outposts were already near the Granny White Pike in back of Hood's left wing. Hatch's division was ordered out of bivouac near the Hillsboro Road to Hammond's left and then to march behind the enemy's back. Johnson's division, which marched over the field from Bell's Landing, first went into the reserves. Around noon, Wilson's riders were arranged in a half-circle from Schofield's right flank behind the enemy line over the Granny White Pike. At this time, the movement of Stiles' brigade, already mentioned, took place. Schofield wanted to have a full division here with which to attack the enemy's back, because he didn't think an attack from the front would be possible or successful. But the position of the enemy with an angle at Shy's Hill did offer the possibility of a successful attack. The advance of Wilson's cavalry from one hill to the next behind the enemy made Hood very nervous, and he repeatedly sent staff officers to Chalmers with earnest encouragement to hold tight to his position. Since he was being too pressured by Wilson, Hood was forced to send Covan's brigade from Cheatham's line to support Chalmers. Bate was ordered, to spread his line left to Shy's Hill, while Coleman, who had been there, was ordered to Covan's vacated spot. Bate's line was now very spread out; the earthworks offered him little protection and were positioned too far away on the ridge of the hills to provide much cover against an advancing storm-charge. The fire from our battery (the 15th Indiana) was so close and too hot to allow any change in the line. Bate's own description of his situation gives us the best information about his position. He said: "The enemy opened a terribly fast and furious artillery fire and kept at it during the day. Around 1 o'clock in the afternoon, he had several batteries move into the orchard of Mrs. Bradford's plantation; these were near the Granny White Pike (Capt. Reed's 2nd Iowa Battery and Coxwell's Independent Illinois Battery commanded by Lieutenant McClaury) and in McArthur's line. These guns shot over both of my lines which formed the angle and their hollow shot exploded at the backs of my left brigade. Another battery was posted on a hill across from me half to my left (this was Battery D, 1st Ohio Battery, Capt. Cockrell in Cox' Line) and fired into the backs of my first brigade. But the battery in front of me, not more than 300 paces away (this was ours, the 15th Indiana Battery in Couch's line) was subjected all day to fire from our sharpshooter's "Whitworth rifles" and must have suffered badly, but could not be shut up. The rifled artillery guns of the enemy were so close to our line that they leveled the earthworks to the ground and for the length of 60 paces, nothing could live on this ridge." (So far General Bate in his report.)

At about 1 o'clock in the afternoon, the guns of the left half of the 15th Indiana Battery were hitched to the artillery wagons and were moved by Lieutenant Adam Kuntz one hundred paces further left and 75 paces closer to the enemy hill and brought into position and again opened fire with shrapnel toward the east side of Shy's Hill. That part of the battery was so close that they could sweep away every attempt of the enemy to defend its front. These guns under Kuntz fired with greatest precision and perseverance, as did the right half of the battery, until the enemy was pushed back by McMillen's charge and fled.

General McArthur could see from his position what damage was being done in Bate's line by the artillery and reported that storm attack up Shy's hill from the position of the 15th Indiana Battery was possible. He wanted to move McMillen's brigade from his division to his right and in front of the line of Couch's division, and then under protection of Couch's guns (15th Indiana Battery) to advance at the place where the steep hill would offer protection and then charge. Thomas supported this plan, and Smith sent notice to Schofield to have Couch be ready to support McMillen's right flank. Schofield immediately gave orders to Couch and Cox; the latter was told to storm the hill in front of his line at the same time. Stiles, from Schofield's corps, was on his right and was supposed to attack the enemy from behind, so that no escape would be possible. Thomas was with Schofield in person, from where he could exactly oversee Shy's Hill and the whole chain of the Brentwood Hills.

In order to understand the entire situation better, we would like back up and turn our attention to the left wing where General Wood was investigating the enemy's position on Overton Hill.

After reconnaissance by Gen. Post, a storm attack was ordered and it was decided to try to turn this daring move into a victory.

The attack of the 4th Corps was given to Gen. Post and his brigade. Col. Streight of Beatty's division was to support Post. Thompson's black brigade from Steedman's corps, supported by Grosvenor's white brigade, was to charge from the east. The artillery of the 4th Corps and Steadman's Etowah Corps Batteries, concentrated their fire now toward Overton Hill. The crashing and banging of almost 300 guns from both sides already in line here sent fire from over the length of two miles. The explosion of the shots made a terrific noise and the view of the battle was a noble sight for anyone who saw it. The roof of the state capitol, about four miles in back of us, was black with gawkers, who watched every shot from both sides. One of those in the crowd told me afterward that from noon until 3 o'clock, when all cannons were in use, it was beyond all description.

Around 3 o'clock in the afternoon, a bunch of sharpshooters charged toward Overton Hill attempting to attract enemy fire to them and to worry the enemy artillery gunners. The attack columns from the line followed them. When they were near the enemy barricades they charged; many reached the parapet, but were greeted by such devastating fire that after short and bloody hand-to-hand fighting, they had to retreat. Their retreat was covered by the rest of Beatty's division and Steedman's reserves. The Union artillery reopened fire and the enemy didn't try to pursue them. Our wounded were brought back to safety. The losses amounted to about half the losses during the entire battle. This attack only showed again that an attack on a barricaded line is always connected to terrible disadvantages and should therefore seldom be attempted. General Post, the leader of the charge was severely wounded. The losses of officers were great, for they exposed themselves unnecessarily by taking their men into the attack without careful consideration.

In the angle of the enemy line, which was held by Bate on Shy's Hill, the situation was different. The lines were, as we saw, under crossfire. The parapet had been leveled to the ground by the guns of the 15th Indiana Battery and our sharpshooters could reach Bate's line. The line of the enemy was thin and the cover of our storming column was protected by the steep side of the hill. All this shows that an attack can be successful and in this case was justified and should have been risked. While our fire on the hill got faster, General McMillen received orders to form his brigade into an attack line in a small low area in front of our guns. This was about 1 p.m. The troops laid themselves flat on the ground as we fired faster and faster and the enemy was no longer seen and was no longer dangerous. Finally around 3:30, McMillen marched with his brigade down the hill that we were on and up the enemy hill. We continued to cover them until they were about 15 paces from the peak. Then we turned our guns to the right. Generals Smith, MacArthur, Couch and others stood on the barricades in thick powder smoke in front of us, and when McMillen's banner was flying on Shy's Hill, Couch's troops on the right and McArthur's left had already followed them a good way to the top. In every part of the line, it now went forward in quickstep and those enemies that didn't want to surrender, saved themselves by wildly running away as best they could.

Wilson's dismounted cavalry had very quickly advanced and conquered one hill after the other, which also encouraged them to new action. Their superior numbers allowed them to go around Covan's enemy flank, which Hood had sent ahead to support Chalmers, and when Wilson's riders came near Schofield's position, they were supported by Stiles, so on the right flank everything was operating in the best order and with the best successes. Wilson was with Schofield and Thomas at the time. When he saw McMillen's progress, he turned and galloped back to his commando. But before he had half covered the distance, the enemy's left flank was crushed like an eggshell.

McMillen naturally had it easy, since Bate's line had been completely ruined. Col. Shy from the Southern Tennessee Regiment lost his life in the defense of the hill, and the hill is named after him today. After the line had broken, Hood didn't have any more troops available with which to reestablish it. From left and right, the enemy fled in wild disorder to the Franklin Pike. At the last minute, young Beauregard, son of the famous general, had an enemy battery under Lieut. Alston drive into position on our right. This fired a salvo at Doolittle's brigade from Cox's division, but their aim was too high and even before they could load again, Cox's troops had gone over the barricade and were around and among them. The whole line west of the Granny White Pike was soon in the hands of Smith's and Schofield's troops. These were briefly held up by an enemy battery of 16 guns, commanded by the young Beauregard.

It didn't take long until we too were on the pike alongside four other batteries. We opened fire on him. The shots had barely been fired when the enemy here too, fled in wild disorder. The horses were unhitched from the guns and the guns remained standing and as Hood said, he was an eyewitness here to how an army that had fought famously from Donaldson to Atlanta, completely unraveled. Not one organized company remained of the whole army. My personal experiences of the day are very fresh in my memory. Around 11 a.m. an enemy bomb exploded so near me that I was knocked down and blood came out of my ears. A little splinter scraped my left temple. Our doctor, having cotton and bandages, stopped the blood and covered the wound, but my hearing, which was even made worse from the thunder of the guns, was gone.

When McMillen's brigade had reached the top, to satisfy our curiosity, I rode with Capt. Wilson of the 19th Ohio Battery to Shy's Hill. Arriving at the communications trench, we met a dreadful sight. The trench was full of dead and severely wounded. One, who looked as if he might be older than 40 yrs., thirsted for water. I had a canteen of good schnapps and also a full water bottle on my saddle. We jumped down from our horses and gave our dying enemies to drink until the water and schnapps were gone. We now rode further to where the enemy had a 20 pound howitzer. Here again was a scene of death and destruction. When McMillen had reached the hill and the gunners were standing by their gun, McMillen's men had given fire with great success. A dead gunner, with the wiper in one hand, had his other arm around the gun barrel. Another lay over the gun carriage and this was repeated so often, that we turned away from the carnage. Then we rode back to our batteries and found a group of prisoners. Among them was a high-ranking officer (General Jackson), who went to Captain Wilson and asked him, whether he had commanded the artillery on the hill. Wilson said no and pointed to me, and said that I had had the honor of commanding the two forward rifled-guns. (Wilson's battery was in reserve.) The general admired my composure and asked if I had served in Germany. When Wilson said no (I was deaf from the wound and from shooting), the Southerner said he was very surprised, since he had expected, because of the excellent placement and effects of the fire from the two guns, to see a former classmate of his in West Point in command. But instead he found a green "Dutch Boy" managing the activities of the two guns. We had to end the conversation because we were ordered to move onto the Granny White Pike as soon as possible. Here we had to cross a small field, where Hubbard's Union brigade had attacked, and were startled to still find many corpses on the battlefield, but their pockets had all been robbed already by corpse-robbers. Having arrived on the pike, we opened fire, as already mentioned, until the flight of the enemy and darkness of night put an end to the battle. Around 7 p.m., General Thomas rode into our camp and gave the officers and men of the battery thanks for their services. He had done the same for McMillen's brigade.

When General Thomas observed the successful attack on Shy's Hill from General Schofield's headquarters, and Smith's and Schofield's corps chased the enemy with loud jubilation and "hurrah", he commented that this of the voice of the American people. The result of this valiant attack by Smith and Schofield on the west side of the Granny White Pike was the capture of 27 guns, 12 battle-flags, capture of four generals (Gen. Jackson being one), a mass of officers of lower rank, along with thousands of regular soldiers, all as brave as soldiers anywhere in the world. They were taken prisoner with their weapons in their hands. So ended one of the large armies in the west on which the Rebels had mainly depended.

After the Battle

When the victory was reached, it was night and a heavy rain streamed down, which made the darkness and the confusion that much worse. General Thomas had ordered General Wood to follow Hood on the Franklin Pike, and the cavalry was to advance on the Granny White Pike until it joined with the Franklin Pike. Then Wilson's cavalry column was to march forward. General Smith and Schofield were to follow Wilson the next day, but few, if any, of the enemy had fled on the Granny White Pike because Wilson had complete control of that road. The mass of enemy troops had streamed through the Brentwood Hills in order to get to the Franklin Pike by the fastest way possible.

Forrest, who tried his best to join Hood as quickly as possible, sent Armstrong's brigade cross country and was able to cover Hood's back. Hood had already sent Reynolds' and Coleman's brigades back from his line before the end of the battle and they had been able to keep Wilson's riders off the Franklin Pike and prevent the majority of Hood's troops being taken prisoner. But Hood had luck in misfortune; during the night, Thomas was awakened from sleep for further orders for the movement of the pontoon train the next morning. He gave instructions to send them on the Murfreesboro Road instead of on the Franklin Pike, as he should have. This mistake wasn't noticed until the next morning. As he was riding forward he asked whether the pontoon train had already passed them on the Franklin Pike. The train was immediately called back from the Murfreesboro Road and quickly sent to Franklin, but the delay was a big disadvantage for the Union troops, while Hood made use of the time to get himself out of our way. We here follow with a description of a pontoon train, as it is used in our army:

As almost everything in American that was taken over from somewhere else is changed and improved, so too the pontoons, already in use for a long time in European armies, underwent improvements here. The linen or canvas pontoons used for a long time in Russia, where copied and improved by us. The length of the boats was usually 21 feet, made up of two side rib-cages...side walls...which were transported on specially built wagons. Our "Pontonniers" introduced the improvement that allowed the boat structure to be transported on a standard wagon and no specialized wagon was necessary. The boat frames would then be cut through and the two parts were connected by hinges and pins (or keys). The pioneers and Pontonniers were called together in Nashville in the winter of 1863-64 and quickly fabricated a large number of these canvas boats, so that by spring, when Sherman started his march toward Atlanta, every army corps had such a bridge for its use. After the Battle of Resaca, when we had to cross the Oostanaula, Etowah and Chattahoochee Rivers, we had to rely on such bridges, which our Pontonniers could quickly set up. Such improvements came from various people, so it is difficult to say who deserves the most credit.

About four miles north of Franklin, Wilson's cavalry caught up to the tail end of the enemy. Knipe's division of his riders attacked the enemy from the front and from the flank, stormed his position and captured over 400 prisoners and their battle-flag. General Johnson crossed Harpeth River several miles downriver from Franklin and forced Hood to leave the defense works at Franklin.

Forrest's cavalry rejoined Hood's army near Rutherford Creek. When Forrest met Cheatham here, he accused Cheatham of being the cause of the defeat. Both pulled out their revolvers and were about to go at each other, when General Bate, who commanded a division of Cheatham's corps, jumped in between them and said, only over his dead body. In this way both men remained alive. On the morning after the battle, the 16th Corps under Smith and the 23rd under Schofield marched after the enemy on the Granny White Pike and that evening reached our camp at the foot of Fort Granger, north of Franklin, and lay down to rest in over a foot of muck. On the next morning we crossed the river to the city of Franklin. Here every house, barn and shed that had a roof on was used as a hospital. The weather turned more bearable and the rain was replaced by hard frost and clean air. We now had an opportunity to look at the battlefield of 30 November. The deep trench to the right and left of the Franklin Pike had been used by the enemy to bury our dead. So that we should see what wild-men the Southerners had become by the war, they had buried all of dead with head down, the bodies covered with dirt and legs sticking out of the earth. In contrast, they had given their own dead a decent burial on the McGavock plantation. Our people were dug up and given an appropriate burial by our troops. In Franklin we camped next to the Carter Creek Pike. The trees on the Bostick plantation, which our fire had reached, showed traces of the hot fight in the last battle.

Since the Rutherford Creek was flooded because of the rains, we had to remain in Franklin a few days. Then we moved with the entire corps to Columbia. Here Hood had been able to establish a strong rearguard from Walthall's division, supported by Forrest's cavalry, whereby the bad roads and weather were helpful to him. In this way, he reached Bainbridge on 26 December. Once again he had luck, for the pontoons that were left in Decatur in November, had come down the river. Hood's own pontoons couldn't be brought forward because of the bad roads, but when our pontoons reached him they were quickly set in place and he was able to get his exhausted troops to the other side. The enemy report relates: As soon as the first bridge was in place, two Union gun boats appeared but were repulsed by General Stewart with a battery of artillery cannons and their bridge was not disturbed again.

On the 17th, when Thomas was in Franklin, he issued orders to Steedman to march to Murfreesboro and go by train to Decatur, to take up his former post in northern Alabama again. At the end of the month, Steedman had arrived in Decatur, Wood with the 4th Corps was near Lexington in northern Alabama and 30 miles south of Pulaski, General Smith was at Pulaski and Schofield at Columbia. Thomas now announced that the campaign was over and all troops would be assigned winter quarters. Other orders from Washington arrived however, which stipulated that he should immediately follow the enemy. The expected march of General Sherman through the Carolinas made it necessary that rebel be given no opportunity to be gathered in front of him. Thomas now prepared himself for a new campaign, to give the enemy in the Gulf States no peace.

The two-day battle at Nashville resulted in the capture of more than 5,000 prisoners, along with 53 guns and a mass of small weapons. Among the prisoners, were four generals: Johnson, Smith, Jackson and Rucker. Along with these were a large number of regimental leaders that had commanded brigades. The losses by death or wounds were small on both sides in comparison to the results. The complete destruction of Hood's army, which was so quickly followed by the end of the war, left us without full reports from the Southern side.

Hood gathered the remnants of his troops at Tupelo, Mississippi and then put a large portion of his faithful on leave and requested to be relieved of further service. He claimed that he did not have such great losses as Thomas claimed and reported that he had 18,500 men in Tupelo, but these claims have not been historically reliable.

General Thomas' numbers of prisoners and deserters during the months November and December are 30,000 men, along with the 72 guns and 300 muskets that he had captured.

Thomas' losses in this battle were 3057; of these, less than 400 were deaths. The 4th Corps had less than 1000 dead and wounded. Of these, two thirds were from the unsuccessful attack on Overton Hill.

Steedman's losses were over 800 men, almost all of which had also fallen in the unsuccessful charge. Col. Thompson's Black brigade had lost 50 percent more than all the other brigades on the battle field. The 16th Corps had lost 750 men in two days. The attack on Shy's Hill was not particularly bloody, for the artillery (15th Indiana Battery) had provided excellent cover. McMillen reported only 118 losses, and of these only two thirds were from the charge up Shy's Hill. The losses in the 23rd Corps were only 150 men and in the three divisions of the cavalry, 329 riders. When we take a look at the whole battle, we can thank the tactical combination of all the forces for such minimal losses. Hood made a huge mistake that he allowed Thomas to get around his left flank on the first day. Had he pulled his troops back to Brentwood Hills right away and then brought Forrest's cavalry into the fight, he would have been able make an orderly retreat with his entire army.

But he waited too long, and by evening he found his good troops fleeing from the battlefield.

After Thomas had received orders from Washington to follow Hood and to continue the campaign, Wood received orders to gather his troops together at Huntsville, Alabama. Schofield, Smith and Wilson were to gather at Eastport, Mississippi. When Schofield was marching to Clinton, to get transportation by boat to Eastport, he received orders that separated him from the Cumberland Army and the activities of his corps were transferred to another area.

Our complete victory resulted in jubilation beyond comparison in all of the North. The president's and General Grant's earlier dissatisfaction had been the expression of public opinion, which then believed that Hood should have been defeated near the Tennessee River, and feared that he would still march to Ohio. Now however, everyone wanted to be the first to bring the victorious General honors and trust in Thomas had been fully reestablished.

Although everything on the 16th went off well, there seemed to an undercurrent of dissatisfaction among the corps commanders that were not part of the Cumberland Army, as a result of the step-motherly handling that the Ohio Army under Schofield and the Tennessee Army under Smith had received, and which are apparent in the public reports from Thomas. Although Thomas had voiced his gratitude to us on the evening of the battle, otherwise we, our battery and McMillen's brigade, as far as a mention of our service is concerned, we could just as well have been on the island of Fiji; not a word was granted us, while the artillery and storm column of the 4th and Steedman corps on Overton Hill were covered with praise. We were successful on Shy's Hill but didn't belong to the Cumberland Army. The others were beaten back and were heaped with honors, while we were passed over in silence. Still, we have the satisfaction that from the Southerner side we given full recognition, for Jefferson Davis in his book "The Rise and Fall of the Confederate States" mentions our position, where we held crossfire on Hood's line. The same is the case in Smith's book, "The War Between the States". Joseph D. Johnson in his "Narrative", and Hood in his "Advance and

Retreat", as well as Bate, as we already mentioned, were full of praise for our battery and also the greatest acknowledgement of McMillen's bravery.

The officers and team of our battery were very satisfied that they had fulfilled their duty on the second day of the battle on Shy's Hill; for our work resulted in one of the few successful storm-attacks on the barricade of the enemy line.

General Stonewall Jackson tried to storm Malvern Hills in Virginia, but it ended in a complete disaster. Under McClellan at Antietam, Hooker, Sumner, Franklin and Burnside tried to break through the enemy line with a frontal charge. Burnside tried the same thing at Fredericksburg, Lee at Gettysburg, Longstreet at Knoxville and Grant too, tried to capture Vicksburg with a charge, even Sherman tried it at Kennesaw Mountain, and here at 3 o'clock on the second day of the battle, Wood tried it; but all the above mentioned assaults were failures, leaving behind a mass of dead and wounded on the battlefield. But here at Shy's Hill it was different and success crowned our work. We used 1926 shots, mostly shrapnel that exploded perfectly. In the artillery, all the members of the team have to work together in order to achieve good results. Our careful fuse cutter was critical to having the shots explode correctly.

During the few days of rest at Columbia, man and beast were well taken care of. Our quarters were now dry, but cold. We protected ourselves from the cold with large camp fires and were not sparing with firewood. Since we had still been on the march at Christmas, we celebrated the holiday as soon as we got to camp. We had plenty of food and firewood, and the days before the New Year 1865 were some of the most pleasant days of our time as soldiers.

In war, the saying, "Ends well, all is well" is more appropriate than anywhere else, and public opinion was certainly with the victor of Nashville. Few people have the character that could awaken such public trust, as did General Thomas. He was highly patriotic and loved his country more than the state he was born in. Although born in Virginia, he wasn't willing to follow his friend Lee and take up arms against the national government that Washington had founded. He was a man of noble ideas; quiet, modest and reticent, who tried to avoid any notoriety. To his superiors he was faithful, to his subordinates fatherly lenient. He did not carry his personal courage for show and he had no fear. These characteristics formed the basis of the affection of his army. His dislike of an independent command kept him in secondary positions, although his rank in the regular army as well as the volunteer army qualified him for a separate command in the field. General Hardee of the Southern Army was in this way quite similar to him. The duties of a soldier, courage and capability of understanding the details of a campaign, were part of him. But to be the object of negotiations in Congress, to be talked about in the newspapers, or to be criticized by 10,000 others, all the while being responsible for plans that could ruin the country...that he hated with all his heart and naturally receded into the background. That was the reason he resisted accepting the position offered him. That these characteristics to a certain extent made him incapable of an independent command cannot be contested. The ambition to always be right, if exaggerated, causes caution and doubt about acting. In such cases, encouragement by the government or the commanding general would be welcome but the complete success of the end of the battle at Nashville can only be attributed to the beginning of the campaign, which the Thomas's staff either intentionally or carelessly left out in their reports. The gentlemen have also done their best to ignore, or better said, been completely silent about the campaign from Pulaski to Nashville.

If we go back to the day before the battle, the 14th, we find that Schofield's suggestion to change the plan was adopted (the original plan was only intended to humiliate the 23rd Corps). With this change, the left wing became the axle of the movement and Schofield's corps that first supported Gen. Smith, was pushed ahead as soon as there was room to our right, and solidly pushed the left wing of the enemy back, thus destroying Hood's plan because he had already gone around that left wing and Hood was forced to pull his right wing back and vacate Montgomery Hill. The capture of the hill by Cooper from Couch's division would not have been possible in the original plan of the 14th, and there is no doubt, now that we have all the reports in front of us, if the actions on the morning of the second day of the battle had proceeded more rapidly, Hood's army would have been defeated and in flight before noon. But Thomas was completely convinced that the enemy, after his flight on the 15th from our left wing, would not come to a halt again until he was on the other side of the Tennessee River. How or from whom the commanding General was led astray, is not to be ascertained in Thomas's reports. Also that he altered his orders to Steedman, Wood and Wilson after talking with Schofield, was not mentioned. All of this seems to indicate that the Cumberland Army wished to take all the credit for the success.

  Here is the place where we, now having all the reports from that time in front of us, to examine more closely everything that happened before. On 8 November, Stanley, who with his corps was stationed at Pulaski, was ordered to attack Hood there. On 19 November, Schofield reached Pulaski and received the same order from Thomas. But when Schofield pointed out to Thomas that Hood was not marching to Pulaski but toward Columbia, Schofield was given authority to use his best judgment in deciding what action to take. In Thomas's report, nothing about that can be found. But his friends shouldn't praise him for things that others have done, and if he had fully acknowledged Schofield for his services and the plan changes, certainly the honor and fame of a general like Thomas wouldn't have suffered in the least. But instead of that, his adjutant reported that Smith's corps didn't reach far enough and for that reason Schofield was ordered to take his corps out of the reserves, in which it had been, and take it into line to the right of Smith. This still indicated that no change had been entered into the battle plan and that we, the 23rd corps, were still in the reserves, while we had actually supported Smith's corps from 6 a.m. on. Had we not already supported Smith from early morning on, it would not have been possible for us in the afternoon to still reach our position on Smith's right.

  Couch's (our) division moved out quickly with Smith already in the morning and around 3 p.m. we were already quite close to Smith's right and in fire, and Cox's division also reached their position early enough to take part in the battle. Schofield said that he had, as also had the 23rd Corps, received full acknowledgement for his services in the battle on the 15th and 16th, but Thomas hadn't given acknowledgement for the change of plan on the 14th, as well as for the information that Hood would not withdraw on the night of the 15th without another battle. Both reports were very valuable for Thomas. Although these little services that he did for Thomas in informing him of the length of the enemy line as well as the length of the attacking column weren't worth great notice, they were important enough that they should have appeared in the official report. For Schofield himself held them to be of significant enough importance that he made a long ride in dark night. After spending the entire day in the saddle, he brought this information personally to Thomas, in order to correct his mistake concerning Hood's retreat.

As is common after a battle, so here too, the government would like to know who, because of bravery or valuable service, was eligible for a promotion after the last campaign. In his reports from 20 January 1865 which covered the entire campaign in Tennessee from Pulaski to Nashville, Thomas makes no mention of Schofield or of Stanley. Thereafter, a telegram was sent from Washington to Thomas asking for recommendations. He answered he would like to see that Stanley and Schofield would be promoted one rank higher in the regular army for valiant service. So Schofield, who had the rank in the regular army of artillery captain, should now become a warrant-major in the regular army capable of commanding four field batteries instead of one, as before. The Washington officials however knew to value Schofield's services better and with Grant's recommendation he received a commission as brigadier-general in the regular army and would most likely have, had the position had been legally open, a major-general. Thomas had received the latter. Schofield and Stanley both had the rank of major-general in the volunteer army, but since both were career soldiers, that rank didn't hold so much meaning for them.

Had Schofield provided similar service for a European government as he had at Franklin for the Union, he would most likely have been awarded the field-marshal staff. Squabbles and jealousy between higher officers are nothing unusual. We remember that after Waterloo, Wellington was commander in Paris and couldn't get along with Blücher. It didn't go any better between the English and French in the Crimea. Italy still hates the French today because of the war with Austria in 1859 and the Prussians and Austrians still haven't come to an agreement over Schleswig-Holstein. The Russians and Romanians in the war against Turkey in 1877 were so at odds that it was expected that they would come to blows with each other. And our three armies that were in battle under one flag at Nashville, where thrown together too quickly and it didn't work. The administration in Washington, which was still dissatisfied with Thomas, had Schofield's Corps move eastward and sent Smith's 16th Corps down the Mississippi to Mobile. Wilson was ordered to gather an enormous cavalry corps of 21,000 men at Eastport. What remained for Thomas personally were the 4th Corps and the "Blacks" under Steedman in his department. Both corps were placed in Chattanooga for further service under observation and with our departure, the envy squabbles against Schofield came to an end. Critics of Thomas claim that he could have had his 60,000 troops oppose and annihilate Hood at Columbia, without having Hood come to Franklin and Nashville, and without waiting for Smith's Corps.

  It isn't to be doubted that Thomas, before his death, deeply regretted his disregard for Schofield and the injustice done to the 23rd Corps, but he was under the influence of his officers who were against Schofield, so that he can't be given all the blame. Just as he was about to place his intentions for the 23rd Corps in the battle of Nashville in the proper light and to make good the injustice against Schofield and his corps, he suffered a stroke which ended his life. No one made use of his influence over Thomas more than General J. B. Steedman, who confessed that he intentionally tried to harm Schofield in his reports. But truth remains the victor, even if some tried to suppress it with false information. In spite of all the injustice that Schofield and his corps had to bear, Thomas still remains one our most noble comrades. He never sacrificed a human life unnecessarily.

  The following little story shows that Schofield didn't seek revenge or desired to pay someone back. He told us that there was a situation at the cadet academy where he spent his last years that almost ended his military career, although he was completely innocent. He is still amazed that his ambitions in that direction hadn't been completely destroyed. He had never doubted the results. It was common at the academy that cadets had to present themselves on 1 June of each year. There were divided into sections and cadets in the second class had to prepare the new cadet for their examination in the middle of the month. Schofield received a section and had to prepare it in mathematics. He said, he had never carried out this task more conscientiously than he did to teach this candidate this branch of science. But in his department there were two boys who were far behind the rest. Not wishing that they should be held back, he took them to the blackboard in an attempt to teach them at the last minute before the exam. During this time, some of his classmates came into the room and started a conversation with the other candidates. Schofield didn't allow himself be bothered, and when the horn signal was given, he went to his chambers not suspecting anything, not knowing what his colleges had done. But one of the candidates, who was not accepted, wrote to his parents about the nonsense that had taken place in Schofield's classroom as the excuse for his failure. This letter found its way to the war-department in Washington and an order soon reached the enrollment commander at West Point to investigate the case. He was acquitted of any personal participation in the joke against the boy who had failed, but it was held against him that he hadn't forbidden it.

When the investigation was over, he was to justify what he did or didn't do. He naturally defended himself as best he could, since he felt he was personally innocent of any intentional action on his part and so was not anxious about the result. To his great astonishment however, he received word from the Secretary of War in Washington that he was being kicked out of the academy. For the first time, he said, he found out what it meant to have true friends. Cadets had taken letters to friends in Washington, so many of them that George Washington would have been proud.

He himself had never gone to see any of the government officials and most likely none of them would have ever heard about his naughty actions except in the war department. The Secretary of War didn't even want to see him until he was finally introduced to him by an officer in the army. Then he said, the Secretary had only extended him the front finger of his hand. This was after he had spent several weeks in Washington. His congressional representative, he said, had received him in a friendly way and had promised to see the Secretary, which he probably had done, but without success. He should name his co-conspirators and then he could perhaps be pardoned. Early one morning, he then visited the "little giant", Senator Douglas, who he had never seen before, and to whom no one introduced him, and explained his situation. Douglas told him that he was not on friendly footing with the government and would prefer not to go to the war department. But at his pleading, the senator said he should return early the next day and they would both go to the Secretary and see what they could do. But Douglas told him further, if he couldn't get it to happen, he would certainly take care of it in the next presidential period. Douglas went into his room, while Schofield waited expectantly outside. Soon Douglas came out again with a smile on his face and told Schofield, "It's alright. You can go back to West Point." The case then went to the war court, where two members insisted on kicking Schofield out. These two were Fitz John Porter, who later as Secretary of War granted Schofield a new hearing, which cleared him of all dishonor. The other was General George Thomas, whom Schofield later so faithfully served in Tennessee and when he became Secretary of War, assigned Thomas to the best department in the United States (California). So Schofield, when he was in that position, repaid bad with good. After a change that neither General Fitz John Porter nor General George Thomas would have expected for the young cadet in 1852, Schofield became the Secretary of War under President Johnson and again under President Grant, and during this time he rewarded, as mentioned, Thomas and Fitz John Porter.

On New Year's Eve, the corps artillery officers were invited to General Schofield's headquarters in Columbia. Here we were served a delicious lunch and punch, which for us, after two weeks of tough going without complaint through deep muck in rain, snow and storms, tasted especially good. After winning such excellent results in the battle, the officers and men were tired and worn out, but in elevated spirits because of our success and in hopes that we would celebrate the following New Year's Day at home. Hood's Western Army had melted down like snow under the noon sun. His battalion columns, banners and guns would no longer be seen by the Union Army in the West again. His disheartened troops crossed the Tennessee River in disorganized groups again for the last time and headed south.

One can imagine that the result of the campaign was depressing for them. In the campaign he had lost almost his entire artillery. He could no longer take his wounded back with him and they fell into our hands. On 4 January we marched again from Columbia to the Tennessee River. Not far from Columbia on the Mount Pleasant Pike, the rebel General Pillow had his plantation, on which his slaves numbered in the thousands. The general had rented out the plantation as soon as he was forced to flee at the beginning of the war. The renter was a Union sympathizer, and had already taken over the plantation before the beginning of the war. While Hood rested at Nashville, General Pillow was at home again but found only a few of his slaves still on the plantation. Although he was a commissioned general in the southern army, after Fort Donaldson, he was no longer entrusted a command of any importance. His military career ended with his surrender of Fort Donaldson.

Our forage-master went to the plantation with three wagons to get corn. After he had loaded, he presented the renter with a receipt and made room for others. At noon, the renter had set the table for various generals. As usual, the conversation turned to a discussion of the behavior of the troops marching past, and if any had bothered him. He said no. But several batteries had loaded buckwheat, and although the quartermaster gave him a receipt, a little Shetland pony that belonged to his son had disappeared. He couldn't say for certain, but believed that it had been taken by the first battery that had loaded there. This would have been the 15th Indiana. When we pulled into camp after a march of 20 miles, we received an order right away from the Division General Couch which read that in marching past the Pillow Plantation, a Shetland pony had disappeared and supposedly it was in our battery. But such a thing was impossible, so I wrote on the envelope that no one in our battery had taken a pony and it was not in our battery. The next day we marched another 20 miles. In the evening we once again received an order, the same as the day before, with the same response naturally. Some of our gunners had inspected the area and discovered that to the right of the pike was an area rich in game where the rich plantation owners hunted. On the evening of the second night we had the pleasure of dining on a roast of game. We rested here several days.

Then we covered the last stretch to Clinton, the end of our trip. On the 14th we were informed that our corps was supposed to go east in order to support either Grant or Sherman. The governments transport fleet arrived a few days later. As soon as the ships or boats were loaded, they started downriver, each time two side-by-side. The boats "Havana" and "Tyrone" along with two barges carried our battery, the 19th Ohio Battery and Cooper's Brigade from our division. It was already dark when we started boarding ship but it was soon finished. As we now were making ourselves comfortable on the salon deck, we heard an Irishman below on the boiler deck cursing and making a fuss. One of the officers, who sat next to me, hollered down what the matter was. "Oh", he said, "Major, come down here and see what the gunners have done! We innocent infantry men have to dig breastworks for these lazy bums, then cover for them left and right, and when we are wounded, we have to bleed to death on the battlefield because there isn't even room in an ambulance, and these gunners have a mule in the ambulance." Naturally that caused a rush there and to our great astonishment we found the much sought-after pony life-size in the ambulance. The Irishman had been looking for some food in the ambulance and found the legs of the pony. It was lifted out and taken to Schofield's headquarters. General Cooper had me come forward and I was brashly and sharply interrogated by him. But no one knew how it happened that the pony was in the ambulance, not the driver nor the cook. Our men certainly didn't know anything.

But General Cooper wanted revenge. On the second morning when we reached Evansville, Indiana on the Ohio River, the first mate of the "Havana" came to me and complained that during the night, one of his overcoats had been stolen. There was nothing to be done but go with him to look for it. To my great joy, the coat was found in the 19th Ohio Battery. The man stated that he had borrowed it to keep warm while he was on guard duty over the horses, which was true. Now I laid the quilt about the pony on that battery too, and I was somewhat relieved when I could tell Cooper that it was likely that the Ohio battery had taken the pony and stuck in our ambulance under cover of some bushes. At the end of our conversation, General Cooper said, that the inventiveness of the Yankees always amazed him. He had been born in Tennessee and had always promised his fellow citizens of the state that private property should be held sacred and especially that of innocent children.

On the next morning we reached Cincinnati and anchored at the foot of Vine Street. Around 10 o'clock, gunner T. of the first gun came to me and asked me for a pass for one or two hours in the city and gave as the reason, that when we had been here two years ago with Burnside's 9th Corps, had made a debt of two dollars at a bar and he wanted to pay it back. We had to reject his request and said the bar owner would have forgiven the debt long ago in his liberality and patriotism. One of the gunners standing nearby commented, T. was the "Boss Liar" in Cincinnati. T. had made himself so fine that anyone could see that he wanted the pass for something else than to repay a bar debt. His buttons shone like gold and in his jacket and overcoat, one could see the cow and horse hair that had been woven into the fabric in some "shoddy"-textile factories in place of wool, which became apparent from much brushing. In order to make an impression, he had borrowed a saber and his boots shone like a mirror. But it was no good, he didn't have a pass. Angry, he sat on a cracker barrel and played with his pocket revolver. In this mood and situation, he was met by gunner S., the Latin student from Kassel.

He made fun of T. and recited Heinrich Heine's song "Die Lorelei"..."I don't know what it is that makes me so sad, etc." The last syllable was barely out of his mouth, when T. shouted; "Wretch, you burned through your father's fortune at the university in Germany when your relatives tried to make a decent person out of you, but had to give it up. And when you no longer could do your nonsense in Germany, you came back here, much to the joy of your parents, to find new territory for your vagrancy. Then, when you left your father's house, you sang "Now Thank the Lord" to your parents. And now you want to annoy me. Get away from me or I am going to shoot you full of holes!" S. sprang up the stairs to the salon in three steps and met our Doctor B. "Doctor! Doctor! Come right away, there is a sick man down here!" Both ran down the stairs and S. pointed to T. Doctor B. asked T. "John, what's wrong." "Oh Doctor", he said, "You can't help me. It's about a pass and time to take care of a little obligation in the city and the lieutenant refused to give me the pass." "Wait, John", said the doctor, "perhaps I can arrange something." The doctor was upstairs again right away and asked me if to allow a messenger to go into the city for him. He had attended the medical college here and would like to send the professor a letter. I granted it, never guessing that I had two liars in front of me. Dr. B. asked me for the services of T. S. the student who often functioned as the company clerk, was ordered to write the pass. S. growled to himself, "That's something, to send such as fancied up boy as T. into the city. Anyone who sees him wouldn't believe he is in the service. He should have sent Lochmüller, Woods or Stevens. He still has unburned powder on his face." No sooner did the doctor have the pass in his hand, he gave it to T., who didn't waste any time, but went into the city. At 3 p.m. he came back. When he was stopped and asked why he was late, he said that the doctors were at dinner and he had to wait for the professors. I never did discover whether Doctor B. had ever gone to the Medical College in Cincinnati.

    S. thought that T. would have had better luck with his pass if he had told the truth right away; that two years ago he had started a love affair in "over the Rhine" in Cincinnati and now marching through again, wanted to visit the "joy of his life" again. But this shows us how depraved people are. Given a chance, he makes up a lie about owning a barkeeper money and because something rotten causes rot elsewhere, the doctor was pulled into it. But there always have to be two...even with lying. T. grinned with his whole face and believed that after this first success that he could expect other favors. But just then the order came to unload the battery and to get into the train made ready for us at the Little Miami depot.

In spite of bitter cold weather the unloading was soon completed, but driving up 4th Street, where the hill was still covered with ice and snow, wasn't so easy. But we reached the depot without delay. Along the way there we were stared at by many onlookers because word had gotten around like wildfire that there were guns and gun carriages spattered with blood. Seldom were the men in a better mood while loading at a train station, and it was never finished more quickly than here. Our S. who always had to have the last word and much to T's annoyance, sang in his bass voice the song, "We bind for her the virgin crown of violet-blue silk...and tie a rope around your neck with pleasure and joy." The German gunners all joined in the song and T. became of the victim of their happy mood.

Before we left Cincinnati, many gallons of coffee were made available to us, and with the help of the station cook, divided out by our quartermaster, which really added to the men's good mood.

A short time after the night passenger train had departed Cincinnati; our train followed and reached Columbus a short time before midnight. We were delayed there for several hours and to protect us from the cold, the quartermaster of our division had fires made in the street near the railroad. Early in the morning our train rolled on toward Wheeling, but around 10 o'clock stopped in the middle of a field. Two deputy sheriffs got on with a search warrant and wanted to search the train for stolen footwear. I sent a corporal along with them. After 30 minutes and came back to our car and reported that they hadn't found anything, not even a pair of new shoes on the feet of a single soldier. Then the two "deputies" wanted to ride along in our car to the next station, but I told them it wasn't possible. The deputies were taken aback and we then asked them about everything; whether they had fulfilled their obligations according to the laws of Ohio and if they were satisfied with the search. The officers said yes and that they were convinced that there were no stolen shoes or boots on the train. Then I told them to get out. "Oh no", said the one deputy, "We are going along to the next station." "No wheel will turn until you leave the train."

was the answer. "And if that doesn't work, we'll tie you to a tree." I told the deputies further that the artillery sons were honored parents, and they better get out and leave us in peace because we are serious. The deputies put on a good face to their bad game and left the train. We later learned what the story was. In Columbus, several cases of footwear had been stolen with the help of the railroad police and the theft was blamed on the soldiers marching through. But the real thieves and the railroad policemen were apprehended and arrested.

We reached Wheeling the next morning. The horses were unloaded here and the men were taken to a large hall which was crawling with pests. We had to put up with it for several days because the rebel cavalry had captured the Baltimore & Ohio Railroad and had ripped up the tracks west of the Cumberland River. Here we had the honor of getting to know General Heinzelmann personally, the commander of the West Virginia Department. Wheeling was the western end of the "National Road" and General Cooper, who was also being held up here with his brigade, thought we could march the rest of the way in a few days, and in passing, give the enemy some blows from the side, instead of waiting until some other troops had driven them from the Baltimore & Ohio Railroad. It is perhaps appropriate to mention that this road is of national importance and to describe it further. In the populated areas of Maryland and Virginia, private companies had already built several good roads at the end of the 18th Century, but the question of connecting the East with the West by building a road over the Allegheny Mountains was too difficult for private investors. Something had to happen to bring the new Louisiana Territory west of the Mississippi River closer. So in 1806, the building of a "National Road" was proposed in Congress and passed. President Jefferson gave his full support to this enterprise. The road began in Cumberland, Maryland and ended in Wheeling, West Virginia on the Ohio River. An older road from Cumberland to Baltimore was connected to the Cumberland Road. The National Road was to connect the largest of the eastern states with the west and was opened for traffic in 1818. This road reached Ohio where the connection by steamboat was possible on the Ohio and Mississippi Rivers through their wide valleys, by which travel to the northwestern states and territories was much easier. The National Road became very important for that reason, and hence was built avoiding indifferent or poor construction. It is very much admired today and one believes that it was built for all time. Maintenance has been considered absolutely necessary and the best methods for repairing it are in use. Statesmen like Clay and Hamilton have dedicated their great attention to this highway. This has been very much appreciated by the large number of coachmen and hotel proprietors who depend for their livelihood on the traffic on the road.

The old stone bridges still stand today as monuments to history and beauty and although they have been in use for almost a century they don't look old. One of these still in best condition is at Grantsville, Pa. It spans the Castleman River with an arch of 80 feet. It rises over the water beautifully and perfectly. The bridge with its approach is 307 feet long and 34 feet wide. All the bridges are like this on the road. Another beautiful bridge which gives it builder honor is the stone bridge near the city of Cumberland over Mill's Creek, better known as the bridge over the "Narrows". It connects two hills between which the creek rolls on over a gravel bed under a simple, large arch.

Naturally, guesthouses of every kind were established along this road. Everywhere there was a need, the need was satisfied and many of the places have become famous in the land for their meals or the owner's obliging service. Although the look of the menus couldn't compare to those of today's hotels, the table was loaded with the best dishes. There is no doubt that the meals served then could hold their own in comparison to today's hotels. In order to get one's fill, it was only necessary to follow the owner's invitation, "Help yourselves!"

These "Taverns" were usually positioned so that they contributed to the "romance" of the road, often on hills with wonderful views, or in a shady corner protected from the sun, protected from public view, cool and inviting the traveler to a longer stay. Each guesthouse had a sign reaching over the road from a tall post, so that the traveler could see it from a great distance. We found such old "taverns" in Baltimore for a long time that were known in earlier times to everyone far and wide.

On the street where one enters the city from the Baltimore road and near the corner of Pratt Street, stood the old "Tree-Ton-Tavern". But the sign has been so hidden by telegraph poles that one can hardly see it.

During the winter, there was much concern for heating the public room, which in most cases was the bar-room. Winter in the mountains was usually quite hard and a big fire in the fireplace, sometimes up to 7' square, was kept going. A regular wagon of coal was thrown on the fire at once to keep the cold out. The landlord himself made sure there was a good fire. Such are the memories that we heard from our ancestors, who made the trip from Baltimore in those days. There was also a well almost every mile. This included a water tank, usually with a stoneware jug underneath filled with the best whiskey that the neighboring plantation or farmer would offer for sale at 12 ½ to 17 cents a gallon to travelers passing by. I myself was witness in Indiana in 1855 west of Indianapolis how the daughter of a wealthy farmer refilled the jugs which had been emptied by the passing travelers.

The great attraction of living close to this road was the continuous activity and traffic. Regular transportation of people was offered by various companies, and the arrival in a village was always the event of the day and drew many curious citizens to have a look, the way people in little villages ran to see the first train that reached the place. The arrival and departure of these coaches were so regular, that someone without a watch could tell the time of day.

Most coaches had relays every 12 miles from each other. Changing the horses was done in the shortest possible time. When the coachman reached one of these stations, he would throw the reins over the backs of his horses and they were unhitched and fresh horses, already harnessed and waiting, would take their place in an instant and with the snap of the whip, the ride continued on at a gallop. Many of these stagecoaches were quite luxurious for the day; the seats were upholstered and could hold nine passengers comfortably.

The seat next to the coachman was the most desirable because of the view. When travel season was at its height, one could see as many as 15 coaches; one behind the other. The greatness of this road was already destined to decline when the canal from Buffalo to Albany connected Lake Erie to the Hudson River and the great northwestern territories were opened to free settlement by immigrants. Before the canal, Baltimore, New York and Philadelphia were the most important cities, but from that time on, New York surpassed the other two. The coachmen and workers on this road were usually men of great honesty and strong of character and were highly respected by the farmers and villagers through which the road passed. Unsavory actions were not tolerated by them and their offspring now belong to the best citizens of the republic. The trip from Wheeling to Baltimore then cost $17.25; now by train first class, $10.

Cooper's wish to march on foot on the road was not approved, and a few days later we were sent on again by train. Having to stop at every switch however, we would have reached Cumberland just as fast on foot. Having arrived there, we were once again in familiar territory, since we had traveled from there to Harper's Ferry in 1862. Our camp on Bolivar Heights in August and September had given us the opportunity to learn more about the history of Harper's Ferry. From a German family by the name of Schumacher that lived on Bolivar Heights, which I often visited, I learned the following about Harper's Ferry and its origin:

Robert Harper, after whom the ferry was named, was born in Oxford, England in 1703. He studied architecture and mill construction in his youth, which became his future occupation. He and his brother became members of a society in Oxford that wanted to settle in Pennsylvania. They sailed on the ship "Morning Star" from London on 1735. Robert Harper went to Philadelphia and married a Miss Griffith and for 11 years, carried out his profession with energy and success. Since he now had money, he bought a piece of land where Frankfort, Pa. now stands. Here he built several houses and a church and called the new village New Oxford. This investment made him a poor man again. In 1746, he sold what little he could still call his own with the intention of leaving Philadelphia to start anew in North Carolina. Just at this time he received offers from Quakers who had a convention in Philadelphia, to settle in the Shenandoah Valley in Virginia. Early in 1747, Harper left his home and friends behind and after a one-week ride by horse, reached Fredericktown,

Maryland; then just a small settlement. Here he met a German peddler by the name of Hoffmann from Baltimore, who was also on his way to the Shenandoah Valley to sell his wares. This man told him about a short-cut through the mountains right where the Shenandoah and Potomac Rivers unite; the most beautiful view and grandiose place that one could imagine. This is now the world famous "Porta" in the Blue Ridge Mountains...Harper's Ferry.

One can travel the wide, wide world and travel to every country, but won't find a more beautiful, romantic place than Harper's Ferry. On 18 March, 1747, Robert Harper crossed the Potomac River and rested for the night on the place now known as Harper's Ferry. He found two settlers here; one was known by the name "Peter in the hole", the other Gutterman Tom, both Germans who had been living there since 1733. Harper bought their property, consisting of a boat, a horse, a log-cabin with garden, an orchard, a few acres of buckwheat and a few acres of pasture. After the purchase was sealed, Peter and Gutterman said goodbye to the new owner and headed west and were never heard from again. Another man by the name of Stevens lived there too. He had come to the area in 1732 with a company under the leadership of a certain Hite, who with 50 others were going to settle in the Virginia Valley and farm. But the manager often brought them in unpleasant contact with Lord Fairfax. Robert Harper bought himself another piece of land in Berkley County for which he paid 20 Guineas. After the land was surveyed by George Washington and George Fairfax, he received the deed from Lord Fairfax in Greenway County, Virginia.

The government of Virginia held a convention in 1763 and passed a law incorporating Harper's Ferry into Virginia. He had made a lot of improvements on his land, built a sawmill and a flour mill, and operated regular ferry service which he leased to William Ready in 1779. He then moved a few miles toward Shenandoah Falls. Shortly thereafter, he wrote to his wife, who he had left back in Philadelphia, that he had become so attached to the isolation and mountain scenery that he decided to make it their home. She then came to Virginia with her nephew Robert Griffith from Bedford, Virginia.

The following winter, 1747, is remembered as the most severe in that region and in spring 1748, the Potomac River had a large flood...so says old documents. The water was so high, that the Harper family had move into a barn on the hill and in the following October there was another flood, which people called the "pumpkin flood".

Thirty years before the revolution, Harper had enjoyed as much satisfaction in human life as a common person can have. But in the short period of four years, his life changed. His brother Joseph died in Philadelphia in 1775. In 1778 his wife died and was buried on the hill, where Harper had donated four acres for a public cemetery near the church. Since Harper's health was deteriorating, on 26 September 1782 he made a will in which he gave the Ferry property to his niece and daughter of Joseph Harper of Philadelphia. She had married a German, John Wagner. The couple held the property "in trust" for their son John Wagner Jr. Harper died on 2 October 1782 and was buried next to his wife. The descendants of Wagner are also buried in the same cemetery. The Wagner family sold 125 acres of the Harper property to George Washington, then President of the United States, for $7066; 2/3 for the use of the national armory (weapons factory). The heirs still received six acres, which were referred to as the Wagner Reservation. But in 1862, the ferry and Wagner Bridge were sold to the railroad. The good water power just above the ferry caused the government to build the biggest weapons factories there and made the place famous throughout the nation, which became even more famous by John Brown's attack and the uproar created by it in 1859.

Arrival of the 23rd Corps in Washington

On the morning of 4 February, we found ourselves in Washington, and the train we had been on for almost five days on the Baltimore & Ohio Railroad switched onto a side track to the "Potomac Flats" near the Washington Monument. We marched to Camp Stoneman right away, about two miles south on the east side of the Potomac River, to join the other units of the division in camp. We had barely made ourselves comfortable when an agent from Indiana, stationed in Washington to satisfy the needs of troops from that state which happened to be passing through Washington, greeted us and took care of our meals. He reported that the governor of Indiana and his staff had settled in Willard's Hotel and that he would be pleased if we would make a visit to him in the evening. After making some preparations, we had our horses brought and rode off to Washington, first furnishing ourselves with a pass and the password to get over the bridge. It was almost 9 p.m. when we reached the hotel. We marched straight to the all-knowing hotel clerk and asked if the governor from Indiana was staying there. He confirmed that but informed us that Governor Morton was at the White House visiting President Lincoln, where we could hardly follow him at this hour. We asked further, whether the governor's staff was also visiting the President. No, he said smiling, they went to "Hooker's Division". "Well", said my comrade, not knowing what "Hooker's Division" meant in Washington, "they've made fools of us tonight. As tired and worn out as we are after fourteen days of little sleep, and to send us here! That's a bit much." As we stood there not knowing what to do, an attendant asked us seriously, "If we wanted to, he could direct us to Hooker's Division". One of my comrades answered, if he thought we were crazy enough to visit Hooker's Division yet at 9 o'clock in the evening, when it will be time to be back in the barracks. The boy grinned and some sword-rattlers (Officers in full uniform with swords, who were making the rotunda of the hotel unsafe) laughed out loud. We were rather taken aback at first. Angered, one our comrades said, "Let us take a drink and go home." We went into the nearby bar room and our comrade asked for the best whiskey in Washington. Glasses and bottles were set up and each poured as much as his thirst demanded. Before we had raised our glasses, one of the bolder ones asked, "Barkeep, say, can you tell us where Hooker's Division has its camp." Potztausend! (Stronger than "gracious me"), you're awfully green. Everyone knows Hooker's Division before he gets to Washington; it stretches from the Treasury to 7th Street...where buxom women do business." If we hadn't had such a colossal thirst, the glasses would have fallen out our hands at this revelation. But we drank up and another comrade bought us another round. Naturally the bartender now gave us the complete history of Hooker's Division. When General Hooker got his division together in Washington, most of the men were New Yorkers. Their camp was not far south of Pennsylvania Avenue. Many were married and it didn't take long before a large portion of their "better halves" were also there. There followed many good and honorable women whose lovers were in the division and these were then followed by the less honorable. The latter are still here today. Though General Hooker and his division took part in the battles at Yorktown and Williamsburg in March, 1863, the name "Hooker's Division" will stick to the region for all eternity.

 Knowing more now about Washington than we had in the morning, we emptied our glasses and made our way back to our camp at Camp Stoneman. Tired and worn out, we stayed in our blankets until the morning sun was high over our heads, and to our astonishment, a messenger stood in front of us and showed us a circular which invited all of the artillery officers of the corps to the White House at 11 o'clock to be introduced to President Lincoln. Now we brushed and polished in order to look as good as possible. At exactly 11 o'clock we were all there. In a real goose march we then went to the East Room and were introduced to the President one after the other to shake his hand. Col. Schofield, our artillery boss, made the introductions. My cheek was still quite swollen. When I stepped forward, the President made some comments. I didn't understand one word he said, but it seemed to be similar to our pastor at confirmation, giving us his well-meaning blessing for the future. What this event was supposed to mean for us, no one knew, for promotion in rank for services in Franklin and Nashville didn't appear likely. The highest rank in an "independent battery" was captain, and since the captain of our battery was a close relative of Governor Morton, General Love and Secretary Caleb G. Smith, there was very little chance that I, without any influence with anyone in power, would get an advancement, and my intention to serve in the regular army after the war, was an impossibility because of my crooked leg, as well as the head wound and the loss of my hearing at Nashville.

Around 12 o'clock noon we got on our horses in front of the White House and looked for the best restaurant in the city in order to indulge ourselves with the delicacies of civil life; good Lincoln had not offered us any lunch. Not far from the Patent Office we found what we were looking for. They were just unloading a wagon full of fresh oysters from Chesapeake Bay; there certainly would be other delicacies there too. We went in and attacked the creative productions of the chef for the next three hours. After having satisfied the inner person, we rode to the Capitol. There the south flag was flying, so we knew that the House of Representatives was in session. We went to Congress Hall and had our representative come to the door. This old shriveled-up warrior, Dumont, under whom I had served in my first battle in Virginia, was very friendly and obliging and showed us every possible attention, even led us into the bar in the cellar of the Capitol, where we had the opportunity to sample really the best whiskey in the country. He asked whether we had a wish from Congress. One of my comrades answered, that he should see to it that our payments were made in gold instead in devalued paper money. No one thought of pensions in those days. Dumont did introduce a bill to that effect but that is as far as it got. Had good Lincoln not lost his life, something probably would have come from it.

Other congressional representatives were equally liberal. One of these representatives promised the Colonel to support his promotion to brigadier-general. This colonel and his regiment had provided very valuable service at Franklin and Nashville. At Resaca and Atlanta he had had heavy losses, but in Indiana there was no vacancy for a brigadier-general at the time. The Koburgs had snapped all those up. The colonel, who provided good service again in North Carolina, was discharged in July 1865.

We arrived back in camp around 6 o'clock in the evening. Another circular from the artillery boss reached us during evening mess, requesting us to meet him at the Willard Hotel at 10 o'clock the next morning. It was wished that no artillery officer would be absent. So, early the next morning we rode back to Washington. At the hotel we threw our reins to the attendants and went in. Here several officers had already gathered, among them our artillery chief, the former Col. Schofield. Brigadier-General Schofield in a brand new uniform was having a conversation with an over six-foot-tall person in a Major-General uniform. Schofield's adjutant was naturally stormed with questions; what it all meant. Yesterday at the meeting with the President, our artillery chief was still seen in a shabby uniform as First Lieutenant of the Missouri Artillery Regiment. Now he had jumped all at once over the highest officer of the regiment. It astonished all of us. Palmer answered, that after the gathering yesterday where the President honored our good service of the artillery at Franklin and Nashville, Colonel Schofield was made a Brigadier-General. The Major-General with whom he was talking to, was General Hancock. We were then introduced to him. "Well", said one of our comrades, "This is a good place to be. We have to stay here, we might still become something. To change from first-lieutenant to general overnight doesn't happen every day."

A wink from Schofield and we were all introduced to General Hancock, one after the other. After a friendly handshake and the usual best wishes, we were invited to follow him to the bar. Here we toasted our new general. After a while, Schofield had another round poured and this time we clinked our glasses to General Hancock.

After we had left the bar and General Hancock, we congratulated Schofield, for which we hadn't found time before. His adjutant led us afterwards into the hotel dining room. Here the table was laden with all the best things that could be found in the market then. One of our American officers began the song: "This is the place I long have sought, what was the cause I had found it not." After we had enough to eat and had spent some happy hours, we rode back to our quarters, without trying to connect with the governor of Indiana or his staff again. On our first day in Camp Stoneman, we had gotten orders to turn our horses and mules over to the quartermaster of the place. After that our men only had to stand watch and everyone in the unit had a chance to visit Washington. The central places where they would collect were the Treasury, the Patent Office, Post Office, Capitol and the shipyards. The Smithsonian Institute had burned down not long before and couldn't be visited. The sessions at Congress however, were the biggest draw. The western veterans had a lot of freedom in Washington. They often visited the theater in the evening. Among the most important that were open then, where the Ford, Wallach's and the National Theater, along with a mass of variety and vaudeville stages.

Finally, the ice left the Potomac and we were ordered to get our new horses from the quartermaster. On the evening of the 17th we were ready for service again. On the morning of the 18th we marched through Washington on Pennsylvania Avenue to the Alexandria ferry at the foot of 7th Street. Our horse teams were the best we had ever had. Here the transport ship "United States" awaited us. We unhitched the teams and the guns and horses were loaded onto an ocean steamer. Loading the horses was very simple; a wide strap was put under the horse's belly with a ring on each end. A hook on a rope goes through the rings. The horse is lifted by steam into the air and let down on the deck of the ship.

The ship didn't look as if it would fare well in a storm. But in three hours, the artillery was loaded. A few horses from Schofield's headquarters were also carried onboard; among these appeared the Shetland pony again that had left us in Clifton. But General Meigs, the quartermaster didn't want to transport him further and he was shoved aside and led to General Meigs' private stable. Since we had a few hours' time before the anchor was lifted, the men and officers had a chance to see the hotel where the Jackson – Ellsworth murders had taken place. By 9 o'clock everything was on board. A short time later the lines were cast off and around 11 p.m., the propeller started turning and we sailed down the Potomac River.

The Ocean Journey to Wilmington

Our ship's captain was a Norwegian, an old seaman; his wife and daughter accompanied him. The other officers and crew were Americans; former whalers from New Bedford. Early in the morning, we reached Hampton Roads and passed right of Fort Monroe and left of Point Lookout and steamed into the open ocean. As soon as the men were subjected to sea air, they lost any appetite. The ocean was very quiet during the day, but by evening the ship was rocking significantly. The men laughed and made fun of each other when one of them made tribute to the sea god. At the dinner table in the cabin, the captain of the ship had the honor chair, his first mate sat on his left and our doctor to his right and me next to him. It was unusual that I didn't miss a single meal throughout the trip, one of the few that was on good terms with Neptune. Our doctor didn't fare so well and already had to leave the table at the beginning. Between meals, the captain's grog was made available to us, which we made good use of.

On the evening of the first day we were nearing Cape Hatteras. Now suddenly the ocean got so rough that one can't describe it. The ship rolled and rocked and the horses were thrown from one side to the other. As soon as the horse lay on the deck, it was completely impossible to get it to stand again. Many had broken their legs. The men were commanded to hold on to the horses, so they wouldn't hit the bulkhead or the boards in front, but it didn't work. The rolling became severe and the storm was like no other. The waves crashed over the ship and it didn't seem to be letting up at all. Several of the men were thrown to the deck. The wood structure of the stalls fell apart and we expected to go down with man and mouse. We asked the captain if there was any way to survive it. Most of the horses lay on their side on the deck. This was the most horrible sight of all. The whole deck was covered with dying horses, and after the stalls broke up, the horses were being rolled together from one side and then to the other. On many the eyes were hanging out. The deck was slippery with blood and no one had solid footing any longer. The rolling caused the hide to be rubbed off the bones and their suffering couldn't be soothed.

Since we couldn't help the poor animals, we went to our quarters, the men in the lower deck and we officers in the cabin. As day dawned, the storm let up somewhat. Now the sailors opened some of the side hatches and those horses that it would be impossible to save were thrown into the sea through the hatches. 36 of our most beautiful, heaviest had to be sacrificed in this way and the others weren't worth the transportation cost to Wilmington. Our men worked all morning with the sailors in the wet in order to save as many of our teams as possible. (The first Monitor went down in such a hurricane in the same area.) The Hatteras storms are some of the worst on either of the American coasts.

The weather on the second day on the ocean was very cold and rough. During the night and on the morning of the third day also; the men had to huddle near the smokestacks to stay warm. But when we reached the gulfstream, it all changed. Here it was warm and the sea was calmer. Since something was wrong with the rudder and the propeller, the few sails that the ship carried were hauled up, and after the men had dried themselves out again, we experienced spring on the coast, just far enough from land that we couldn't see it. As modest compensation, the ship's kitchen served a good meal. The ship could only make slow progress with the sails. The sailors worked day and night on the rudder and propeller. Since healthy people always have to be occupied in some way, the men helped, just to have something to do. A young signal officer tried in vain to find someone to play cards with on the third day, but there were no gamblers in our battery. In order to satisfy him, the ship captain's wife said she would try, although she could hardly speak English. When the day came to an end, she had won $200 from the lieutenant. On the next morning the young officer wanted to play again, but she was so sick that he never saw her again as long as he was on board. On the afternoon of the fifth day, the young signal-lieutenant had to disembark, since we had reached the end of our trip. Since the battery stayed on board until the next morning, we noticed that the wife had recovered again as soon as the gambling lieutenant had left the ship.

About the time it was getting dark on the evening of the 24th, we passed the mouth of the Cape Fear River. The waves were once again as high as hills and the ship rolled horribly. The next morning we had a view of Fort Fisher with 60 war-ships and monitors at anchor. The towers of the latter looked like smallpox victims from hits of enemy balls. During the day we were brought to South Inlet. Here we had to transfer to a flat-bottomed lighter, since the harbor in Wilmington is too shallow for deep ocean vessels, which is why it was so valuable for the blockade-runners. The large warships couldn't follow so the entrance to Wilmington stayed open until we took procession of the forts: Fisher, Casswell and Anderson.

When we left Washington, everything there was still covered with ice and snow. But at Smithville, our first sight of land, it was more spring-like. The green was already showing through the sand and everything looked fresh. The shore south of the entrance was strewn for miles with the ribs of stranded blockade-runners, for as soon as they were chased by the fleet and couldn't reach the harbor, they ran aground on the sandy shore and the sailors got away on dry land. The shore and the low land on the west side of the Cape Fear River were very built up and valuable. The impression of prosperity was apparent everywhere.

The enemy under General Hoke had already cleared out of the area but the blockade runners hadn't gotten the news yet that the city was now in Yankee hands. Two loaded ships had entered on their way to Wilmington during the night without the least suspicion and were taken by our troops. Wilmington was one of the most important harbors in the south, since it was from here that the confederates could still get luxury goods which they usually paid for with cotton. It brought the place a lot of profitable business. But this last artery of life for the south had been cut off with our capture of the harbor. The biggest losses fell to the English who had the illegal commerce entirely in their hands. A newspaper in Wilmington had written that the losses to Wilmington wouldn't nearly be as significant for the south as it would be for the British, for the Southerners would now keep their gold at home and would spend it on domestic products.

But the citizens of Wilmington didn't believe the paper. Two days before the capture of Wilmington, the price of gold was at an all-time high and no business was carried out in confederate money afterwards.

As soon as we reached the wharf, we left the ship but our horses were so ruined that we only had teams for two guns. As we moved these to camp, one after the other, we received orders to deliver all our horses and mules to the quartermaster. Other batteries were in the same position and there weren't any teams available. For an indefinite time we would be without teams, so we could enjoy the vacation that we hadn't gotten in almost four years. The men made good use of it, and since we had plenty of provisions, we lived wonderfully and with pleasure.

There wasn't any shortage of deep-water fish, oysters, froglegs and other delicacies from the sea and land. For 50 cents paper money we could get a whole drum of oysters. We could get buffalo fish for almost nothing and the splendid weather turned Wilmington into a blooming garden already in early March and our cook had fresh peas. Nature seemed to be welcoming us more than the people here. In a junk shop I noticed two strong young men that, judging by their age, would have been expected to be in the Southern army. The father and storeowner said they were Englishmen and didn't have anything to do with this spectacle. Inquiring further, I learned that the place was full of Englishmen who were getting rich on the blockade runners. The Americans living there had bought as much cotton, turpentine, pitch and tar as their southern paper money could buy (certainly not dumb).

The most horrifying sight for anyone, but especially that a soldier could witness, was the arrival and exchange of our prisoners. This took place a short time after taking Wilmington. No pen can describe the sight. Thousands starved to skin and bones, tattered figures with sunken eyes, strong men before, moving slowly with frequent pauses to rest, (if they hadn't collapsed already just from joy), through the streets and sat down along the side-roads staring half unconscious at their approaching comrades and only begging for something to eat. The torments of Andersonville had robbed them of their senses. Even today one shudders at the memory of the inhuman treatment there and will never forget it.

Two brothers from the 118th Ohio Regiment served in the same company. One was taken prisoner. When the other was walking through the street in Wilmington, he looked into the face of one of those freed, who was sitting by the side of the road holding a piece of bread and some meat in his long thin fingers with even longer fingernails. Traces of scurvy had been left behind; the dry, long hair hung over his face, and his bones could be seen through the tattered clothing. Andersonville had turned a strong, lively young man into a ruin. "My God, John, is that you?" The brother was instantly at his side, tears streaming down his cheeks. As in a dream, the unfortunate man turned his face to the speaker and with trembling, bloodless lips said, "Yes, I think I am he, and aren't you George? Please bring me something decent to eat. I am hungry!" After several days of care, his mind was completely restored.

I made a friendship with a comrade named Schäfer from the 82nd Illinois Regiment, who was prisoner in Andersonville for 21 months. Later he lived in Breese, Illinois. His legs had almost rotted off and he was in the hospital in Wilmington for a long time. All the sentimental statements gushed out in speeches on both sides at gatherings and reunions, sound very strange when one remembers the misery of the poor prisoners.

Wirtz, the commander of the prison, could have posted Dante's words over the gate at Andersonville: "He who enters here, leave all hope behind." With Captain Wirtz we see again how a family was divided by the war. His brother served for four years as veterinarian for the 6th Indiana Battery on the Union side, while the other played slave-driver at Andersonville. The South still parades its knightliness, daring and unbending courage. But in this proud presentation he forgets the inhuman treatment of prisoners in the southern prisons, where the only friend of the Union soldiers was insanity and death.

The capture of Wilmington was followed by many of the residents seeking to establish a good connection to the new administration. Most of these were older men or strangers, since the youth were in the army. Many of them acquired passes to protect themselves from the provost marshal. One morning, one of these old men furnished with a pass, found several recently freed prisoners in his courtyard and in blunt words told them to get off his premises. The poor wretches hardly understood him and continued to lie in the sunshine. He threatened to report them to the provost marshal. A lieutenant passing by heard the threat and asked him to repeat it. "I'm going to report it," said the officer, "and will spare you the bother. You men, stay here until I get back." When he returned he had an order to take possession of the house as a hospital for the sick and worn-out freed prisoners. In a few hours, the house was full of residents. I took a look at this home for the starved prisoners and how comfortable they had made themselves on the fine carpets.

There were still many families living in Wilmington, but no occupations for the older men and female members of the whites and their foodstuffs were coming to an end. Since they hadn't been able to turn their cotton, turpentine, pitch and tar into cash, Uncle Sam had to jump in to help so that our former enemies didn't starve. One morning, my duties took me to the military supply depot. Here a group of needy had gathered, and to my surprise, one only saw a few old, half-crippled former slaves and no young, strong blacks, but many whites which looked as if they had been wealthy before; many women in silk dresses with baskets in their hands, now willing to carry home themselves what they had received; probably something that had never happened before.

Since we didn't have any duties and our quarters had been set up in the middle of town under shady trees, many of the men turned over their rations to the neighboring families and had them prepare meals for them. In this way, a number of families could share the meals. There were several German families living in Wilmington. These traveled as soon as possible to visit their families in the East.

As soon as the released prisoners were in condition to travel, they were given leave and transported to the North. But nothing is sadder in the history of the war than the sinking of steamers loaded with these poor veterans. After all the suffering that a man can bear, and then while traveling home so full of joy, they had to give up their life in a storm on the coast. That happened to the ship "General Lyon", to the "Sultana" on the Mississippi and on the Ohio, a portion of the 9th Indiana Battery died in the waves on their way home.

The Bombardment of Fort Fisher

We got ahead of ourselves with telling about landing our battery and we would like to go back to describe the capture of Fort Fisher, Fort Anderson and Wilmington and their occupiers in more detail. Among the most important secondary operations in Sherman's campaign from Savannah north, were the captures of the North Carolina coast and of Wilmington, as well as the transfer of Schofield's 23rd Corps to North Carolina. The second attack on Fort Fisher was made about the same time as Sherman marched out from Savannah and Schofield's Corps moved north from Clinton on the Tennessee River. Two months later, Sherman had his whole army together again, with the exception of the 4th Corps. In its place he got Terry's 10th Corps, while the 4th Corps remained in the West. The city of Wilmington was the most important harbor for the South and was situated on the left bank of Cape Fear River, about 30 miles from the ocean. At the mouth, the river runs parallel to the coast and the sandy spit of land known as Federal Point is five to six miles long but only one mile wide.

Fort Fisher stands on the end of this spit and was built up of sand held together by swamp-grass and on the land side, an earthwork stretched all the way across the spit from the river to the ocean. The parapet was 500 yards long. On the ocean side the wall was 1300 yards long and the corners were protected by batteries on both ends which could protect the front of the fort with crossfire. A little island, Smith's Island, lies right in the mouth of the river, making two entrances possible. Fort Fisher and Fort Buford cover the entrance on the north side of the inlet, while Forts Caswell and Johnson provide protection for the main entrance. A little village that pilots and fishermen lived in lay under the guns of Fort Johnson. Lush leafed oaks gave the village a peaceful appearance, whose residents risked the greatest dangers in the dark stormy nights or thick fog during the day to carry out their piloting services on which the South's trade depended. Fort Fisher didn't only protect the nearby island, but a channel and the narrows of the river were also completely under the control of its guns. Once the fort was in our control the Wilmington harbor would be closed to the South. It was for this purpose that it was built, since it was self-evident that an army would land in the north out of reach of the guns. The land side of the earthwork was built very strongly, with greatest care and exactness.

The parapet was 20 feet high with only a shallow trench on the outside. The sand had been thrown up from the inside; in the middle was a little citadel which functioned as the entrance to the fort. Two guns were stationed in bastions to protect the trench in front of the earthworks. On the front of the outer works, 21 heavy guns and three mortars were positioned. In front of the palisades, mines were systematically arranged that were to be fired electrically. Very heavy cross-traverses, a dozen in number and running out about 25 feet perpendicular to the main line, rose ten feet above the heads of the gunners. They were very strong and hollowed out as casemates which served both as magazines and for protection of the men, should they be driven from their guns by an attack of the fleet. A large magazine, several houses for provisions and barracks were built in similar fashion. The front toward the ocean was similar but not so strongly built. The guns here were arranged in batteries which were connected to each other by a parapet for the infantry. Twenty-four guns were placed here, among which was a 150 pounder Armstrong Cannon that had been donated to the Confederacy by the "Manchester Friends of the South" and sent from England. The gun mount of this huge cannon was made of mahogany; the other guns were usually eight and ten inch Columbiads, as well as heavier moveable guns here and there. The entire garrison was made up of 2500 men under Col. Lamb, but General Whiting was also present at the surrender of the fort.

The first attack on the fort in December was not successful, but Admiral Porter, as well as other officers of the army were of the opinion that the fort could indeed be taken. This led to a second attempt to capture it not much later.

General Terry became commander of a division and a brigade of the 24th Corps and one division of the 25th with two field batteries. A fleet of transport ships brought them and an occupation unit to a rendezvous on the North Carolina coast. When they met up with Admiral Porter's battleships, severe storms on the coast prevented a landing until 13 January, when they went on land under the protection of the fleet. The shore here is only a narrow beach, about a few hundred yards wide, which can be reached from the mainland through Myrtle Sound. Debarking was accomplished between 8 a.m. and 4 p.m. by means of several hundreds of small boats from the fleet with several steam tugboats, even though the coast was quite rough. To cover Terry's rear, it was decided after considering several alternatives, to form a line all the way across the spit about two miles north of the fort. This was carried out by Pain's division and Abbott's brigade. The interior of Federal Point and a portion of the peninsula along the river is a flat swamp, in which pine trees grow and thick brush covers the ground. First, an artillery line was established at some distance from the fort, the flanks of which touched the swamps, but these were so flat that they offered no cover. A communication trench was therefore made from the ocean to the river. Under the protection of the fleet, Curtis's brigade from Ames's division was sent down the river toward the fort and so they reached the little unfinished earthwork on the west end. General Terry with other officers, among them Col Comstock from General Grant's staff, who had been sent along on this campaign as chief-engineer, made a careful inspection up to within about 600 paces of Fort Fisher. Curtis had been along on the first expedition in December and as a result of this inspection, he was convinced that the attack had to be made from the north, which then was carried out. Admiral Porter was asked to maintain continuous bombardment of the earthworks in order to destroy the palisades in front of the trenches so that the columns would have nothing that could hold up an attack. After a conference it was decided to attack at 3 p.m. on 15 January, which was to be made by General Ames with his division. The admiral ordered a column of sailors and marines under the command of Commander Breese to land and attack the bastion at its corner from the land and from sea. Admiral Porter fired at the fort irregularly throughout the night and in early morning of the 15th he formed 60 battleships and cannon-boats in a half-circle toward the shore and opened a regular systematic bombardment of the fort. The method used here was slow but certain fire by which one after the other of the traverses was destroyed, toppling the guns and destroying them.

One part of the fleet directed its fire toward the palisades. A regular hail of heavy gunshot was sent to the fort itself. Many of these balls (11 and 13 inches in diameter) forced the infantry of the fort to seek protection in the bunkers of the fort, while the southern cannon gunners tried in vain to counteract the northern fire from the ships. One after the other their guns was put out of action. By the time assigned for the assault, only a few of the large cannons were able to provide any service. About two o'clock, a sharpshooter line, equipped with shovels, was sent forward, and in no time they had shoveled some protection for themselves in the sand not more than 175 paces from the fort. The enemy infantry now mounted the parapet and opened fire with their muskets on Curtis's advancing line, which came within 100 paces. These too, made cover for themselves in the sand as quickly as possible. Curtis again made a charge forward to a little elevated place in front of the fort, while Pennybecker covered him and Bell's brigade took over Curtis's first position. The fleet now received the signal to redirect their fire and Curtis's brigade now attacked the same bastion near the river where the ground was swampy and where the palisades were still standing in some places. But a unit of Pioneers stormed ahead and soon reached the road and didn't stop until our troops had swarmed over the parapet and made their attack from behind the first traverse. At the same time, the sailors and marines from the ships under Commander Breese, stormed the bastion, but the enemy brought a field gun into the bastion and another into the outer works which were fired on Breese's men. At the same time, the enemy maintained fire from the parapet toward the advancing seamen. Since their position didn't have any of the protections that Ames' men had used, they were driven back with heavy losses. On the river side, Pennybecker's brigade advanced to give Curtis support. He stormed the palisades, and from the earthwork reached the river taking many prisoners. It came to hand-to-hand fighting in which the garrison was slowly driven back from one traverse and bomb shelter to the next. Col. Pennybecker was severely wounded in this fight. Bell's brigade now was ordered to attack and was positioned inside the fort. But the excavation of the sand to build the parapet had left many pits in the fort, and the magazine and the ruins of the warehouses and barracks also provided protected places for the enemy, so that the advance of Bell's brigade was very slow and difficult. Each traverse formed a new fort inside the other. At about 6 o'clock, six traverses had been captured. Terry now ordered Ames to support Abbot by making an assault from the ocean side. Through this, Abbot captured the fort from the land side. Ames now captured one traverse after the other on the ocean side that was still in enemy hands, which delivered the entire fort into Union hands. In the last charge, General Curtis was wounded in his head and Bell died from a bullet received while leading his brigade in the last assault. The remainder of the enemy garrison retreated to Fort Buchanan, followed by General Abbot, where late in the evening, General Whiting and Col. Lamb surrendered their men to the Union troops as prisoners.

During the attack of the fort, General Hoke of the enemy infantry tried to attack General Payne from the rear, but the marines under Commander Breese that had been repulsed earlier, were sent against him and after a little skirmish, Hoke pulled back and left the garrison of Fort Fisher to its fate. The fight against the parapets was very serious and lasted a long time. Losses were very great in comparison to the numbers of men taking part, especially of officers; more than fifty of these fell in this battle. The number of common soldiers was more than six hundred. As soon as the charges were made, the battleships could offer no further support. The advantages that the enemy had inside the fort with the traverses and other defense-works, made the work for Ames just as difficult as the Russians had made it for the French at Sevastopol. The attack of the marines from the ships, even though repulsed, still served as help for the infantry, for it distracted the defenders from the main assault. Fire from the battleships had also destroyed the connections between the mines and the electrical batteries, for no explosion took place during the attack. The victory was very significant, and much more valuable in that, after Butler's failed attack on this same fort in December, he had testified to the Congressional Military Committee that it never could be captured. The enemy immediately vacated the forts near Smithville and all the armament was captured by the Union troops, which together now amounted to 169 guns as well as a mass of smaller weapons and provisions, along with over 2000 prisoners. The harbors were now in our possession and it meant the end of the blockade runners. General Hoke, the commander of the district, now barricaded himself and the remainder of Whiting's division on a line from Myrtle Sound to Cape Fear River about two miles above the southern end of the sound. Directly across from him on the right bank of the river was Fort Anderson, a very strong earthwork, and from this point on, the river was full of torpedoes (mines) and full use was made of anything that could keep the Union fleet and army from advancing.

General Schofield met with General Grant at Fort Monroe and both visited General Terry at the mouth of the Cape Fear River for a conference with Admiral Porter about the next actions in the North Carolina department. The result of this conference was that Wilmington would be the first focus of attack in this campaign, so that a new base for Sherman could be established, in the case that he needed to collect his army south of Goldsboro. After this could be accomplished, it would be necessary to open up the road from New Berne to Goldsboro and to get the railroad working again, and then bring the two army corps, the 10th and 23rd, together in time to connect with Sherman's army in order to take part in the closing battles of this great campaign. After Schofield had returned to Washington after this meeting, he boarded the transport ships with Cox's Division on 4 February and had another part of his corps follow later as soon as ships were available. A terrible hurricane around Cape Hatteras kept the transport ships two days longer at sea but the division landed at Fort Fisher without any further disturbance on 9 February. The fort showed signs of the terrible sea battle, the inner walls of which were evenly studded with large, rust-covered balls 13 – 23 inches in diameter.

On 11 February, Schofield's army moved toward the enemy and so close, that it had to use its entire forces in order to hold him back. In the next night, our troops tried to lay a pontoon bridge over Myrtle Sound, hoping to get behind Hoke. But the weather was so stormy that the boats could not be brought to the shore. The night was completely dark and terribly cold and the hurricane blew through every opening in the shoddy uniforms which some supplier had cheated the government with, so that the troops were chilled to the core. The high tide and breakers made progress extremely difficult. The sand which wasn't washed by the water was too deep and loose for wagons to be used, and where the waves were washing over it was impossible to do anything, so the attempt was given up completely. Before the designated position could be reached, the moon rose and illuminated the battle fleet on the high seas and also showed the enemy the advancing troops. The enemy, now with eyes and ears open, moved to prevent our attempt to cross the sound. Schofield then tried to move to the right bank, where at least there was space to maneuver, even though the area was swampy and covered with little ponds. The troops consisting of two divisions and a brigade all under the command of General Cox were now led to the other side with orders to march to Fort Anderson and try to get around it. The battleships with their far-reaching guns were already bombarding the fort, and a section of the fleet had been commanded to open fire again, as soon as the infantry moved forward on land. Schofield had his headquarters on a steamer and could in this way go from one shore to the other as circumstances required. On the 16th, more troops were moved over the bay, as well as some field artillery batteries and a little wagon train. On the 17th, Cox's division advanced and after about three miles met the enemy cavalry and with sharpshooters forced them back to within two miles of the fort. He formed a line with his right flank on the shore and made a connection to the fleet. During the day, the infantry had covered ten miles. On the next day, the advance was renewed and the enemy was driven into its defense works. Reconnaissance showed that near the main fort, a defense line for the infantry extended several miles at a right angle to the fort, which could only be gotten around by a long detour. The line was further protected by abatis and enclosures for the enemy artillery, which opened fire with shrapnel as soon as the Federal troops were within gunshot. General Cox made a little trench here for two brigades and with two others marched to the pond to where Ames' Division was supposed to push through to him. The detour that he had to make was about 15 miles and it was almost dark before the distance through the swamp to the point of the pond had been covered.

The enemy managed stiff resistance with its cavalry but then one unit advanced around its flank and after a difficult crossing through the swamp reached solid ground and took possession of the other side. During this, the battleships had been bombarding the fort and the two brigades continued action from their position. During the night the enemy vacated its line and more troops advanced quickly on the west side of the pond, in order to complete their task. Here he received the news that Fort Anderson had been occupied by our troops and ten heavy artillery guns had been captured. The enemy retreated on the right side of the river as far as Town Creek, destroyed the bridges and made the roads impassable. On the other side of the river he withdrew to a strong position across from Town Creek, which was protected on the east side by a swamp. General Terry followed Hoke on the east side of the river and in order to strengthen him, Ames' Division was sent to him, while Cox followed the enemy to Town Creek. (Town Creek is a deep, impassable river with swampy banks, furnished with dikes near the banks so the area could be used for growing rice.) A long line of earthworks had been constructed on the north side of the river before Fort Anderson had been abandoned. In this there was room for a moveable artillery gun and two smooth-bore cannon. A brigade of Hoke's rebel division was supported by some other regiments who defended the earthwork and removed the planks from the bridge. The artillery could sweep the long path which led to the bridge through the swamp.

Henderson's brigade marched to the corner of the low area and a strong skirmisher line worked its way through the swamp to the bend in the river. After cautious scouting up and down along the river during the night, a little flat-boat was found which had been used for harvesting rice. The north bank of the creek was held by Hagood's enemy brigade on the hill near the bridge. Behind this, the terrain again ran into swamp and rice fields, which were bordered by woods. Cox's intention was to get his troops across with the flat-boat below the bridge. The war ships in the Cape Fear River stayed with the troops as they advanced and cleared the river of the torpedoes (mines). They were also prepared to fire on enemy positions as soon as they could reach them with their guns, but after Fort Anderson had been abandoned, the enemy had chosen positions that couldn't be shot at. Early in the morning on the 20th, Henderson moved against Hagood with his brigade, while the other brigades got themselves over the river in the flat-boat little by little. The boat could only carry fifty men at once and the swamps and dikes were impassable for draft animals. The officers on horseback left their horses behind. It took the entire morning for Casement and Sterhl to get their brigades across.

Henderson's sharpshooters had gotten so close to the creek that the enemy didn't dare look over the parapet. The enemy Whitworth cannons were put out of commission by our fire. Moore's brigade followed and around 3 p.m. Cox had three divisions on the north side of the swamp through which they had marched. The enemy had completely relied on the swamp being impassable and hadn't even stationed outposts. The divisions now marched quickly toward the west until they crossed the road that led to Wilmington. This action brought them within two miles behind the enemy. Moore's brigade was sent further west in order prevent any escape. Casement's and Sterhl's brigades now prepared themselves for the assault. The enemy brigade was under the command of Simonson, since Hagood was absent. These gave good resistance but were beaten into fleeing and he and 375 of his men, along with two field-guns, were captured. The rest of the brigade fled on the road that Moore was supposed to have covered, but didn't arrive in time to do so. The bridge was repaired during the night and Cox marched further the next morning.

Hoke offered Terry stiff resistance on the left side of Cape Fear River. For that reason, the columns under Cox on the right side of the river were ordered to cautiously advance on Wilmington, and to use the Wilmington & Manchester Railroad in order to take possession of the Brunswick Crossing, which is the name of a tributary river across from Wilmington, forming Eagle Island. Around noon, Mill Creek was reached. The bridge over it had been burned and repairing it so that it was passable for artillery delayed them by a few hours. Here the image of the freeing of the slaves took place in front of our eyes. The blacks of one of the largest plantations let themselves go in wild jubilation when they saw our troops. The white owners had naturally fled. The available forage and foodstuffs were of course requisitioned by the troops but the tools and furniture were hastily taken by the former slaves. It would have given a probate-judge a headache to give a just decision, for each of the female slaves claimed items that had belonged to the mistress, but which they had considered their own since before the John Brown putsch at Harper's Ferry, and had only waited for the day when they could hear "Lincum Gun Boats in year Jubilo and Jubilum" when the "Master" would flee. They divided up the entire estate as if there never would be another dark day in their lives; but 24 hours later they were taught something else, for they were now confronted with the serious question of how were they to live.

As soon as the bridge had been repaired and the soldiers fed, they proceeded in a rapid march to Brunswick Ferry. The ruins of the railroad bridge were still smoking, since it had been set afire just that morning. The enemy had a pontoon bridge at the ferry, but in its haste hadn't destroyed it completely and it was quickly repaired. While that was happening, several boats were used for the crossing. The island was about a mile wide, but already a complete swamp. A small causeway had been thrown up through it to the city ferry, where two guns could protect the entire road. One of our batteries was brought into position there in order to cover the unit on the island. The explosions of shrapnel shot in the city proved that our guns could now reach them and this sped up the withdrawal of the enemy from the city.

The report that Hoke had received significant help and was now giving Terry a hard time, caused Cox to withdraw his troops and send them to help Terry. But since Cox had evidence from the smoke that the enemy was vacating the city, he only sent one brigade to help Terry and reported to Schofield why, but since a quick report and connection couldn't be made through the swamp along the river, it was midnight before an understanding between the two was established and other messages were sent by Schofield to support Cox's decision to remain on the left side of the river. Hoke's action against Terry was only to cover for the retreat he intended to make during the night, and Wilmington was captured by Cox's troops early the next morning. In this way, our troops celebrated Washington's Birthday with a new victory.

Since many connections to New Bern made it more valuable as a base for Sherman's army than Wilmington; among other things that deep draft ocean ships could reach Morehead and Fort Macon, while the mouth of Cape Fear River only allowed shallow draft boats through, and the railroad tracks between the harbors and New Bern were still usable for about 40 miles. There were also some locomotives and cars there, while nothing of that sort had been left behind in Wilmington. New Bern was also quite far on the way to Kinston and the railroad tracks over the Dover Swamp were still usable and the repair of this railroad would be easier and cheaper.

Since Sherman had a reliable base at Wilmington in case he would need it, Schofield dedicated his attention to rebuilding a better line from New Bern to Goldsboro. Our transports brought those of Sherman's troops which had recovered and been released from the hospitals from Washington to New Bern and Ruger, who now commanded a completely new division, was added to the 23rd Corps. The old garrison in the military district yielded another division.

On 26 February, Cox was relieved of his command at Wilmington and ordered to go to New Bern by sea to carry out the intended plan. Col. Wright, Sherman's main railroad repair engineer, was also commanded to New Bern to direct the rebuilding of the railroad. As soon as Cox arrived in New Bern he organized his troops. The recovering soldiers were divided into battalions, keeping companies together as much as possible and then combining them into organized divisions. Two divisions were created this way and General L. R. Palmer and General C. P. Carter became commanders of them. On 1 March, Classen's brigade from Palmer's division was sent forward about 16 miles to Core Creek, and on the next day Carter's division was sent after them so that work could begin right away. The enemy only had one brigade in this area, but Cox had so few vehicles that he had to limit himself to the protection of the railroad construction. There were only about 50 wagons in his district and all of these were needed for railroad construction.

About three miles below Kinston runs a large river, known as the Southwest River, which crosses the railroad and a highway that goes to New Bern. The upper portion of the river runs almost parallel to the Neuse River and all the land between the Neuse and the Trent Rivers, 30 miles long, is a swamp which is known as Dover Swamp in the lower section and as Gum Swamp in the upper part. It was important to have control over the Southwest River, for the elevated banks on each side of the river were the only dry land in the whole region and formed the main highway through the Neuse Valley. It was reported that Hoke had reached Kinston with a large enemy division and it was rumored that other support troops were on their way. It was also known, that an enemy gun-boat was in Kinston. It was therefore worthwhile to retain possession of the banks of the Neuse River. In spite of the prospect of few provisions for his men, Cox led his two divisions to Wise's Forks in the upper portion of the swamp on 7 March. Palmer's division covered the railroad on the right and General Carter's division on the left and guarded the Dover Road. Both were parallel to each other about a mile apart. The 12th New York Cavalry Regiment was the only mounted troops that belonged to Cox's command, and was deployed to patrol to the left of the road about five or six miles to the crossing of the Southwest Creek. The river was not passable at this time. An old road, known as the British Road, ran parallel to the creek and a mile from the position of our troops. Col. Upham of Carter's division with two regiments was pushed forward to the junction with the Dover Road in order to cover the road from the left. Our actions had attracted enemy artillery fire at us from the other side of West Creek, while we occupied the position at the railroad and the crossing of the Dover Road, but a chain of the outposts had been established along the river which reported that all the bridges in this stretch had been torn down and that enemy outposts were stationed on all the side roads. Ruger's division was ordered to Gum Spring at the end of the next section of the railroad which was to be rebuilt and was only three miles from Carter and Palmer's line, which they were to support in the case of an emergency. General Schofield reached

New Bern from Wilmington, and on the 8th had a conference with Cox and the other generals that had positions at the end of the railroad. Early in the morning, rapid artillery fire was heard from the left of our front line. Ruger was sent in rapid march to support Carter. Cox realized that the enemy had attacked Upham without warning, but since the men were almost all new recruits, they had not been able reorganize themselves again after they were driven apart. Upham however, led his own troops (the 15th Connecticut) back in an organized fashion, but most of the others were taken prisoner. Carter's line was partially behind barricades and this division met the enemy without being able to take advantage of what usually follows an initial assault. Palmer was ordered to quickly move a brigade forward on the left to support Carter and with another part of his division to make a strong fake attack at the crossing of the creek that was in front of him.

The prisoners that were taken belonged in part to Stewart and Lee's Corps from the Tennessee Army that had stood opposite us at Franklin and Nashville and Bragg's attack was limited to Upham's brigade. Carter's division at Wise's Fork's held the enemy back with the help of one of Palmer's brigades, until Ruger arrived at the battle area. This division held a line between both flanks and barricaded itself by cutting down trees. A fairly good breastwork soon covered the whole line. The region was covered with swamps and impassable brush which limited the view. Bragg's initial success made him think that he had driven Cox's entire corps back, but the main line hadn't been reached by the enemy. After he became aware of this, Bragg organized his troops for a second attack. Bragg was personally in command of the enemy troops. With him were also troops under Hoke that earlier had served in North Carolina.

Since Sherman was rapidly moving northward, Johnson, who had been rehabilitated, ordered Bragg to combine the troops that were in Goldsboro with those portions of Hood's army that had arrived in Smithfield and with them attack the Union army under Schofield and Cox advancing from New Bern in the hope of destroying them. Then he was to reconnect again with the main parts of the enemy army at Goldsboro in order to attack Sherman again with combined forces. But the attack had restricted itself to

Upham's commando and was very easily repulsed. Information from the prisoners indicated that three enemy divisions had made the attack, so Schofield ordered Cox to be very alert and defend himself until the other portions of the 23rd Corps had arrived at the battle area from Wilmington, which was expected the next day. Schofield himself returned to New Bern in order to speed the support troops on their way.

During the 9th, the skirmishers carried on a lively confrontation. Bragg rebuilt the bridges behind him and tried to send units forward on the right side behind Palmer. This was prevented of course, but it made Palmer anxious. On the morning of the 10th, the enemy made a strong assault on Carter's front and left flank. Since that was expected, Carter had significantly extended his flanks and deployed sharpshooters. As soon as the attack was made, McQuiston's brigade from Ruger's division, which was in reserve, was ordered to move in quickstep to Carter's left and the enemy was greeted with shrapnel and grapeshot by the artillery, as well as certain infantry fire, and after making the effort to capture the line in vain, the enemy had to retreat again.

McQuiston followed him from the flank and took several hundred prisoners. But now the enemy attack focused on Ruger's center and McQuiston was pulled back from his chase after Hoke to support Ruger, whose line was very weak. Palmer also had to send several battalions from the right and with this Ruger was strong enough to be able to repulse Hill and Clayton. During this attack, Schofield reached the battle area again from New Bern. As soon as he became aware of Bragg's stubborn attack, he sent urgent orders to Couch to bring his commando there in rapid march. Bragg realized then that further attempts were useless and retreated during the night back to Kinston where he had left a small unit, and then with the others, marched to Goldsboro to join Johnson's entire forces which would be thrown against Sherman. If we are to believe enemy information, the Southern general had about 15,000 men here, which in Bragg's opinion was enough to manage a victory, which is also what he wrote to Johnson. He had left New Bern with more than three divisions, but the bitter experience that the enemy made each time he confronted Schofield's troops in the East or the West, didn't allow much hope that he could make a successful attack with insignificant forces, even though the troops he was fighting against weren't regularly organized ones. The losses of the Union army were 1257 men, of these, 935 from Col. Uphams' commando had been taken prisoner. The other 322 were either dead or wounded as they defended themselves from Bragg's assault. No part of the main line ever was in enemy hands. The character of the battle was a destructive repulse from strongly defended barricades. The prisoners that were taken by our left flank number 266, which shows clearly that Bragg's losses were the same as Schofield's, even including those from Upham being overrun, which can only be attributed to the carelessness of the outposts.

Schofield's troops were constantly working on rebuilding the railroad and Kinston was recaptured on 14 March. One unit was ordered to restore the highway and Colonel Wright was also supported in rebuilding the railroad bridge and tracks at Kinston. The ironclad steamer which still lay at Kingston was burned and sunk, and its ribs were all that remained of the southern fleet which once was active on the ocean and rivers. When Kinston was taken by our troops, Schofield ordered Terry to go by train from Wilmington to Goldsboro. Terry reached Faison's Station 20 miles south of Goldsboro on the 20th and was now in connection with Sherman's army, on whose orders he reached Cox's bridge on the 22nd, from where he guarded the base of the great army. The Neuse River was cleared of all obstacles and steamboats reached Schofield's camp on the 18th. For several days, provisions were collected, but on the 19th, the dull rumbling and thunder of the cannons could be heard, which later was learned to come from the Battle of Bentonville, more than 20 miles away. On the 20th, Schofield marched to Goldsboro, which he reached on the 21st. After a few days of rest, the great army under Sherman was together and ready for battle. This campaign from Savannah was just as romantic as the earlier one from Atlanta, which we will now describe.

General William Tecumseh Sherman.

Sherman's March through Georgia

When Sherman took leave of his officers in Rome, Georgia, after they and their troops had been ordered to Tennessee, it was his opinion that if Hood did not follow him, the troops under Thomas would have some heavy battles ahead of them, but he also knew that other than Hood's army, the South didn't have any forces with which they could confront Sherman's march through Georgia. Even before starting his march, he informed his subordinates that the purpose of his march was the capture of Columbia, South Carolina, and at the same time the destruction of everything that could serve the South in their continuation of the war. The war would end after the capture of the capital of South Carolina, since as soon as one state of the Confederation was separated from the others, the separated state would no longer contribute money or men to the southern cause. The anxiety over their families that would now be within our line would cause the southern soldiers to desert. The credit of the South would be damaged and their paper money would become worthless, thereby cutting them off from foreign help. Sherman also thought that General Lee would leave Richmond and find a more central location, from which he would have better connections to the other states in the south. Then he would have a large enough army already in place that could hold Lee back until General Grant could get there with his troops. In order to carry out this plan, it was necessary to establish a base on the seacoast, for the one at Chattanooga had already been abandoned in the beginning. In order to separate the southern states on the Atlantic coast from those on the Gulf coast, it would be necessary to completely destroy the railroads in Georgia. The army could provide for itself from the land as it marched through, but as soon as they halted, provisions would have to be there, or they would starve. The residents of the regions they would be marching through would be against them, so it would not be possible to requisition enough provisions from the citizens to provide for an army on a long-term basis and the destruction of that which wasn't used made such requisition unthinkable. This made a rapid march to the ocean necessary. He himself didn't know yet if unforeseen circumstances would drive him to the Gulf of Mexico or to the Atlantic coast. He had told Washington that our fleet should expect him at Morris Island at Charleston, at Ossabaw Sound just south of Savannah, or at Pensacola near Mobile.

On 12 November, the connection to the North was cut off. The railroad bridge at Altoona was dismantled and brought to Chattanooga. From the crossing of the Etowah River to Atlanta, the railroad was systematically destroyed; the iron foundries, machine workshops and all factories in the city of Rome were burned down. On the 14th, the army came together at Atlanta. Sherman's forces consisted of two army corps from the Tennessee Army under General Howard and two corps of the Cumberland Army under General Slocum; the first was designated as the right wing and the other as the left wing. The strength of the forces, according to reports on 10 November, was 59,000 men, but those called back from leave and new recruits arrived so quickly that on the day the march began, he had somewhat over 62,000 men under his flag. Much attention was paid to having only the best and healthy men along on the march, for in enemy country Sherman couldn't use any sick men; he also didn't want his artillery or his wagon train to be incapacitated by weak horses or mules. For every 1000 men he had a field-gun and every battery had four guns, and eight horses for every gun and caisson. In his wagons he carried rations for 20 days and 200 bullets for each man. Whole herds of cattle for meat rations came along on the march. As these moved forward, the herds grew ever larger. At the withdrawal from Atlanta, naturally all the buildings erected for quarters, hospitals and workshops had to be destroyed, since the national troops no longer had any use for them. This was done thoroughly.

On the morning of the 15th the march was set into motion; each wing went a different way, one to Macon, the other toward Augusta, but both wanted to reconnect with each other at Milledgeville, the state capital. Sherman himself, stayed in the left wing which followed the railroad from Atlanta to Augusta, from where he could better lead his forces. After leaving the mountainous region, the terrain depends on the path the rivers take.

The Savannah River, which forms the boundary between South Carolina and Georgia, flows generally to the southeast in a straight line toward the ocean. The Ocmulgee and Oconee Rivers, forty miles from each other, flow the same direction about forty miles apart but join together after about 200 miles to form the Altamaha River and this runs into the ocean near the border with Florida. Another important river in the state is the Ogeechee, which flows for about 50 miles about 20 miles from the Savannah River, before flowing into it. Sherman moved between the Ocmulgee and the Oconee Rivers, but had his right wing march on Macon Railroad line. The object was to confuse the enemy and to drive back the cavalry and the state militia which had gathered at Love Joy Station. Howard's right wing marched by way of Jonesboro to the Ocmulgee Crossing at Planter's Factory. The 17th Corps marched further east toward the same place. Kilpatrick covered the wing with his cavalry and pushed the enemy skirmishers back to Love Joy. The old barricades there were manned by two brigades and two guns. Kilpatrick had his riders dismount and assaulted them successfully. He continued his successful attack until near Forsyth on the Macon Road, then turned and crossed the Ocmulgee with the infantry.

Each army corps had a pontoon bridge. The forward guard of the army reached Planter's Factory on the 18th but the bridge that had been erected here was continually in use so that it wasn't until the 20th before the rear guard had been able to cross it. The approach to the bridge on the east side was steep and slippery from the rain, which made it difficult and time-consuming to get the wagons over. The advance guard was only a few miles north of Macon when the rear-guard made it over the river. Kilpatrick made a fake attack on Macon and reached the railroad east of the city, where he captured a train which he destroyed and then tore up the tracks and rendered it unusable for several miles. While he held the road, Howard's infantry marched toward Gordon, a station twenty miles further east on the Macon & Savannah Railroad.

We will now turn to the left wing under Slocum, with whom Sherman himself was at that time. We find that this part of the army had dedicated itself completely to the destruction of the Atlanta & Augusta Railroad and had already done this as far as

Madison, 70 miles from Atlanta and had destroyed the bridge over the Oconee River 12 miles further. At this point the two wings were the farthest apart from each other and it was 50 miles in a straight line between Slocum's right wing and Kilpatrick's left. Slocum was now instructed to march straight south to Milledgeville, where the entire left wing of the 23rd came together. The little enemy forces there were easily driven off and retreated over the river without destroying the bridge. Slocum took possession of it right away so we could use it in the future. Sherman's advance from Atlanta caused Beauregard to bombard all the officials of the Confederacy with telegrams; he informed them that he had ordered General Taylor in Alabama to have all available troops march to Georgia, but Taylor didn't have any troops; he did come to Macon on the 22nd himself, where he met with Governor Brown and his adjutant Toombs, who had just fled from Milledgeville in order not to be captured by Slocum's marching columns. The only battle-ready troops opposing Sherman were Wheeler's cavalry, the Georgia Militia and a few volunteer companies. General Howell Cob had the impressive title of Commander of the Confederate Reserves, but no reserves were on hand. General Hardee had been in Macon on the day before and had voiced the opinion, that Sherman's army, which now extended from the Oconee Bridge to Planter's Factory, would either march to Augusta or Savannah, and that Macon was not in danger, and that Smith should quickly march eastward, in order to throw himself between Sherman and Augusta, and to block the road with felled trees, while Wheeler's orders read that he should continuously pester the flanks and rear of Sherman's army in an attempt to prevent his rapid advance. Orders from Richmond had united all the southern forces in Georgia under Hardee's command. In response he hurried to Savannah to strengthen the defense works there and to be in communication with Augusta, Charleston and Richmond.

      From Corinth, Mississippi, Beauregard demanded that the citizens in Georgia should throw themselves against Sherman with unified forces, to destroy all roads and provisions; then Sherman's army would starve in their midst. He wanted to encourage them further by telling them that he would soon be coming to help them.

At the same time, he ordered Hood to advance to Tennessee, since it was the only effective action that he could still take against Sherman. In Milledgeville, the state government was still in session as Sherman was marching nearer and passed a general mobilization order with the claim that the Union troops would murder everyone and burn everything down, but this law came too late and failed in its purpose because there was no more time in which to organize troops, if there had even been material available for such a thing. It was only a sign of desperation. Had the residents actually been willing to destroy the roads, Sherman would have made them understand that the property of anyone that would do this, could expect no considerate treatment, for resistance against a large army would only result in greater trouble for the unfortunate people of the area. The people had already been tired of the pressures and difficulties of the war for so long that they had lost any courage for more sacrifices. In spite of the great distress of the residents, the political quarrels did not end and the opponents of Governor Brown's administration made use of their absence, in which Vice-Governor Wright, who was at the same time General of the Southern Army, made a proclamation in Augusta, that he as acting-governor would only be ruling the part of the state to the east of the Oconee River, and would give orders there. The citizens should place themselves under his command, but this demand wasn't successful since everyone from the Georgia Militia that was still together, was ordered by Governor Brown to Savannah which they reached on the 30th. In truth, the communications from Augusta to Macon by couriers were disrupted while Sherman's army marched through.

While the Southern leaders held their war conference in Macon on the 22nd, a division of the Georgia Militia under General Philipps marched to Gordon, following Hardee's orders. At Griswoldville, after they had marched eight miles, they ran into Walcott's brigade of Wood's division by chance. This was the rear-guard of Sherman's right wing. Walcott was pushing Wheeler's cavalry back at the time and seeking to get information from Macon when he was attacked by Philipps. Phillips brought his four brigades into the fight and tried to get around Walcott's flank, which only had two guns and had to retreat at the beginning of the attack. Philipps, who had far superior forces in infantry and artillery, renewed his attack several times only to be pushed back each time. After some hours of heavy fighting and the loss of 600 dead and wounded, he retreated from the battlefield. On the Union side, General Wood (who was there) reported a loss of 94 dead and wounded. Walcott received a leg wound in one part of the battle and Colonel Catterson of the 97th Indiana Infantry Regiment became commander of the brigade, both officers offered praiseworthy service in the battle. Philipps' attack was needless, since if Walcott had been pushed back, two army corps under Howard were behind him. Phillips had orders however, to advance to the railroad until he received the order from General Smith in Macon to retreat. This was given as soon as Smith learned of the bloody battle. The division was then sent by train to the end of the line in this region at Albany. From there they marched 60 miles to Thomasville on the Savannah & Gulf Railroad, where Toombs had gotten transportation for them on the railroad, on which they now rode on to Savannah and could report for further service to Hardee on the 30th.

Hardee's orders to Wheeler now read that he should oppose Sherman's advance on any of the roads. Wheeler marched therefore south from the Central Railroad, swam through the Oconee River and reached Sandersville on the 26th and now stood directly in front of Sherman's main column. Kilpatrick now had to accommodate himself to Wheeler's movement and following Sherman's orders, moved to the front and to the left in front of the infantry, since there wasn't any enemy on the right flank after Wheeler had crossed the Oconee River. Sherman lost no time in Milledgeville and marched further on the 24th. After he had passed Sandersville, he reached the Central Railroad at Tennille and destroyed the tracks as he advanced toward Davisboro. From here, the left wing moved in the same direction toward Louisville, crossed the Ogeechee River before reaching the village, and camped here on the 29th. During this time the right wing destroyed the railroad from Griswoldville to Millen, so than nothing of the railroad remained. The crossing of the Oconee River near Ball's Ferry by the right wing under Howard was difficult because the river had rushing, high water and the ferry boat couldn't be used.

In addition, Wheeler's cavalry made great efforts to prevent the crossing from the other side. A unit of the engineer corps was able however to lay a bridge two miles above the ferry. As soon as a portion of Blair's corps reached the other side, the artillery swept ahead on the main road and forced the enemy back. The pontoons were then placed at the ferry and the advance of the right wing continued. When the army left Milledgeville, Kilpatrick received orders to make a fake advance with his cavalry quite far north; he was to destroy the railroad bridge over Brier Creek near Waynesboro and then move quickly to Millen in order to free Union soldiers that were held prisoner there. Kilpatrick marched toward Augusta on the main road. Wheeling learned about this movement and gathered his troops together on a road that led there, from where he could attack Kilpatrick from the Brier Creek swamps. But Kilpatrick had according to orders departed from the main road and was already far along on the way from Warrenton to Waynesboro before Wheeling learned anything of the change. Murray's brigade formed the rear-guard for Kilpatrick's corps and in the evening they camped quite far from the main column, near a place called Sylvan Grove.

Wheeler learned of their location and around midnight attacked both regiments, the 8th Indiana and 2nd Kentucky, and drove them out of their camp. These defended themselves but were ultimately driven back on the other portion of Murray's brigade. Although Wheeler tried very hard to destroy Kilpatrick with his superior forces, and made several assaults on back and flank, he won no advantage other than preventing Kilpatrick from burning the Brier Bridge and forced him to turn toward the southwest after destroying two miles of the railroad. Kilpatrick learned here that the prisoners in Millen that he was to free had been marched off, so he continued his march toward Louisville, where he rejoined the main army. One brigade after the other now had to function as rear-guard, which still had to fight with Wheeler daily. On the 28th, Kilpatrick barely escaped capture because he had foolishly set up quarters for the night some distance from the main army. As watch, he had the 9th Michigan Cavalry Division with him. The enemy forced itself between him and the main force and it was only through great effort that he was successful in hacking his way back to rejoin them. The narrow road and bridge over Buckhead Creek were protected by Colonel Hatch with the 5th Ohio Cavalry Regiment and Wheeler was energetically repulsed there, the bridge was destroyed and Kilpatrick barricaded himself on Reynolds' Plantation. Wheeler made a strong attack here with all his forces but was repulsed and Kilpatrick could rejoin the infantry unhindered again. Wheeler had three divisions and bragged that he had driven Kilpatrick to flee with a loss of 200 dead, wounded and prisoners. Kilpatrick, who was dissatisfied with the result, received permission after his men and horses had rested for a few days, to advance against Wheeler on the Louisville and Waynesboro Road. Supported by Davis's division of the 14th Corps, he attacked Wheeler near the village and drove him in gallop from three barricades through Waynesboro over Brier Creek. Wheeler admits that he could only carry out his retreat with the greatest of difficulties, and claims as his excuse that the entire 14th Army Corps had attacked him. But Baird's division of the corps wasn't even involved in the battle, although it can't be disputed that their presence nearby was of help to Kilpatrick, in that he now attacked Wheeling with more energy and self-confidence, which he probably wouldn't have risked otherwise. He would have been able to use the cavalry more on his flank because his center was secure with the infantry. The village of Millen was reached on the 3rd by Blair's corps. Sherman was with him, and the railroad from Augusta to Savannah was here completely destroyed. Three army corps now marched on the narrow space between the Savannah and Ogeechee Rivers. Osterhaus, who commanded the 15th Corps, marched on the right bank of the Ogeechee River in two columns several miles apart. Howard, the officer of the right wing was with Osterhaus and was not held up by the enemy. From Millen, the march went forward in organized form without further delays. Wheeler's cavalry kept a safe distance away and soon crossed over to the left side of the Savannah River. The region now got sandier and provisions got noticeably sparser. All noticed that they were getting close to the coast where little provisions could be found. On the 9th and 10th the columns came near the defense works of Savannah. Davis' corps stood on the Savannah River, William's, Blair's and

Osterhaus' extended the line to the right near the Ogeechee River. Cavalry units and practiced scouts were sent out on foot to make contact with the fleet and to destroy the Gulf Railroad. This was the last connection of the city with the South.

The destruction of the railroad between the South and Richmond was very important in Sherman's eyes and he was not sparing in efforts to accomplish that completely. A battalion of laborers was chosen and provided with tools to pry the rails off the ties and make them unusable. The laborers were always busy, but the infantry too, was trained on the march in the methods of destroying it, and the cavalry too, was active. The constant skirmishing on the front and flanks kept the riders constantly busy. Usually a division would march along the tracks, stack their guns together and form long lines along the tracks and on command, remove the spikes and lift the pieces of rail high in the air and let them fall again on command. Obstacles would be made from ripped-up ties and whole rails were made hot and bent and all rail traffic was destroyed. In this way, 10 – 15 miles of track were destroyed each day; as well as demolishing machine shops, stations and bridges. The destruction of the railroads by Sherman's army was drastic and for hundreds of miles nothing remained other than the track bed to show a wanderer where the railroad had been. If the South had wanted to rebuild the railroads after Sherman's march, the workshops would no long have existed and the blockade of its harbors made it impossible to import new materials. The destruction work in the South was complete. What the South itself hadn't destroyed was destroyed by the northern army. A mass of blacks joined the march and accompanied it, much against the wishes of Sherman, who then had more people to feed than the army was responsible for feeding, and hence didn't pay much attention to them. The common soldier encouraged the blacks to go along, who willingly suffered all privations to follow the "bluecoats" and live on what the soldiers gave them. No complaint was voiced as long as they were allowed to follow "Linculms" people, who would certainly lead them to that place where they could live in excess. But as the lower and less cultivated land was reached, they became an ever greater burden on the army, especially for the left wing, which now alone was subjected to attacks by the enemy. General Davis, the commander of the 14th Army Corps finally had lost all patience since no attention had been paid to his orders to these people to stay at home. He had the pontoon bridge over Ebenezer Creek removed before the blacks had gotten over it. The river couldn't be crossed without a bridge but these poor creatures had set their hearts on freedom and in their fright that they would now fall into the hands of the Southern cavalry, with a wild cry they plunged into the water. Some could swim, others not, and many drowned in spite of the soldiers trying to help them in any way possible. Everything was done to save them from a wet grave. This shows that the blacks preferred to die in freedom than to live in slavery.

When Savannah was reached, all the run-away slaves that had come along with the column, where taken to an island where they were added to an already existing colony that had been officially established there by the government. The Freedman's Bureau later became a necessity because of the run-away and freed slaves. It had been Sherman's plan to feed the soldiers from the land that they marched through. Gathering food became an entertainment for the soldiers at times. What was taken on the march was only supposed to be taken if it was really needed, so it was necessary to forage every day wherever they found themselves. About 20 percent of every regiment would move out every morning to forage and those from each division tried to stay together as much as possible in order to support each other in case the enemy attacked them. Toward evening they were to rejoin the main column. Soon foraging was the "Beau Ideal" of the advancing army, and as self-confidence and wagons grew to an amazing height, no organized line of pickets could drive off the enemy cavalry as quickly as could the foragers. Only troops in a trench or behind barricades could keep them from advancing, and when they swarmed around on the flanks to carry out their job and an enemy cavalry showed up, it was a show to be seen. From here and there, out of barns, smokehouses, kitchen and gardens of the plantations, individual foragers driving their mules piled high with harvest from the gardens, smoked and fresh meat, fowl, etc. dashed toward the safety of the main force. As soon as one of them met another, one would drive both mules to safety while the other would shoot from behind fences and trees at the enemy with his far-reaching Springfield rifle, which was far superior to the rifles of the enemy riders.

If pressed too hard, the foragers would retreat until enough of them had gathered to form up in a regiment's column that could oppose the enemy. He then would pull back believing that he had driven the skirmishers back to the main column, while in reality these were still miles behind. The foragers then went back to work and only rarely were Wheeler's riders able to break through the energetic sharpshooters in order to get near the main column of the advancing army. As soon as the army made camp in the evening, they found the provisions train waiting for them. It was so regular it was as if they had been delivered by a scheduled railroad train. They collected all the farm animals that could be used by the army. As soon as a mule or artillery horse became incapacitated as the result of hard work through a swamp for example, fresh teams were at hand and by the time we reached Savannah the draught animals were in better condition than when we had pulled out of Atlanta. The orders for the foragers were that they were not to enter any house that was still lived in, or to take any private property that wasn't needed by the army. In the best disciplined divisions, this was also carried out. But discipline is not everywhere the same in the army and in an army of 60,000 men, one always finds those that are robbers by nature and officers that also take part in the thievery, which is a terrible misfortune for the people that are affected.

General Kilpatrick left behind a bad impression. His own immorality had a demoralizing effect on his troops, even though his best officers tried to control it. His energy and cleverness were always sufficient to defend himself against Wheeler's dozen brigades, and the valuable service that he performed made General Sherman inclined to ignore his infringements. Kilpatrick several times got himself and his men in danger of being captured or driven apart, but he was always able to save himself from night attacks. He would jump on the best horse or mule, without a saddle, and then gallop in his nightshirt to the front line and attack the surprised enemy like a reckless devil. His men would follow his example and would soon drive the enemy into fleeing.

The stragglers...and there were countless...were very burdensome for the army. There always were differences in the armies. In many brigades, regiments had a guard behind it that prevented men from falling behind. The provost guard (military police) marched behind everyone and arrested anyone who tried to get out of line and reported officers that didn't hold their men together, but whenever the army started marching again, the stragglers would become more numerous and many didn't reach their commando for several days, thereby avoiding the heavy work that their comrades had to do. These "army bums" were just as numerous in the southern army as in the Union forces and southern citizens demanded strict laws against these delinquents. Responsible persons sent specific accusations to the secretary of war in Richmond. Leading newspapers in the south demanded the firing or execution of the responsible officers, since they caused more havoc than their enemy, the Yankees. It is unlikely that war can be made without criminal activity, but we can at least congratulate ourselves that the injustices were only against property and that murder, rape and other inhuman crimes were not committed. The majority of officers and men worked hard during the march to build bridges over rivers, or log roads through swamps, pulling the artillery guns and wagons out of the muck when they got stuck or tearing up the railroad tracks. Those that were usually only seen in the evening were the foragers who worked for everybody. They would come into camp with all sorts of carts, often in grotesque clothing, causing quite a bit of merriment on occasion. Once in a while one would see an ox harnessed to an elegant carriage, or a horse harness with silver ornaments on a mule bringing a load of food into camp. Weather was usually good, with just a little snow in November, but in December it was warm. If camp was made in pine forests, the men sitting around the campfire would toss burning pine cones at each other and all sorts of other things to fight boredom. On the whole march an atmosphere prevailed of, one could almost say, cheerfulness, even though one wasn't free of difficulties, and now when the men recall these days at their reunions, they are usually pleasant memories. That usually reaches a climax when the song

"As we were marching through Georgia" rings out from strong men's voices.

The Capture of Savannah

Savannah had 25,000 residents at that time. It is situated on the Georgia side of the Savannah River and was the home of wealthy people, which made it one of the most pleasant cities of the South. The region is sandy and lies about 40 feet above sea level about 15 miles from the ocean. It is as close to the harbor as it is possible to build a city. To the south, a distance downriver from the city, the ground gets lower to almost sea level. The whole coast is low and is divided into many islands. The high ground on which the city was built is almost an island in the swamps, 6 miles wide and 8 miles long. There are other high spots here and there in the area. On these are the homes of the owners of the rice plantations, which are usually laid out in the swamps.

The Savannah and Ogeechee Rivers get closer to each other as they near the ocean. The tongue of land that separates them is hardly more than 10 to 15 miles wide for a length of 50 miles. Both rivers border rice swamps which surround the city more than three miles to the northwest. Alongside these flows the Little Ogeechee River past the city in a southwesterly direction. The rice fields provide natural defense for the city. On the other side of these are the Salt Creek Swamp and the Little Ogeechee River and a defense-line was completed to the bridge of the Atlantic & Gulf Railroad. The roads running into the city were narrow dikes, just high enough so they could be used when the rice fields were flooded.

The Savannah River is wide from the city to the ocean and contains various little islands. Right in front of the city is Hutchinson Island, significantly larger than the others. Next to it is Argyle Island, ten miles long, with little Anslow Island to the west of it, and for a long distance the river has three channels. Before Sherman moved into the eastern portions of Georgia, Savannah only had forts on the sea, but after the capture of Fort Pulaski in 1862, these were moved closer and consisted of individual forts. In these were 10" Columbiads, mortars up to 32" and several howitzers which could be used in case of an attack. The mouth of the Ogeechee River is known as Ossabaw Sound, the mouth of the Savannah River as Tybee Sound and the inlet half-way between them is Wassaw Sound. These were guarded by our fleet under the command of Admiral Dahlgren so that no time would be lost connecting with Sherman when he reached the coast. The main fleet and military station was Port Royal, about 20 miles further northeast at the mouth of Broad River. General J. G. Foster had his headquarters in Beaufort, where he had stockpiled masses of provisions for Sherman in order to deliver them as soon as he could be reached.

Hardee was not willing to defend the inner defense line if he could avoid it. In order to do that, he had to give up the Charleston Railroad, for it crossed the river about 15 to 18 miles above the city. Once this portion of the railroad was given up, his only connection with the North would be by the Union "security road" and Hardeeville, a station in South Carolina about six miles from the river, would be the end of the railroad. The security road which Hardee later used to in order to get out of Savannah leads to a ferry close to Hutchinson Island and then runs for a long distance northward through rice fields, which protect it from attack.

Hardee didn't have any provisions with which to hold out during a siege even if he had been willing to risk it. It would have been very difficult to bring in provisions 15 to 20 miles over a single road. His first intention was to establish a road between the Savannah and Ogeechee using the Charleston Railroad and holding it. He had chosen a very good position for it behind the Monteith Swamp. Individual earthworks were built along the line and artillery and infantry were stationed there, but Sherman rendered them useless. He had ordered Howard with the 15th Corps to position themselves on the right bank of the Ogeechee River and flanked the earthworks so that Hardee no had a choice but to destroy the railroad and to pull back to the inner defense line of the city.

We now turn back to 29 November, when General Taylor, with the help of Toombs as State Adjutant, led the state militia to Savannah, which now were the only support troops available in the Confederacy. Never was help of more usefulness in a dire situation than these measures. Taylor rushed to Savannah and conferred with Hardee, but on the 29th a report came that a division of Union troops under General Hatch had landed at Boyd's Neck on Broad River and was marching toward Grahamville and the Charleston Railroad 20 miles away.

General Foster had ordered this move in the hope that it could help Sherman, and if Hatch had been successful in reaching the railroad, it would have eliminated the possibility of Hardee of retreating out of Savannah. The Georgia Militia had only signed up for service within the state, but Taylor and Toombs put their heads together and to Hardee's joy, arranged with General Smith to have the trains redirected to the Savannah and Charlestown Railroad. When the Georgia Militia awoke they were at a station near Grahamville in South Carolina, and without knowing it, were now in service to the Confederacy instead of the State of Georgia. While the Southerners proceeded with the greatest energy, Hatch, on the Union side, had stopped his march even though only a small troop of enemy cavalry was posted between him and the railroad; in so doing he failed to make use of his opportunity, for Grahamville on the railroad was only ten miles away. When he advanced on the next day, Smith with his Georgia troops were ready for them and made use of the swamps near Honey Hill for their position, a place that could only be attacked by using the dikes which could easily be covered by artillery. Hatch tried a flanking movement but the Southerners set fire to the fields of very dry broom straw. The flames swept through the fields and forced our troops to seek protection in the river. Hatch advanced again and drove the enemy a mile and a half back to his barricades. Several brilliant assaults were made here but were repulsed by the enemy. During the night, Hatch pulled his troops back to their own earthworks at Boyd's Neck. The Confederates reported a loss of 50 men, while the Union forfeited 700 men. This is new evidence again that desperate leaders will gamble the lives of their men by first being too cautious and later by throwing them into battle like a crazy man.

The result of the meeting between Hardee and Taylor was that the latter sent a true report of the situation in Savannah to Richmond. The Southern government had caused Hardee to believe that Sherman wouldn't undertake anything in South

Carolina until he had established a new base on the coast and that it would be easier to advance on the roads between the rivers instead of marching through the many swamps to Charleston. They expected then, that Sherman would attack Savannah and advised Hardee to be ready to vacate the place before he was completely surrounded. Hardee's troops could then join Bragg's forces which had gathered at Augusta, and then with their combined forces and the garrison of Charleston and other parts of the Carolinas, confront Sherman on his march to the north. The intention and understanding of the situation was correct, but the mistakes having just taken place are the reason this advice couldn't be followed. Taylor wrote later that it was clear that without an army with which they could come between Sherman and Lee's rear, their cause was lost as soon as Sherman moved.

Hardee had assigned his troops for the defense in the following positions; the Georgia Militia under General Smith, along with 20 guns, was posted from Savannah past William's Plantation to the central railroad station; General McLaws' division with 29 guns was to hold the road to Louisville and the lines toward Shaw's Dam; General Wright commanded the left wing and reached from Shaw's Dam to the Gulf Railroad Bridge over the Little Ogeechee River and had 32 guns of heavy caliber, along with 11 field artillery batteries with 48 guns under Colonel Jones. These were spread out in positions where they could be most effective. The forts and stationary cannons on the ocean side were under the command of Colonel Anderson. Of these, Fort McAllister was the only one that could be attacked by the Union troops, and will be the only one we will more closely describe.

It lay on Genesis' Point on the right bank of the large Ogeechee River and covered the traffic channel of Ossabaw Sound and also protected the important bridges of the Gulf Railroad over the river. It was a strongly built fort with the main facade toward the river which it was intended to protect. The back of the fort was also strongly built for infantry and artillery enclosures which usually accommodated seven heavy guns and eight lighter field guns on a barbette inside the parapet. The river was mined and before Sherman had arrived, subterranean structures in front of the land side of the fort had been constructed and its communication trenches protected with palisades. The fort had been provisioned for 50 days, in case it was necessary to make it independent. The garrison was made up of 200 men under the command of Major G. W. Anderson. Just upriver of the fort, the river made a double bend. A straight line over both bends was less than a half-mile in length, while the river traveled nine miles to reach the same spot. In almost a straight line over the widest part of the bend, about two miles further, was Cheve's Plantation with its rice mill and on the other bank of the river was the fort in the corner on higher terrain. The land sloped down to the south to a broad salt swamp, over which sand and the ocean could be seen.

Hardee's troops numbered about 18,000 men in all, of which 1000 were sick in the hospital and should be subtracted. He also had the residents of the city, which he could lawfully use as a folk-militia and which were already in service as per a proclamation by the mayor on 28 November. This was the situation in Savannah as Sherman surrounded the town on 10 December. A few days were necessary to get all the various army corps into position, but by 12 December, the region between the Savannah and Ogeechee Rivers was completely occupied. The outer left wing of Jackson's division of William's 20th Corps touched the river and the other divisions extended the line almost to the Central Railroad. Here Davis' 14th Corps joined them and reached over the Ogeechee River near Lawton's Plantation where it connected with the right wing of Blair's 17th Corps. The 15th Corps (Osterhaus) completed the line to the Ogeechee River near King's Bridge, a structure 1000 feet long, which the enemy had destroyed but the pilings still stood. On orders from General Howard, the chief of the engineer corps, Captain Reese, had the bridge rebuilt. It was ready for traffic on the 13th. At the Central Railroad tracks, the outposts under Slocum were sent ahead to the three mile stone and the barricade line was a quarter mile closer to the city than Howard's troops.

The prospect for provisioning Sherman's army from the land had gotten slim and the foragers failed to bring in any animals or wagons loaded with foodstuffs. Bread was now baked from what had been brought along and rice was the only thing that the land could still provide for the troops. Sherman's main task therefore, was to establish a connection with the fleet and a base by means of transport ships between Ossabaw Sound and Port Royal. General Howard had sent a reliable scout, Captain Duncan, with two comrades to the sea. Duncan managed to reach Admiral Dahlgren but that wasn't known until two days later. Kilpatrick too, had sent a patrol ahead for the same purpose, but the Ogeechee River couldn't be used until Fort McAllister was in our hands. The Kings Bridge had just been restored when Sherman had sent Howard orders to storm the fort with enough forces to capture it, since he believed that the quicker this was done, the less loss of life there would be. Hazen's division of the 15th Corps had the honor of making the assault and early on the morning of the 13th, the troops crossed the bridge and marched forward on the right bank of the river and reached the neighborhood of the fort around noon.

General Howard had erected a signal station at Cheve's rice mill on the left bank of the river and had positioned a section of twenty pounder Parrot guns there to cover the rear of the troops. Sherman and Howard were both at the signal station and in communication with Hazen. They could see the ships of our fleet from there. Hazen's people had captured an enemy advance guard that was able to tell them where the mines were in the road. These were removed and a brigade under Col. W. S. Jones which had been sent ahead arrived there already in the early afternoon and marched to within a half-mile of the fort. Jones wanted to attack right away but Hazen thought it would be better to attack the fort with a portion of every brigade in his division. It took a while to get all of these into position. The reserves were stationed at the place where the mines had been, and three regiments from every brigade were ordered to attack. Col. W. S. Jones brigade was left, Col. Oliver's in the middle and Col Theodore Jones' on the right. The latter found it very difficult to reach his position and it was almost five o'clock before the signal to charge was given. A short time before, the garrison in the fort had made an abatis as additional protection on the land side, but didn't have time to remove the tree trunks from which the branches were taken. These trunks now offered protection for our sharpshooters, who could now get so close to the fort that they could shoot down the gunners at the guns, so that they couldn't use the guns against our people.

During this time, Sherman and Howard were very anxious and saw the setting sun from their station at Cheve's Mill. They now ordered Hazen with signals, to hurry forward. A little dispatch boat from the fleet came as near as it was safe and the captain asked if the fort was already in our hands. This took place just as Hazen gave his troops the signal to charge. Sherman answered; "Not yet, but it will be in ten minutes." The brave charge of the line fulfilled that promise after a short, hand-to-hand fight; the parapet was taken by all our troops at the same time. The assault was made with just a thin line, which pulled together as soon as the charge began without being delayed by the abatis, the palisades or the trenches. The greatest losses were caused by mines which exploded just as the trench was reached. A portion of the troops reached the outer flank where they could get around the palisades and where the corner of the fort didn't have so much cover. At the time it was also low tide, which gave the attackers an advantage because the palisade didn't reach the water. Within fifteen minutes it was all over and the national flag was flying from the parapet from which the rebel flag had been taken down, while the victors fired shots in celebration. Hazen's losses were 24 dead and 110 wounded, the total loss of the garrison was 48. There was no formal surrender, but the officers and men of the garrison, laid down their guns as soon as they knew they were overpowered. Colonel W. S. Jones was mortally wounded in the attack and command of the brigade passed to Colonel Martin of the 111th Illinois Regiment. The capture of the fort was of greater importance to Sherman than the taking of prisoners. The Ogeechee River was now open and large ships could come up as far as King's Bridge in the rear of his line, and the question of a base on the coast was now solved and Sherman could send the joyful message to Admiral Dahlgren, General Foster and General Grant at City Point by means of the dispatch boat. Even before morning, Sherman had heard from General Foster, but he couldn't proceed against Fort McAllister because the mines had not been removed yet. Sherman traveled out in a small boat to Foster's steamer and met then with Admiral Dahlgren in Wassaw Sound. The Admiral accepted Sherman's plan right away and tried to get shallow-bottomed ships in order to carry provisions for Sherman's army to King's Bridge. Foster reported about his efforts to reach the Charleston Railroad through Hatch. This hadn't been successful in spite of having a position from which his guns could reach the railroad. He wasn't able to sit in his saddle because of an old wound, which was a great disadvantage since his presence at the front line was necessary then. Although this position was only one mile from the railroad, this was used the whole time by the enemy as far as Hardeeville, from which point a connection could be made to Savannah over the dikes. The trains usually ran during the night throughout the whole week, until Savannah was vacated by Hardee and his troops.

Foster was ordered to capture the railroad and Sherman returned on the morning of the 15th to Howard's quarters. During this time many reconnaissance trips had been made by the corps commander, who had studied Hardee's movements carefully and had taken provisional steps to deal with the flooded rice fields in front of the city by improving roads and draining them with canals, mainly into the Ogeechee River. Until the water had receded significantly, one could hardly consider an attack, since columns on the dikes would have little prospect of success; the wounded would drown in the flooded fields, and this unnecessary sacrifice of the men couldn't be justified. In the night of the 11th, General Williams of 20th Corps had moved a portion of the 3rd Wisconsin Regiment onto Argyle Island and the rest of them on the following morning. While this was taking place, three enemy war steamers tried to come down the river but were driven back by our batteries. One of them, the "Resolute" was driven unto the bank and the crew was taken prisoner by Colonel Hawley of the 3rd Wisconsin Regiment. Hardee had more cannon boats below on the river and their presence made it inadvisable to use pontoon bridges until there was better protection available for them. Through an unfortunate mistake, the "Resolute" was burned by our men, when it could have provided valuable service for us in transporting provisions. The rebels had gotten all flat-boats and barges to safety and considering the great danger that our troops would be exposed to on the South Carolina side, it was probably better to trust Foster's ability to attack the railroad. Great quantities of rice were found on the island and for several days these were the entire provisions that were available for the men, while the rice straw served as the only forage for the horses. Colonel Carman moved with the other part of his brigade to the other side of the river on the 16th with Wheeling's cavalry trying to prevent the landing on the South Carolina shore. On the right side, Howard was building wood roads toward the new depot that was being built at King's Bridge and he hurried to get the rice fields dried. His divisions, as did Slocum's, made haste to build earthworks for the big siege guns that were expected to arrive from Port Royal, since field artillery couldn't compete with the enemy's heavy guns. In many places the spruce trees provided protection for the Union troops, as it had been observed that if such a forest was a half-mile deep, the heaviest of the enemy guns couldn't penetrate through it. Giant oaks surrounded the plantation mansion, covered with the long-haired moss typical of the south. In combination with the tents of headquarters placed between them, it made a really beautiful picture.

A mail steamer had waited on the coast with our mail and Sherman received letters from Grant which had been written on the 3rd and 6th of December in which orders had been given to build a fortified camp and then to send the rest of his soldiers by sea to Grant to be used against Richmond. Sherman answered in detail, that he would like to follow the order of the Commanding General, but it had been his plan to capture Savannah and then march to Columbia. But on the same day that Sherman wrote, Grant wrote that it was perhaps better after all, to allow Sherman to proceed according to his own plans. Halleck also wrote that according to the wishes of the government, he was willing to allow him to carry out his own plans. So, the original object of the march was retained, but since the dispatches of the 16th and 18th from General Grant didn't reach Sherman until after the capture of Savannah, the result was not so drastic as it could have been if he had immediately taken his left wing over to the South Carolina side of the river or if he had made preparations to lay siege to Savannah, from where he could easily have withdrawn his troops as soon as transport ships could have reached him and taken his army to Grant. For that reason he relied more on Forster's advance in South Carolina and limited Slocum's advance on Argyle Island, which allowed him more flexibility in withdrawing. Sherman knew better than anyone that such an advance was dubious. He gave orders to Colonel Poe, the chief of the engineering corps, to build the fortified camp near Fort McAllister, which could be held on to according to Grant's wishes and ordered the corps commanders to carry out the siege with all earnestness. In hopes that this daring action would also affect enemy morale, he sent Hardee a formal demand to surrender the city on the 17th. Naturally, this was rejected, but it was clear that the Southern commander did not want to be trapped in the city. The question was only, how long could he remain there without endangering his withdrawal. Beauregard had reached Augusta and was in command of all troops and agreed with Hardee and Taylor's plans, as had been sent to Richmond. General S. Jones, in command at Charleston, was ordered to Pocatalico to keep the railroad open. A ship's bridge was built over both branches of the Savannah River to Hutchinson Island and then over to the South Carolina shore. During this time, the previously flooded rice fields were getting drier and Howard and Slocum had their siege cannons in position. People from their divisions built light bridges that could be carried from place to place and could be thrown over canals. All other preparations for an attack were being made.

On the 19th, Carman's brigade was taken over to the South Carolina shore and a strong defense position was established at Izard's Mill, but the fields here were still under water and the bridge had been burned down, so the advance was not easy. This movement however, convinced Hardee that his retreat could no longer wait and he started to vacate Savannah by sending a strong unit over to hamper Carman's advance on the dikes. Since he recognized the danger that Hardee's flight could cause and was still hoping that Foster's advance could still make Hardee's escape impossible, on the 18th Sherman rode out to Foster, who wasn't able because of his wound to come to Sherman's camp. On the 20th, Sherman was on Hilton's Head, where he ordered Hatch's division to advance. He was about to go back to his headquarters in the night, but the boat that he wanted to board had been delayed by a storm and then went aground at low tide so that it wasn't until the evening of the 21st that he returned and found Savannah already in the hands of his troops. Hardee had completed his retreat on the 20th and on the 21st, Geary's division of the 20th Corps, which was closest to the city, moved into the city vacated by the enemy. Sherman's dispatch to the government in Washington reached Lincoln on Christmas Eve and the news was considered by the public to be a Christmas present of immeasurable value. The morale value of the march through Georgia was significantly amplified by the capture of Savannah, one of the most important ocean harbors for the South. Hardee's escape was a disappointment, but he had only been able to take his field artillery along. The heavy guns in position or in storage, 250 in number, became the booty of the victors. 31,000 bales of cotton also fell into our hands and were turned over to the treasury.

    The Southern armies pulled back to Charleston first. From there the Georgia Militia was sent back to Augusta to be relieved from the regular southern forces and then to continue service to the State of Georgia, which was in keeping with the conditions of their enlistment.

Confederate General William Joseph Hardee, (1815-1873)

From Savannah to Columbia
The Burning of Columbia

Secretary of War Stanton visited Sherman as soon as the news reached him that Savannah had been captured, and informed him of the intentions of the president concerning the cotton that had been captured, the abandoned plantations and the run-away blacks. It was then that Sherman learned of the government's plans concerning a peace treaty, in case the residents of the South wished to consider such a thing. The General however, focused strictly on concerns of purely military nature and prepared himself to continue his march through the Carolinas. After his troops had received new clothing, the guns and wagons had been taken care of and provisions had been distributed, he was again ready to march and the first movements forward were made already in January.

General Howard got his first wing together at Beaufort in South Carolina, some by transport ships, and some by marches on foot on the Union Road in the same direction. The left wing under Slocum was ordered to march up the Savannah on both banks and rejoin in Robertsville, South Carolina, while Howard was to march to Pocatalico and drive Hardee's troops over the Combahee River and occupy the area. Howard's movement toward Beaufort would leave the impression as if he was heading toward Charleston, while Slocum would head toward Augusta. The enemy would be in doubt as to what Sherman's intentions were, while Howard's troops would be in excellent positions from which to march to Columbia, which was actually the plan...to reach that city at the beginning of the campaign. Although at Pocatalico he was already 50 miles in that direction, his base was still at the ocean. It was the same case for Slocum, for Robertville was near Sister's Ferry and the foraging wagons could all be fully loaded, even if the connection to Savannah was destroyed.

General Hogan had returned to the army and commanded the 15th Corps. The sick and wounded officers and men were shipped by water to the north, while those already recovered returned to the army.

Sherman's plan was to make it appear that he was advancing on Augusta and Charleston, but he actually wanted to march directly toward Columbia and then attack Goldsboro, where he hoped to connect with Schofield who was coming from New Bern. The capture of Fort Fisher and the advance of Schofield with the 23rd Corps gave him the certainty that it would be a success. He was also certain that no significant enemy force could oppose him until he had crossed the Fear River. Then he could expect Lee to come from Richmond to oppose him even before Grant would follow him with the Army of the Potomac. Grant however, had his eyes open to such a movement and extended his line out west of Petersburg, so that Lee wouldn't have any straight routes to the south. Since Lee was now forced to march west and then south, he would never be nearer to Sherman than Grant was himself. The main plan of this campaign was rapid forward movement with as few confrontations as possible until a new base and connection with the supreme commander had been established. The route that Sherman would have to take was determined by the topography of the area, which is low and sandy with many swamps and rivers, connected by long highways on which a small unit of men can easily hold a whole army back. Almost all of the rivers in South Carolina flow parallel to the Savannah. In order to avoid the many crossings it was necessary to march through the terrain between two or more rivers. Sherman also intended to destroy the railroad, much as he had done in Georgia, to prevent the enemy from gathering troops in front of him. For that purpose he marched northwest between the Combahee and Savannah, as if he was going toward Augusta, in order to destroy the Augusta & Charleston Railroad at the point it crossed the Edisto River. He could cross this river then without any difficulty and no other river would be a hindrance until he reached the Saluda River near Columbia. This was the route that Sherman took, with the exception of a side trip to destroy the railroad twenty miles north of Orangeburg.

The reports that Generals Taylor and Hardee had already sent the enemy government in December show how precisely they had predicted Sherman's march. As a result of the news of the horrible defeat that Hood had suffered at Franklin and Nashville, Beauregard had asked to be relieved of command, at least of command in South Carolina and Georgia so that he could devote his full attention to the Tennessee Army and the Gulf states. He also suggested that Charleston may have to be abandoned and that Hardee should gather all his forces to confront Sherman. He ordered that all cotton be removed from the city, and where this was not possible, to burn it. This was in agreement with the procedures of the Southern Government concerning the most valuable staple of the country. On the National side, one tried to preserve such cotton as came into our hands or had been sent from the southern harbors, but that which fell into enemy hands again was burned. It was often the case that both armies, if in doubt as to which army it would fall into the hands of, tried to burn it so that neither would have the advantage of it. The rebel general at that time, Joseph Wheeler, had offered Sherman that he would preserve cotton, but then Sherman should guarantee protecting other property as well. Sherman simply answered; "If you don't burn the cotton, I will."

    Vacating Charleston was certainly a bitter pill. Beauregard called it a terrible calamity and a sensitive blow to the South, but moving his brave garrison out of the town would be a more severe blow to us. Now that we know how the southern generals thought, we come to the conclusion that the Confederate Government waited too long with the abandonment of the city, until it was too late to make use of the forces to oppose Sherman. Sherman surprised everyone with the rapidity in which he made his move to the north. Even after Hardee had pronounced the Salkehatchie Swamps to be impassable, Sherman marched right through them, covering on average ten to twelve miles a day. The weather was against him; it rained every day. The Savannah was so flooded that it was three miles wide at Sister's Ferry and long piling bridges had to be built to connect the pontoon bridge with the banks. If uprooted trees now were driven down with the current, it was difficult to protect the bridges. The Union Road on which two of Howard's divisions were marching was under water and the whole region looked more like a lake than habitable land. At the end of January, Howard had his whole wing together, with the exception of Core's division from Logan's corps, but he couldn't get through and had to join Slocum in order to cross the Savannah on his bridge. This action did not lead to any battles because Hardee had decided to position his troops in a line on the Combahee and Salkehatchie Rivers. Force's division was supposed to make a fake advance, ten miles below the railroad bridge, as if he intended to cross the Combahee River with the intention of moving toward Charleston.

After this took place, he was ordered to march northward in the expectation that Slocum's and Kilpatrick's cavalries had reached Sister's Ferry and were ready to join the movement as soon as Howard had reached the crossing. About the time that Sherman began his march, the Southern officers gathered in Augusta in order to decide on details of a plan with which they wanted to move against Sherman. Beauregard, Hardee, Hill and Smith were all in attendance and after counting up their forces, thought that they could move against Sherman on 4 February with a force of 33,500 men. They didn't count the state militia as part of that and also had no hope of getting new recruits. The conscription period had run out and the people that weren't already in the service were chased away in fright and terror because of the presence of the Union troops. As Hardee later related, everyone knew it was only a matter of time before the Confederation would break up but the politicians couldn't appear before the public with the truth. The prospects weren't encouraging but Beauregard, mentally and bodily broken, had to take over the command and make arrangements to confront Sherman and resist him.

During the time they were making their plans, Sherman marched on ahead and the opportunity to gather a force together with which to confront him had passed. On 7 February, Howard reached the Charleston & Augusta Railroad at Midway Station and on the 12th had crossed both branches of the Edisto River and had destroyed the Columbia branch of the Orangeburg railroad. Butler's enemy cavalry division with two field batteries was all that Hardee could oppose Sherman with. These joined with Wheeler, burned the bridges and tried to hold the long highway through the swamp, but Sherman's most forward divisions were usually strong enough to repulse the enemy without suffering large losses, so that road building wasn't disrupted. Sherman's 2500 wagons rolled on without delay. Beauregard now had only one road on which to move the remnants of the Tennessee Army through New Berry and Chester toward Charlotte in North Carolina, while Hardee waited for the hour in which he would have to vacate Fort Sumter and Charleston, the cradle of the rebellion, in order to still use the only railroad through Florence to Cheraw so that the gathering of forces that had been planned in Augusta, could be achieved in Raleigh, the capital of North Carolina. General Hampton was sent from Virginia to South Carolina to command the cavalry there, in the hopes that his personal influence would animate the people and to achieve what hadn't been accomplished through proclamations and mass-recruitments in Georgia. But the only result of his presence was the arousal of the controversy whether it had been his or the national troops that had set fire to Columbia which turned his most beautiful home into ashes.

The daily log of Sherman's march through South Carolina would tell an interesting story; how the Pioneer Corps overcame the obstacles of the rivers and swamps. Oesters marched the troops through rivers that were actually swamps, through muck in which the water reached to one's armpits, with the cartridge pouches around the neck and muskets held above the head. "Swamp" is the appropriate word for these rivers when we remember that passing the Salkehatchie River at Buford's bridge, the river had 15 separate branches, every one of which had to be bridged over before Logan's 15th Corps could get over it. Anyone, who can remember how difficult it is to get guns and wagons over muddy roads, can imagine how much work the troops had here. The rebel General Joseph E. Johnson said, when he heard that Sherman had successfully crossed the swamps, there never had been another army like that since Julius Cesar's time. The roads through the swamp were all paved too, with heavy blocks and small trees, which contributed to sinking the blocks in the mud. That was continued until the miles-long wagon train had gotten over it. One can imagine the amount of work necessary to accomplish that. How disappointed the southern generals were, who had believed that Sherman would wait in his base camp until the rainy period was over and the rivers had fallen again.

While the march through Georgia is remembered by the troops as romantic and pleasant, the movement through South Carolina will remain unforgettable as a daily battle with the elements. The strong will of 65,000 men with a common cause overcame all the obstacles over hundreds of miles and will stand out brilliantly in history as the modern Hercules's of our time.

After two weeks of marching, hard work and skirmishes, the army had reached the Saluda River, just upstream of Columbia. The Augusta Railroad had been destroyed for 50 miles from Edisto to Aiken. The Columbia branch, five miles south of Orangeburg to the Congaree River, about 30 miles, was rendered unusable for a long time. These great and long stretches in the center of the southern line, split up the southern forces and the destruction was so great that they wouldn't have been able to rebuild them again so easily. It took only a few hours for Sherman to secure a crossing over the Saluda and Broad Rivers, which unite just above Columbia to form the Congaree River. It was easier to cross the first two rivers than the latter, since the Congaree is bordered by the Caw Caw Swamp, which is very long and wide and made reaching it almost impossible.

When the national troops advanced, the southern cavalry set fire to the bridge after spreading it with resin and tar, so that the fire would destroy it quickly. It burned so quickly that the enemy rear guard couldn't pass over and had to gallop away on side roads in order not to be taken prisoner. In Columbia they burned down two train stations and accessory buildings, one each on the south and north sides. Long rows of cotton bales lying in the middle of the street were cut open and set on fire, since Wheeler followed the custom that nothing of value be left behind for the enemy, and businesses were broken into and looted.

Before Sherman had entered Columbia, he had ordered that residences and private property, universities, libraries, hospitals, poor houses and such things should not be destroyed; but arsenals, foundries, machinery factories and such were to be destroyed. This order was similar to that issued at Savannah, but here the result was quite different. The wild chase through the South, where the troops had to work hard and were exposed to all dangers to life, and where they had to get their food from the land through which they marched, had broken down their discipline so that they were on the verge of rebellion, and their anger against the enemy was not lessened by the sight of the birthplace of the war. The stragglers even marched to the front to take part in the fun.

General C. R. Wood's division of Logan's corps and Stone's, all Iowa troops, had the honor of being the first to occupy the city, the other troops marched through and camped outside the city. A strong wind blew the burning cotton in all directions. With hand squirts and pails, the troops and citizens tried to get control of the fire. As usual at fires, so here too, one of the merchants gave the fire-fighters a whole pail full of whiskey. Soon the fire was something secondary and the whiskey was the main thing. The wind grew stronger and the fire became more dangerous. Sherman and Logan reached the city, the mayor presented himself and was informed of Sherman's order about private property, but by this time the Iowa boys were already under the influence of the whiskey. General Wood naturally replaced them, poured the rest of the liquor on the street, and arrested the drunken soldiers. The wind didn't seem to let up and in a short time there was a hurricane and the burning cotton now broke into bright flames. A nearby barn caught fire, which then spread rapidly and there no longer was a chance of putting it out. Sherman himself was there and kept the whole division at it, trying to put the fire out, either by damping the fire or containing it. Most of the houses in Columbia were built of spruce wood and it was soon a sea of fire. Unfortunately, some of the drunken soldiers remembered their sufferings as prisoners at Andersonville. Many of these had been released from there and now satisfied their anger by trying to raze the city to the ground as punishment for keeping the state in the rebellion. Drunken soldiers, army stragglers and criminals freed from prison, formed a very dangerous gang and the fire which had started by chance, caused destruction without limit. When the situation became clear to General Howard, he brought in a brigade from Hazen's division, and with mounted bayonets swept through the city arresting all disorderly persons, white, black, citizens and soldiers. Around midnight the fire storm ended. The fire found no new material and the largest part of the city lay in ashes.

Sherman regretted this very much and tried to do what he could to make the situation for the residents easier. He gave them a large herd of cattle and other foodstuffs to lessen their need and ordered the city administration to distribute them to the needy. No one more than Sherman intended to destroy public property that could be of advantage to the enemy, but here the intention was to not increase the suffering of those not involved in the war. The southern government immediately proclaimed that the destruction of Columbia had been done according to plan, but no action was more closely investigated than the fire storm, which produced the following facts. Orangeburg was also partly destroyed by fire after the cotton stored there was set afire by the rebel cavalry so that it wouldn't fall into our hands. But this place, as well as Hardeeville, Grahamville, Gillissonville, McPherson Ville, Barnwell, Blackville, Midway and Lexington, were all destroyed by their own troops and then were blamed on Sherman, although Kilpatrick tried to leave behind only chimneys without houses and to see the country turned into desert. Even a harmless comment made by Sherman in a letter to Halleck, was used by the enemy as evidence that Sherman marched through the south with fire and sword. His orders to his troops at the beginning of the campaign were that all citizens were to be treated well on the march from Atlanta to Savannah, as well as from Savannah to Raleigh. That shows he wanted to treat the Southerners well and only to destroy what was of help to the rebellion. The city of Atlanta stands today as witness than many of their original buildings are still standing, but train stations, machine shops and military warehouses as well as factories and nearby houses were destroyed by fire. Every war is a plague, but the cries that our civil war with its gruesomeness was worse than any other does not match the facts. In Columbia there was a gunpowder factory, an arsenal, government work-shops, and a mint to produce paper money. All these were destroyed on 18 and 19 February, for their remote position had protected them from the fire in the city. On the 20th, Sherman marched on, leaving behind a community overpowered by terrible losses and astonished at the awful change which had come about in just a few days, and were only saved from starvation by the provisions that the national commander had distributed to them.

Surprise Attack against Kilpatrick and the Battle of Averasboro

The actions during the beginning of the march had not taken many lives. Although skirmishing continued without letup, here and there serious resistance was made, such as at River's Bridge on the Salkehatchie River, where Colonel Wager Swayne lost his leg to a cannon ball. Usually wooded areas provided safe cover for the troops and units that were sent up or down the river a few miles, repeatedly pushing the enemy back so that the main column could continue to march on uninterrupted. After Columbia had been passed, the terrain changed and became more rolling, the streams smaller and easier to cross, plantations were in larger numbers and more prosperous, and the foragers collected more provisions. The 15th Corps turned onto the Charleston Railroad toward Cedar Creek and destroyed about 20 miles of track on the left bank of the Congaree River. Howard now turned his column toward the north to overtake Blair's corps, which had marched forward on the railroad to Charlotte and destroyed a forty mile stretch of railroad from Columbia almost to Winnsboro. The only remaining railroad leaving Columbia was the branch west to Abbeville and this was assigned to Slocum, who with his left wing and cavalry destroyed a similar distance to what Blair had totally destroyed on the Charlotte Road. Part of the army then turned toward Winnsboro, where they doubled Blair's work and leveled 15 miles of the North Railroad to the ground. Sherman's main purpose in destroying the railroads here was to make any connection between Beauregard and Hardee impossible. He also wanted them to believe that he wanted to march to Charlotte so that the enemy would not gather its forces together near Raleigh. The Federal columns were now redirected straight east, they crossed the Catawba River and marched toward the Great Pee Dee River and Cheraw. While the cavalry covered the left wing, the outermost right wing made a visit to Camden. During this movement between the two rivers, the wings of the army were often as much as forty miles from each other. During this time it rained almost without a break, but the swamps weren't numerous. As soon as Hardee heard about Sherman's attack on Columbia, he withdrew from Charleston and his troops were transported by train to Cheraw, bringing with them much public and private property to safety. The large amounts of cotton still in Charleston were burned in the warehouses. The fire also destroyed a large part of the city, a magazine full of gunpowder and ammunition also blew up and cost 200 curious bystanders their lives. Dahlgren and Foster had their eyes open on the coast and on the 18th occupied the abandoned and ruined city.

Hardee had strong defense works at Pee Dee behind Cheraw, but as usual, Slocum got around these works too, and the right wing under Howard moved into Cheraw on 3 March and took as booty 28 field artillery guns, 3000 small weapons and a large mass of prepared ammunition and goods for the use of the army. General Wade Hampden, in command of the southern cavalry, had been misled by Sherman and first marched toward Charlotte but reached Hardee after a long round-about way before Hardee crossed the Cape Fear River at Fayetteville. On the 11th, he withdrew from the place before Slocum reached it and on the same day, the 14th Army Corps under Gen. Davis moved into the city. The remnants of Hood's army had gathered in Charlotte and since Hampden wanted to move back into his position confronting the Federal Army, he marched unexpectedly in the night of the 9th to a little place called Solemn Grove to confront Kilpatrick's cavalry corps. Kilpatrick had positioned his three brigades on a crossroads to support each other, but the enemy came. Atkins and his brigade were ahead and although he tried hard to reach Spencer and his brigade during the night on side roads, he wasn't able to warn Spencer of the attack from his side. Kilpatrick was with Spencer, and Hampden, now certain of success, attacked Spencer with Butler's division just before daybreak. The attack was totally unexpected. The house in which Spencer and Kilpatrick were resting was surrounded and a battery of field artillery near headquarters fell into the enemy's hands. The whole brigade took flight and sought shelter in the swamps. Kilpatrick managed to escape half-naked and without a weapon. His tough riders were rough and used to unusual fights and as soon as they had some protection, they joined with the wagon train guards and with volunteer snipers they attacked Hampden, whose men were busy looting the captured camp. Kilpatrick recaptured his guns and opened fire on the opponent and turned a retreat into a victory. Spencer and his staff had barricaded themselves on the second floor of the house and were now happy to be unexpectedly freed by their friends. Atkins, guided by the thunder of the battle, reached the battle-field when everything was over. So also Jordon's brigade and an infantry brigade that Slocum had sent when he heard the battle. In spite of Kilpatrick's cool-headedness, there would have been very little chance for Spencer's brigade to regroup after its flight if they hadn't been able to reorganize under the protection of the dismounted wagon train guards, who were armed with rifles, muskets and bayonets under the command of Lieutenant Colonel Stough of the 9th Ohio Cavalry Regiment, which wasn't far from the main camp. When the enemy saw the shiny gun barrels and bare bayonets in the early morning light, they shouted: "The infantry is here!" The noise caused consternation and much confusion among Hampden's troops. Kilpatrick's attack followed then and the tide turned. This fight wasn't significant but shows the character of cavalry skirmishes which here and there bring a bit of life into the plodding movements of the army. Hampden was able to free some southern prisoners and claimed to have taken 500 of Kilpatrick's men prisoner. Kilpatrick claimed to have only lost 200 men however.

Enemy losses were heavy, especially of officers, but the number isn't reported. Over one hundred dead and many wounded remained on the battlefield, which shows that Southern losses were greater than Kilpatrick's. The arsenal and weapons factory in Fayetteville, which had been built by the national army before the war and significantly enlarged by the rebel government with the addition of machinery that had been moved from Harper's Ferry at the beginning of the war, was thoroughly destroyed by Sherman. It was here that the victorious columns could again hear the whistles of the steamboats which established the connection with Wilmington by way of the Cape Fear River and news of the reserve army which Schofield was bringing to Sherman. He was approaching in two lines, having believed that Sherman would have to march down on the right bank of the Fear River to establish a new base camp, but Hardee's retreat northward and the certainty that Kinston would be in our possession, left no doubt that he would be connecting with Schofield at Goldsboro. He didn't know that Bragg intended to make a surprise attack on the corps under Cox that was coming from New Bern and believed that his own march forward would cause all enemy units to focus their efforts against him to stop his progress. He intended to march with his left wing upriver as if he were trying to reach Raleigh and then suddenly turn to the right to connect with Schofield in Goldsboro.

The news that General Joseph E. Johnson was again in good favor and in command of the enemy troops reached Sherman at Cheraw on 3 March, but the appointment had already been made on 23 February, at the time when the Union troops were still at Winnsboro. The rebel government then was convinced that Sherman wanted to march to Charlotte in order to destroy the railroad and the supplies stockpiled for the army there. The greatest efforts were being made to gather supplies by railroad for the army and this was the only railroad still functioning. Almost four months of foodstuffs and clothing had been stockpiled there.

The Southern Congress in its desperation had appointed General Lee to Supreme Commander of all their armies and he had recalled Johnson out of his seclusion to lead the troops that were supposed to stop Sherman's advance, since the backdoor to Richmond was only shut tighter with each of Sherman's advances. Jefferson Davis, the president of the Confederacy, had often stated that he would never put Johnson in command again, but the responsibility now was on Lee and he had to give in. The news that Johnson was reappointed, served as a warning to Sherman's army that they could now expect stiff resistance. Officers as well as men were of the opinion that Richmond had finally taken the right step, but they were also convinced that it was too late for anyone to save the rebel cause. Sherman believed that Johnson would be able to oppose him with 45,000 men, among them Bragg's troops in North Carolina. This most likely was in agreement with what the Southern leaders determined during their meeting in Augusta.

Hardee's 18,000 men from Charleston were already fused together after vacating that city and the South Carolina and Georgia militias had been sent home. The cavalry had experienced heavy losses and the remainder of Hood's army had gotten smaller as it marched northward. When Beauregard made his rough estimate at Charlotte, he had 26,000 infantry and artillery and still had 6,000 cavalry men on whom he could depend. Johnson was convinced that Sherman would go by way of Fayetteville and after leaving Beauregard with some troops in Charlotte, he went personally to Fayetteville to meet with Hardee and Hampden, and gave orders to pull the other troops together at Smithfield. It was around this time that he sent Stewart's and Lee's corps in combination with Hoke's corps under Bragg against Schofield near Kinston, believing that he would have enough time to pull all the troops back together again to confront Sherman before he could reach the Neuse River. This plan was certainly the best, but he didn't have the troops with which to carry out the plan, no matter how much effort was made to be successful.

Sherman was waiting for shoes and clothing to arrive in Fayetteville from Wilmington, his army was almost naked and barefoot, but he couldn't get anything and then went on ahead. Slocum's columns with the cavalry put a lot of pressure on Hardee and on the 15th took Colonel Rhett, the commander of the rear guard, prisoner. He attacked Averasboro, where Hardee had barricaded himself on a hill between the river and the swamp. Slocum now ordered Jackson's and Ward's divisions of the 20th Corps to spread out in an attack line. Kilpatrick was in the right wing. Sherman was present and gave instructions to send a brigade of infantry to the left in order to attack the enemy's flank. These orders were quickly carried out and Taliaferro's enemy division fled and didn't reorganize until in the rear where McLaws' division had barricaded itself. The main assault fell on Rhett's brigade, which had lost its commander the day before. This left more than a hundred dead on the field and lost over two hundred prisoners. A battery of artillery was also taken. William's division moved now toward Hardee's second line but darkness put an end to the fight and during the night Hardee retreated. The next morning Sherman moved further. The Union forces lost 77 dead and over 500 wounded at Averasboro. Since Sherman had enough work with our own wounded, he left the Southern wounded in the field hospital with their Southern doctors.

The Battle of Bentonville

The days following Averasboro will forever remain unforgettable to those involved, as being the most difficult and strenuous of the entire campaign. The continuous rain made the already bad roads virtually impassable. For that reason, Sherman had changed his marching orders at Fayetteville. He assigned four divisions to each of the wings, and although a bare minimum, he thought he had enough forces in each wing to be capable of holding the enemy back if it attacked, until he could pull his troops together. In spite of great effort, the columns became quite separated while marching on the terrible roads. On the morning of the 19th, two divisions of Davis's 14th Corps were about eight miles from Bentonville, a small village just south of Mill Creek, a little tributary of the Neuse River where the north-south road from Smithfield to Clinton crossed a road from Averasboro to Goldsboro. Two divisions of William's 20th Corps were eight miles further behind. Kilpatrick had followed Hardee with his cavalry and was somewhat behind Williams' corps, making his way toward the main column. Howard was on the right with his four light divisions on parallel roads to the south, often six to twelve miles apart. The slowly moving wagon train was advancing further back on side roads. Sherman believed that Hardee's actions at Averasboro had only been carried out to keep him from advancing toward Raleigh until Johnson could collect all his troops in one spot. That Hardee troops were alone in the battle seemed to indicate that Johnson wasn't yet capable of risking a battle until he had been able to connect with the others at Goldsboro. Sherman didn't know however, that Johnson's column from New Bern with Bragg in charge was already in front of him and that Hardee's action at Averasboro was done to give Bragg time to unite with him before Schofield could join Sherman.

The Southern commander was in contact with his subordinates by telegraph from his central headquarters and on the morning of the 19th knew better than Sherman what progress Schofield's two columns had made. Johnson could make his plans with full knowledge while Sherman was feeling his way in the dark. If Johnson only wanted to make a defended retreat, all he had to do was carry out his attack quickly; twenty-four hours later it would be too late, for Slocum and Howard would have been reunited at Cox's Bridge, and Terry with his two divisions of the 10th Army Corps would also be there. Johnson could either defend himself in that position or attack if he wished to. He knew that on the 17th Sherman was marching from Averasboro toward Goldsboro and that Hardee was resting at Elevation, about two-thirds of the way from the last battlefield to Smithfield. Bragg had reached Smithfield and reports from Hampton were that Slocum's two corps were about a day's march away from each other and about the same distance from Howard's troops; these would be marching past three miles of his flank near Bentonville. It seemed to him that there was an opportunity to attack Sherman's corps individually and he sent orders to all to get together a Bentonville on the 18th. Sherman disliked having his troops so separated from each other, but in order to feed them from the land, he was forced to do that, and for the same reason, he had to stay in motion until he could establish a connection with his base by the railroad that Schofield had restored. But he told us too, that he was certain that Johnson would remain on the north side of the Neuse River in an effort to prevent him from crossing same. This conjecture had led him to leave Slocum's line and to march to Howard. His habit was always to be with the threatened flank until the danger was past. With this movement to the right wing he also hoped to come into personal contact with Schofield and was closer to the point at which he would have to look for a place to cross the Neuse River in order to march to Goldsboro. His calculations were correct but, as usual, the unexpected stepped in. It probably would have been better if Slocum had stayed with Davis's advance until William's 20th Corps had defended itself, but everyone was so certain that Johnson wouldn't be moved to attack. But Johnson's calculations were also incorrect in this. He wanted to attack Slocum already early in the morning, but the maps were, as usual, incorrect and Hardee was too far away to make the march in one day after he had received the orders to do so. For that reason, Hampden was ordered to make Slocum's road impassable in order to prevent him from reaching the crossing before Hardee could get there. The enemy cavalry under Wheeler was therefore always in front of the line of Davis's corps as they were moving forward on the 19th and had also erected barricades at various places from which they offered strong resistance. Carlin's people were in the lead, his foragers to the left and right of the road. They found it impossible to drive the enemy away so that they could gather provisions. This led to some meaningful speculation that this wasn't just resistance from a rearguard, but Carlin pushed forward and Hampden pulled back slowly and it soon seemed evident that the defense was only cavalry. Sherman made his way to the right flank. Around midday a staff-officer caught up to him and reported that the defense only consisted of cavalry, but thunder of the artillery was now faster and indicated that the battle was more serious.

If one marches south of Bentonville, a country road branches off from the Clinton Road about one-half mile before reaching the Goldsboro road. This turns toward Averasboro, producing a triangle, each side of which is about a half mile long. Hoke's enemy division was the first to reach the place and received orders to march about 700 to 800 paces further on the road to Averasboro. Here he halted and set up a barricade with one wing bent back somewhat near the open angle toward the road on which Davis was marching closer. Stewart with his own corps and Lee's corps took a stand next to him and put up barricades across the road that they had arrived on with a distance to the line of about 400 to 500 paces. From this point the first wing was extended forward facing the cultivated farmland of Cole's Plantation. When Hardee reached the area, he sent Bate with two divisions of Cheatham's corps and positioned them on the outer right, and Taliaferro's division was moved forward to support Bate. The other division (McLaws') was sent forward on the left flank on orders from Johnson. The center of Johnson's position was not on the Averasboro Road but on the corner of the Cole's Plantation, the two wings extended forward from this point, the middle of the left wing crossing the road that Davis was marching on. The right wing was hidden in a thicket and extended forward in order to encircle the approaching troops if these had passed west of the Cole Plantation. This plantation was an impenetrable thicket with woods and swamps, out of which little rivers flowed out in all directions.

Around noon, as Carlin's division of Davis's troops slowly pushed Hampden's cavalry back, they reached the barricade crossing the highway. Hobart's division had spread out in battle formation somewhat sooner and crossed the road on which a battery of artillery was moving. To the right of the road one could see nothing, for it was brush and jungle, but one could see the enemy line on the left which seemed to be retreating to the west of Cole's Plantation. Still believing he only had enemy cavalry in front of him, which he had already followed for five miles, Buell ordered Davis to make a detour to the left across the open fields of the plantation and to attack the enemy's flank. Hobart's sharpshooters however, discovered a line which opened fire on our troops and reached our flank, and Hambright's brigade spread out on Hobart's right. Carlin now advanced with his two brigades intending to storm the barricades in front of him but was met with such disastrous fire that he was soon convinced he wasn't just dealing with the cavalry here. Carlin took some prisoners, among which was a Union soldier who had signed up with the Confederates to avoid imprisonment. From him it was learned that General Johnson was present here with his entire army.

Slocum soon reached the field, and after consulting with Davis ordered Morgan's division to take a stand to the right of Carlin; Mitchell's and Vandever's brigades in front and Fearing's in the second line. Strong picketer lines kept up fire toward the enemy while the troops in the line tried to erect barricades for protection. It was now about 2 p.m. when Slocum reported to Sherman on the situation, who then sent Colonel McClurg from his staff to quickly lead two divisions of William's corps to the field.

Buell's brigade could only slowly make headway through the swamp, and the cracks and rattle of musket fire warned him that a storm-assault was going on. Hardee had moved Taliaferro's division toward Bate's right and on Buell's flank. Bate now stormed Buell from the front and from the side and Buell's brigade was overpowered and had to quickly retreat. This attack was imitated by Stewart's division, which now swept over the Cole Plantation and attacked one after the other of Carlin's brigades from the side and from behind and pushed them from the field. But our people didn't let themselves be hunted so easily, since they weren't used to retreating and the enemy crossing the field was severely punished. Slocum's batteries positioned next to the Cole residence, cleaned them up terribly. Added to this was crossfire from Hobart's infantry. Step by step, the enemy advanced. Every regiment of Hobart's defended itself as it pulled back to follow Carlin, always forming a new line and behind new barricades, until the brigade had been driven a full mile back. Now the enemy came in a storm down the highway and captured the battery. Mile's brigade was also driven back from the line and every connection between Morgan and Carlin had been broken. General Davis, whose battlefield talents were so brilliantly displayed here, galloped to Morgan and ordered Fearing to move his brigade quickly to the left and spread out parallel with the road and then storm the enemy flank.

It was as if Fearing had been made for this job. During running there he changed the front of his brigade and drove before him with the points of their bayonets whatever came into their way until he had reached the highway. There he formed his line and directed his devastating rapid fire and forced the enemy on his right into the swamp. The crackle and thunder of the fight moved Williams to quickly get the troops of his corps into the battle. Robinson's brigade from his division was the first that arrived at the battlefield and they formed themselves over the road in front of the residence of the Morris Plantation, about a mile from the Cole Plantation. The terrain was somewhat higher here and the artillery of the 20th Corps went into position here as soon as they arrived. Robinson joined with Fearing's left and Bate attacked the line repeatedly, first going forward and then going backwards, until Hardee pulled his center back somewhat due to the flight of his troops. The other portion of Morgan's division wasn't idle while Fearing was under such heavy fire. His first assault on Hoke's division had shaken up the latter's forces and Bragg, who was commanding this flank of the enemy forces, asked for support. Hardee had just reached the battlefield and Johnson ordered McLaws to support Hoke, while Taliaferro was positioned behind Bate, as already mentioned.

Morgan was not able to break through the enemy line but had been able to keep his line together and he used the pause that resulted from Stewart being bloodily pushed back in the center, to strengthen his line. Cogswell's brigade from William's corps reached the battlefield about 4 p.m. and was sent into the line to the right of Fearing, but the line was still too short to reach Mitchell, whose line was bent back somewhat so that it exposed a small flank. Shortly after 5 p.m., another general attack was made against our line again and continued until it got dark. Hoke's division stormed Morgan's barricade but was bloodily repulsed. Vandever's brigade resisted the assault and captured the battle flag of the 44th North Carolina Regiment, but the enemy found the opening between Morgan and the other part of our line and charged Cogswell's line anew. He bravely defended himself but some were able to get through. These wanted to attack Morgan from behind. But Davis warned Morgan by McClurg, who was almost taken prisoner. Mitchell and Vandever turned toward the enemy and chased him into fleeing. The 14th Michigan Regiment that had captured a flag in the last assault had the same luck in this and took the flag of the 54th Virginia Regiment as they attacked the enemy from the rear. The enemy had wasted all it forces against Davis's 14th Corps, and since Johnson knew that strong reinforcements would soon arrive for the Union side, he ordered Hardee and Bragg to pull back their troops as soon as the wounded could be taken care of. After dark, a group of the enemy attacked Mitchell from the rear, but was greeted with a salvo, after which they dropped their weapons and fled to safety. Hardee's wing occupied the north side of the Cole Plantation, but early in the morning, Bragg's wing was pulled back until the line was a closed straight line instead of the open angle, the left touching Mill Creek, focused toward the east to the area from which Sherman was expected with Howard's Corps. Slocum's report written before the battle at 2 p.m. reached Sherman at 5 p.m. Sherman intended to gather all his troops together on the following day, unless he had to retreat. He didn't change his plan at that time other than to order Kilpatrick to remain with Slocum instead of marching to the right, but around 2 p.m. on the 20th, Sherman received a message from Slocum by which he was informed of the heavy fighting at the end of the day. A courier was sent immediately to Hazen's division, who was with Howard's wagon train and was closest to Slocum, with orders to immediately go to Slocum's aid. The other divisions of Logan's Corps were at Fallen Church, where the roads, on which both wings of the army were marching, crossed. These were instructed to march at daybreak. Blair's Corps, marching on the Wilmington Road, was also called back. Hazen reached Slocum at daybreak and found that the whole left wing was now together and formed a very good defense line that had been organized by Howard, in which Carlin had collected his troops before nightfall. At noon, Sherman had reached the place with the leading regiment of Logan's Corps. The rest of the day was spent creating a line through woods and swamps. Lively skirmishing was kept up and the connection to Slocum completed. Hazen was positioned to the right of Morgan, so that he could join with Logan's Corps as soon as it arrived at the battle site. The entire enemy line was protected by a little steam that flowed through a deep swamp. By Johnson's masterful genius, his line had created a barricade protected by an abatis and just as complete as those in Georgia with which he had always opposed our every movement. His position was only provisionally for the defense of Bentonville, and he only wanted to hold the bridge over Mill Creek until his wounded had been taken care of and he could safely pull his troops back to Smithfield. Slocum's wounded were numerous enough to fill all the ambulances and Sherman believed that he could drive Johnson out of his position more easily by a maneuver than by an assault. He limited himself then to advancing toward his opponent, mainly with his right, where Blair's Corps had extended Logan's line. Schofield received orders to march immediately to Goldsboro. Terry was sent forward to Cox's Bridge and was to try to take control of the crossing over the Neuse River. Shortly after noon on the 21st. General Mower moved through the swamp and since he encountered only weak resistance, two brigades were sent ahead until their shots could reach the bridges behind Johnson. This action had no connection with the other parts of the corps and wasn't noticed by Howard until he became aware of Mower's position from the rapid fire of Johnson's reserves. This was a dangerous situation, and if the action had been done with the approval of the commanding general, it could have produced good results.

Johnson first threw Wheeler's cavalry against the division and followed with Lowry's (formerly Cheatham's) division of the Tennessee Army, which had just reached the battlefield. Howard ordered Blair to support Mower and instructed Logan to advance. He captured a line of trenches for sharpshooters and Logan's troops barricaded themselves within fifty paces of Bragg's front line. The topography of the area was so unknown however, that the full advantages of Mower's movement couldn't be utilized. He was called back because Sherman was concerned about safety. Since he was aware that Johnson would have to retreat and that he himself could gather his whole army together north of the Neuse River, he preferred this instead of plunging into a general attack in a place where he was surrounded by thickets and swamps. Later he regretted not having supported Mower's move. With better knowledge of the region, he would have done that, but his caution was better than an impulse, for as it was he was sure of his thing, with the exception if Johnson had already completely withdrawn from the place. The loss of life in a general assault on enemy barricades would have been terrible and couldn't have been justified.

  The enemy army kept the bodies of troops together that were originally part of Hood's army until the surrender a few months later. Stewart's, Cheatham's and Lee's Corps had their complete lists of divisions and brigades. The usual method of calculating the strength of the enemy was the number of brigades, which the prisoner's represented, but in this case the information caused us some confusion, which likely was the intention. For this and other reasons already mentioned, Sherman overestimated Johnson's forces and not willing to take chances, hurried to get his troops together which would give him superior strength and allow him to bring his campaign and the war to an end without having to sacrifice lots of lives in a large battle. Johnson withdrew his troops during the night and on the 22nd, Sherman marched on, following him. Schofield had marched into Goldsboro on the previous day. Cox's 23rd Corps was positioned north of the city and covered the road to Smithfield. Terry's 10th Corps reached Cox's Bridge on the same day and laid a pontoon bridge there. On the 23rd,

Sherman reached the place at the head of his troops and now had all his forces together, numbering almost 100,000.

The losses during the battle were heavy. On the Union side, 1604 men were rendered unfit for duty, 1196 of them belonged to Slocum's command and among them was General Fearing, who was severely wounded. In the assault on the Southerner's center, the enemy left 267 dead and 1625 prisoners in Sherman's hands. Johnson said that Slocum had 35,000 men in the battle, while in reality Slocum only could bring 12,000 men into the line on the 19th. Johnson said he only had 14,100 men available for the attack in his infantry and artillery, but his official report on 31 March shows 22,000 infantry and artillery and 5500 cavalry. Since his army had been freshly organized, he did not have any sick men. If we now subtract prisoners and wounded, we can assume that Johnson led 22,000 against Slocum's 12,000 into the fight. Had Slocum held back, after learning that Johnson was here with his whole army, until the other division had gotten closer, Johnson himself would have had to march through a mile of swamp which would have served as protection for Slocum. A charge against an unknown line is always risky, and in such a swampy wilderness, it is as if one runs into an ambush. Johnson had barricaded himself and was prepared to withstand an attack and it is certain he would only have slowly retreated. But in the end, the left wing managed to get out of its dangerous situation with honor and flags flying.

Stoneman's Ride

We would now like to present an overview of Sherman's military division, a part of which was now commanded by General Thomas, to better understand the last actions. Following Grant's and Sherman's wishes and orders, the army under Thomas after the Battle of Nashville was to follow the enemy in an active winter campaign in Alabama and Mississippi in order to keep its scattered troops from having enough rest in which to reorganize. Both generals hoped that General Thomas would march through Alabama and Mississippi just as Sherman had marched through Georgia and that Thomas would then reach Mobile, as Sherman had reached Savannah. Thomas was then to join his army with those of General Candy and in so doing, establish a supply base on the Gulf of Mexico. Since General Thomas didn't believe that his troops were ready for such a campaign, General Grant became convinced that he would have to make a new plan. He would send A. J. Smith's Corps along with Knipe's Cavalry Division by way of New Orleans to help General Candy, by which he hoped to achieve the same result by having Candy make a significant march on Mobile. Schofield's 23rd Corps was ordered to the East Coast and Thomas was to limit himself to cavalry skirmishes under General Stoneman in East Tennessee and the Carolinas, and under General Wilson from Florence and Columbia in central Alabama. Under any circumstances the intention was to develop such actions in all parts of the war territory so that no department of the enemy army could get support from another area.

Before the armies of Ohio and Cumberland had been united (the latter under Schofield, before he was sent to North Carolina), Schofield had ordered General Stoneman, commander in East Tennessee, to drive back and destroy the forces of the Southern General Breckenridge, who had carried out a raid to benefit Hood. Stoneman moved out of Knoxville on 9 December with two brigades of cavalry under General Gillem and General Burbidge and in a short time cleared East Tennessee of the enemy and followed his advantage by marching up the Holston Valley to Abingdon, Wytheville and Saltville. At the last place, he destroyed the salt works which were of great value to the south and against which raids had been often carried out without success. At the town of Marion, extensive iron works were burned down and in Whyte County, the lead mines were completely destroyed. Two railroad trains were captured and the railroad bridges and tracks destroyed for many miles. A great mass of provisions fell into the victor's hands, ten field-artillery guns and several hundred prisoners were taken. Breckenridge had to flee to North Carolina and at the end of December, Stoneman returned to East Tennessee.

In order to carry out General Grant's plan, Thomas ordered Stoneman to march through the Smoky Mountains with his cavalry to South Carolina to destroy the railroad connection between Columbia, South Carolina with Charlotte, North Carolina, to keep the enemy out of the way of Sherman's advance. Grant had expected that his orders would be carried out immediately, but it seemed that nothing in the West worked as planned. After long preparation and delay, the march wasn't set into motion until 20 March when Sherman had just reached Goldsboro and this action for his benefit was no longer necessary.

Stoneman was therefore ordered to make another march to Lynchburg, with the goal of making the railroad that he had destroyed in December, completely unusable for the expected retreat of Lee's army from Richmond. General Thomas also received orders to reposition the 4th Army Corps in East Tennessee, in order to hold up Lee's move, in case he tried to escape the Potomac Army by this route. Stoneman's riders consisted of Gillem's Cavalry Division which had three brigades under Brown, Palmer and Miller. The enemy had taken possession again of the upper valley of the Holston River with a small brigade of riders under General Jackson and local militias companies. The railroad bridges had been rebuilt for Lee's use. On 26 March, Stoneman was again in Jonesboro in the outermost northeast corner of Tennessee and here reached the valley of the Watauga River and followed it on the mountain cliffs through which the river snaked to Boone County in North Carolina. Here he crossed the Blue Ridge Mountains to the upper reaches of the Yadkin River and with a swing northward, reached the New River and

Wytheville. This long round-about way brought him to the rear and flank of his opponent Jackson.

In Wytheville the provisions for the southern army that were stored there were completely destroyed and units burned all the bridges on the railroad for more than 90 miles almost to Lynchburg. This work continued until 7 April when Lee was cut off from his supplies stockpiled in Lynchburg by General Grant's army on the 2nd after Union columns took possession of the railroad between Burk's Station and Danville. The rapidity by which Lee's army was surrounded at Appomattox didn't allow him any time to try to escape and the knowledge that Stoneman had destroyed the last of the provisions at Lynchburg, sped up the surrender on 9 April.

On that day, Stoneman had gathered his brigades together on the border of North Carolina and marched south along the Danville & Charlotte Railroad, which was the line on which Johnson and Lee were going to join each other in the case that Lee could escape from General Grant at Burkeville. He passed south through Germantown to Salisbury. From here he sent out detachments to the left and right to destroy factories and stores of provisions for the southern army. One of these raider columns almost took Jefferson Davis and his cabinet prisoner at Greensboro.

On the 12th he captured Salisbury in a brilliant attack. Almost all of the southern troops were taken prisoner here. They had all given up hope after Lee's surrender on the 9th. The capture of army supplies in Greensboro was exceptionally large, and had the actual situation in Virginia and North Carolina been known, much would have been spared destruction, but based on the information he had then, all army provisions were to be destroyed.

The enemy troops under Gardiner and Pemberton were driven together and 1300 men were taken prisoner, 18 field guns and 10,000 weapons for the infantry, as well as immeasurable supplies of ammunition, foodstuffs, clothing and blankets that had been stockpiled here for Lee's army fell into Stoneman's hands, and as already mentioned, were destroyed. From Salisbury, after destroying the railroad bridges for many miles, he marched back to East Tennessee. On the way there he heard about Sherman's and Johnson's ceasefire, and later Johnson's surrender on 26 April.

General Wilson's March through Alabama

The march that General Wilson made through the state of Alabama was quite extensive but it wasn't until 23 March that it was set in motion. Grant had hoped to see Wilson and his army in the saddle by 20 February or shortly thereafter. The cavalry was divided into four divisions and gathered at Gravelly Springs nine miles below Florence in Alabama on the Tennessee River after Hood had withdrawn from the area. Exercises and preparations kept him busy every day, one division under Hazen had to relinquish their horses to Knipe so that he could go across country from Vicksburg to connect with Candy in Mobile and could join Wilson's advance on his right wing. The other three divisions were commanded by Generals Long, McCook and Upton, but the march started too late to hold back any part of Hood's army in Alabama, for the remainder of the southern Tennessee Army was already at Kinston under Bragg opposing Schofield again, later marching to Bentonville against Sherman before Wilson's column even started moving on 23 March. But General Taylor gathered the reserves and militias under the conscription laws of the southern states together and Forrest too, was very active in recruiting and re-arming the cavalry anew in order to get them into serviceable condition. He managed to get four divisions together under his command, which gave him the confidence that he could successfully oppose Wilson and drive him out of the states of Alabama and Mississippi. Taylor was obliged to put one unit against Candy in Mobile, but this didn't weaken Forrest's strength because the latter always expected, based on his earlier actions, to be the first in any place, which was his idea of the pinnacle of the art of war. In order to be the first in any spot however, it is also necessary to have troops near the threatened point, which was now not possible for Forrest.

The only surviving arms factory in the South was at Selma. It stood on the north bank of the Alabama River, about 150 miles above Mobile in the center of the most fertile region of the state where sugar cane grows best. The river is navigable and the state also had a railroad connection to the coast by way of Demopolis and over Talladega with the Northeast. On this railroad, about 50 miles northward, lies Montevallo, which then as now, was the center of the largest ironworks which delivered a better quality of iron. Forrest's riders were scattered over the central and eastern parts of Mississippi, from where they were getting better horses and where deserters and the conscription laws were most strictly dealt with. Jackson's Division of Forrest's Corps had its headquarters at West Point on the Mobile & Ohio Railroad, and Chalmers was near Columbus, Mississippi, two of Roddey's brigades were near Mobile but Roddey himself was on advance-guard duty with his other brigade in northern Alabama. Buford's Division had been so decimated in the Nashville battle that only a few remained and Crosland's Brigade was the only unit of troops from that division still capable of taking part in the campaign. There was one more brigade from Chalmers' division under Wirt Adams on the way from Jackson, Mississippi to Columbus, but this was ordered to guard the Mobile & Ohio Railroad. For this reason, it was not possible for Forrest, under the best of circumstances, to lead more than 8000 riders into fire against Wilson's 12,000 core troops. Wilson had made good use of the time it took him to make preparations and a train of 250 wagons were outfitted for quick movements to carry ammunition and small rations such as coffee, sugar and salt. Meat and bread were to come from the land. A pontoon train of large size accompanied the train and almost 2000 dismounted cavalry served as guards for the vehicles. The three divisions moved forward on three different roads but reunited again at Jasper, 90 miles southeast of Tuscumbia.

The reports that Wilson received here urged him to speed things up. He had the bread sacks of his men be filled up and leaving the provisions train behind, he marched as quickly as possible to Montevallo. Roddey's enemy brigade wanted to hold him up at Elyton, but without success. McCook was ordered to let Croxton's brigade go ahead to Tuscaloosa to destroy supplies, public property and a military school. Croxton captured a railroad bridge at Hillsboro before the enemy could reach it, and his column marched over it and reached Montevallo on the 31st. Roddey's brigade and the militia units under General Adams got out of the way as General Upton advanced. In the surrounding area five iron foundries and as many coal mines were destroyed. Wilson did not waste any time and marched rapidly southward. Crossland's enemy brigade had joined Roddey and Forrest personally tried his hardest to be there too, but the large column under Wilson didn't give him any rest by attacking the enemy wherever they gathered to defend themselves. In this way Forrest was driven fourteen miles back to Randolph on 1 April. On the next day, when the Union troops under Wilson reached Randolph, they captured an enemy courier and were able to learn about the positions and movements of the enemy. He learned that Forrest was personally leading the troops in his front line, but Jackson's division had been forced to join him by Croxton's Union brigade at Trion, 30 miles northwest between the Cahaba and Black Warrior Rivers. Wilson also learned that Chalmers' division was at Marion, about 30 miles southwest of Forrest and was marching toward Selma with the intention of crossing the Cahaba close to his present position. Croxton sent Wilson a message that he would follow Jackson and try to engage him in a battle. So it seemed that Wilson had reached all the places first and with the largest forces.

McCook was now sent out to join with Croxton in the attack on Jackson. McCook crossed the Cahaba at Centreville, driving the militia guarding the bridge apart, and then marching on toward Trion, but when he discovered that Croxton was no longer following Jackson, since the latter had much superior forces, he returned back over the bridge to the east side of the river and burned the bridge. Jackson now, not being able to march over the river, was forced to move all the way forward to Marion before he managed to get across. Wilson no longer feared that Jackson could join up with Forrest north of Selma and marched with renewed energy against Forrest, who had chosen an excellent defense position for himself six miles north of Plantersville. Luck was with Wilson again, as it usually is with the bold; through an error in a telegraph message, Forrest believed that Chalmers was behind him on the Selma road and ordered him to march to Randolph. This dispatch was sent to Chalmers from Selma. This officer was marching upriver on the west side of the Cahaba, separating himself from his commander instead of coming to help him. This error reduced Forrest's forces to two brigades of cavalry and a little unit of militia under Adams.

So that the troops under Wilson had an easier time moving forward, Upton's and Long's divisions were directed onto different roads to Randolph, where they reunited near the enemy position. Long was the first to arrive and didn't hesitate to attack. His advance guard attacked on foot and broke through the first line of Roddey's brigade. He now sent in a battalion of the 17th Indiana Mounted Infantry to cut down the fleeing enemy with their sabers. Roddey's brigade was driven together and the brave "Hoosiers" galloped through the enemy line, turned to the left and rode through their line again. Their losses were an officer and 16 men killed or wounded which fell into enemy hands. Captain Taylor of the 17th Indiana Regiment lost his life in leading his men into this heated fight. Galloping after the enemy, he personally attacked Forrest, severely wounding him by saber slashes and blows from his pistol. Then Forrest shot him through the heart with the last bullet in his revolver, so that he fell dead from his horse.

Upton's riders now arrived on Long's right to help. This movement broke up Forrest's line and it left the field in wild disorder and fled toward Selma. Three artillery guns and 200 prisoners fell into Wilson's hands. Around midnight, Forrest met Armstrong's brigade from Chalmers' division. These he sent to Selma and he ordered Chalmers to immediately send his division to the same place. Wilson's actions provide evidence of how valuable time is in such a campaign. After beating him on 1 April and chasing him for 24 miles, he marched at daybreak on the 2nd and reached the outer defense works of Selma at noon, just early enough to prevent Jackson and Chalmers from being able to unite with Forrest. Forrest met here with his superior and department commander. Taylor was just about to leave Selma by train to Demopolis to see with what he means he could help Forrest from that city. The train on which Taylor was fleeing had just about reached the city border when Wilson's column appeared, just early enough to shoot a few salvos in his direction, but he was able to escape. Forrest spread his little garrison out along the long line of earthworks and the militia, now made up of boys between 14 and 18 yrs. old and old men between 50 and 65 years, who were so demoralized that Forrest couldn't trust them. The defense-works were strong and well-built, with good trenches, palisades and heavy artillery guns. Steamboats and railroad trains had been loaded with weapons and supplies for the Southern army to take them to safety; for in the present situation in the South they were worth their weight in gold. The last trains and ships were now gone and residents of the city had been left to their fate.

As soon as Wilson reached the town, Long's division was positioned on the right and Upton's on the left, but it was almost dark before the lines had been established and the enemy line had been investigated. The plan was to overwhelm the enemy by getting around them on the left through a less-guarded swamp area, but Long heard that he was threatened of being attacked from behind and sent a regiment behind to guard his pack-train and the horses he had left behind. He then stormed with the main portion of his division directly at the enemy breastworks. The noise of the attack was the signal for the other troops to also attack.

The boldness of the attack terrorized the demoralized Southerners and after a short fight, the enemy line had been captured everywhere and Wilson's troops streamed into the city from all sides, while the enemy troops fled in indescribable disarray. Forrest had once again exposed himself to all the dangers of the common soldier, but it didn't help and during the night he managed to slash his way through with some of his best men and the more prominent officers to the Montgomery Road to the east. During the night they marched around the Union cavalry and reached Plantersville by morning, the town he had just left the day before. After resting for a few hours, he led his people to Marion, but here he was confronted by McCook's troops, who were on their way to join Wilson in Selma. To save time, he left behind some pickets and went around to the left of the Union troops and after a night ride, crossed the Cahaba River and joined Chalmers' and Jackson's cavalries on the morning of 4 April.

Wilson's success was immense thanks to his intelligence, his rapid movements, his immediate assaults, and of course, his superior forces were all of great value. He could usually anticipate how his opponent would move and because of that, could attack being sure of success. Forrest had now found in the last days of the war, an opponent that destroyed him with his own tactic; being first in a place. 40 guns, 2700 prisoners and war materials of immeasurable value fell into Wilson's hands, but the greatest losses to the South were the arsenal and weapons factories. Wilson now kept busy with the construction of an 800' pontoon bridge over the Alabama River. The work was difficult because the river was deep and with a strong current, which made it dangerous. After destroying the factories, public workshops and supplies, he decided to march first to Montgomery and then to the state of Georgia and finally to join Sherman's army in the Carolinas. The southern militia consisting of boys and old men only presented a weak defense.

    As soon as the troops had reached their camp in Selma, Brigadier-General Winston was named commander of the area and he was ordered to destroy anything that could be of value to the rebel government. General Upton was ordered to march at daybreak the next day to establish a connection with McCook's Division, which was expected soon on the road from Centreville. The latter was guarding a long wagon train. The plan too, was to draw Chalmers' cavalry to the west side of the Cahaba River by Upton's movement and to annihilate him there. The capture of Selma had put Wilson in possession of all the supplies for the enemy in the entire Southwest and was a bad blow to the Confederacy. It was now open to Wilson to march in any direction he chose. The craftsmen in Wilson's cavalry were working day and night in the workshops of the city under the command of staff officers of the Engineer Corps to construct the previously mentioned bridge to the south side of the Alabama River.

    Upton and McCook reached the city with their long supply wagon train on 5 April, but there was no news from Croxton's division. McCook had been successful in a march against Centreville, but when he reached Scottsboro, he found Jackson's enemy division opposing him with superior forces in a strong position, so that it seemed too risky to attempt an attack. After a sharp fight with his advance guard, he retreated back to Centreville, burned the cotton factories in Scottsboro, burned the bridge over the Cahaba River and withdrew back to Selma, convinced that Croxton would show up by some other route and would be fully capable of defending himself in any attack by the enemy. On 6 April, the bridge over the Alabama River was hurriedly put up under the personal oversight of the head of the Engineer Corps, Major Hubbard. On the same day, General Wilson had a conference in Cahaba with General Forrest concerning an agreement over the exchange of prisoners; but Forrest wanted all the advantages of the exchange for himself, with the explanation that those prisoners in his hands would soon be freed by Wilson anyway, so no agreement was reached. But Wilson heard enough to be convinced that Croxton's command would soon reach him in the best of order. For that reason he tried to transfer all his forces to the south side of the Alabama River as soon as possible. The river was climbing and the weather was changeable and rainy, so with almost superhuman effort the Engineer Corps managed, with the help of General Upton, General Alexander's and Wilson's personal staffs, to finish the 875' bridge and Wilson's entire corps was on the south side of the river on the morning of 10 April. The current was so strong, the bridge broke up several times, and General Alexander had been in danger of drowning. Wilson now had all his troops together, with the exception of Croxton's brigade, and convinced that the enemy would have no further benefit from the possession of Selma since Forrest had previously destroyed the 25,000 bales of cotton there, he set off on his march toward Montgomery with the intention of proceeding on to Georgia, the western parts of South and North Carolinas, and uniting with Sherman's army in southwestern Virginia to march against Lee's and Johnson's rebel army there. Enough horses had been captured in Selma that all the riders with no horses could be in the saddle again. The unnecessary wagons were burned; the remaining pontoons were also destroyed because they would no longer be needed after crossing the Alabama River.

The "contrabands" (run-away slaves) which were fit for service, were mustered into regiments under capable officers, and these strong youths, organized into companies, marched on foot from 35 to 45 miles daily.

On the march from Selma toward LaGrange, McCook's Division marched in front. The rain made the roads almost impassable and a little troop of Rebels had destroyed several bridges. This all made progress forward difficult. Early on the morning of the 12th, Wilson's advance guard reached Montgomery. The mayor and city father's surrendered the city to the victorious Union troops.

The Southern General, after retreating to the city, had burned 90,000 bales of cotton that were stored here, worth almost four million dollars, and then retreated to Mount Meigs on the Columbus Road. Five artillery guns, a mass of small arms, as well as ammunition and provisions, all fell into our hands. The 4th Kentucky Cavalry Regiment under Colonel Cooper was designated as the occupation force of the city and destroyed what public property still existed. Major Weston and a small unit from this regiment made a quick attack on Wetumpka and captured five fully loaded steamboats by swimming the Coosa and Tallapoosa Rivers. These were taken back to Montgomery and completely destroyed. On the morning of the 14th the march continued and General Upton was ordered to head straight to Columbus. The brigade under LaGrange was ordered to rapidly march to West Point, thoroughly destroying every railroad bridge along the way there. Wilson hoped to secure the crossing of the Chattahoochee River on this road. The brigade under Winslow followed Upton on the road over the Tuskegee River. McCook remained a few more hours in Montgomery with a portion of his division until he had destroyed what remained of public property. A short time after LaGrange left camp in Montgomery, he met a small enemy department under Buford and Clanton. He drove these together and took 150 prisoners. At about 2 p.m. on the 16th, General Upton, with a unit under Alexander, met enemy outposts on the road. These quickly retreated by way of Girard over the Chattahoochee to Columbus. After Upton had secured a position on the lower Montgomery Road, he sent a unit by a round-about way to the bridge about three miles upriver from the city. There he made a personal reconnaissance and found the enemy in a strong position protected by earthworks, which protected all bridges on both sides of the river. He had already decided to attack the defense works on his side of the river with the troops under Winslow which were at hand instead of waiting for the 2nd Division which was marching toward him.

Wilson reached Winslow's Brigade around 4 p.m. and found the troops on their way to the positions that Upton had assigned them, but because of a misunderstanding, Winslow didn't reach his position until sundown. Upton suggested to Wilson that he wanted to attack the defense works at night. General Wilson seemed to think it was a good plan and gave the necessary order. Three hundred men under Col. Noble of the 3rd Iowa Cavalry Regiment (he was later Interior Minister under President Harrison) were dismounted and sent forward in skirmish lines under heavy artillery fire. The 4th Iowa and 10th Missouri were to be ready to help in the reserves. At 8 p.m. just as Noble's troops were ready to attack, the enemy opened up with terrible rifle fire as well as the four field guns. The General's Upton and Winslow were present as Winslow's troops under Noble marched forward, sending rapid and devastating fire from their Spencer rifles. They forced their way through the brush and abatis and drove the enemy back to its outer defense line, which was first thought to be the main line. During the whole time that Noble's men were exposed to heavy enemy fire, General Upton sent two companies of the 10th Missouri under Captain McGlasson forward in gallop up the road to insure Noble's success and to take possession of the bridge. These reached the inner dense line and before the enemy became aware of them, they had already captured the bridge leading to Columbus.

As soon as all available troops had reached the position that Colonel Noble held with his dismounted riders from the 3rd Iowa Cavalry Regiment, General Upton went forward with his entire command and pushing aside all resistance by the enemy, took possession of the river and railroad bridges and placed guards throughout the entire city, taking 1200 prisoners, 52 field-guns already in position to fire at us, and a great mass of small weapons and war materials fell into our hands as well. Our losses under Colonel Noble were only 24 dead and wounded. The success is attributed to the great bravery and bravura of those taking part in this night raid. When we remember that the entire attack was made only by the cavalry, without the encouragement that the men would have had, had they known about the great events in Virginia, and since the occupation of Columbus can be considered the key to Georgia, this battle cannot be valued high enough.

As soon as the supplies and all workshops and cotton of possible use to the enemy had been destroyed, the march continued. The abandonment of Richmond and Lee's defeat were soon common knowledge everywhere and the march to Macon had lost all military importance and there was nothing to show for the brilliant and instructive tactics against Forrest. Strategically it was completely against the healthy principal that had guided the first part of the campaign. Two thirds of Forrest's riders still remained between the Cahaba and Tombigbee Rivers, and Mobile was not yet in our possession. His actual march should have been further west and south and not toward the east and north. But the Confederacy had lost its strength and fell apart on all sides. Their president feared for his life and fled; it was Wilson's luck that he had troops in southern Georgia and captured and made him prisoner. Mobile was soon captured. Suffering from his wounds and even more from frustration that his military career had ended with such a major defeat, Forrest gave his word, let his faithful veterans return to their homes and advised them from now on to be as good citizens as they had been good soldiers and to resign themselves to the new situation and the triumph of the national government.

The Advance from Goldsboro toward Raleigh Johnson's surrender and the end

On 7 March, two columns of Union troops marched from Wilmington under Terry and Couch, to assist Sherman and Schofield. Terry followed the railroad bed to Goldsboro while Couch marched through spruce forests and swamps toward Kinston. Intending to cut off the troops from Wilmington hurrying to help Cox, the enemy had set the spruce forest on fire, which prevented General Couch's division from directly marching toward Kinston and forced them to build new roads through the swamps. As soon as the flames reached the resin-filled trees they immediately became columns of fire never less than 30', and sometimes more than 200' high that lighted up the night in an awe-inspiring way and caused an impenetrable cloud of smoke during the day. It seemed that the Southerners would be willing to destroy the earth to forward their cause. But the elements were good to the Union forces and on the 10th, it rained for several hours with such strength that the fire was dampened. The rain however also made Couch's progress forward impossible, because the wagons were always up to their axles in the swamp. On the evening of the 10th, Couch learned that Cox had thrown Bragg back at Kinston and that he no longer had to hurry. Couch reached Kinston on the 13th and after three days of rest, the combined forces marched under Schofield, as already mentioned, toward Goldsboro, where on the 21st they were joined by Terry's troops from Wilmington. On the same day, Terry's left wing connected with Kilpatrick's cavalry corps from Sherman's army, which on the 19th had defeated Johnson's whole army. On the following day, out in the open we could see troops steaming in toward Goldsboro from every direction of the compass, over meadows and fields, on horse or on mules and also on foot, individually or in platoons. Sherman reached Goldsboro himself on the 23rd. The 23rd Corps paraded past his headquarters in parade march. He wore the same tired look from overwork that he had worn at Rome, Georgia, when we separated from him in October. He was asked to give a speech and he said a few words: He said that the war would be over in three months and then we would have the welcome march home to the North ahead of us. You can imagine that this talk was applauded and brought the men into such a mood that they sang the song; "When Johnny Comes Marching Home". After the so-called "Sherman Bums" reached Goldsboro, a portion of the main army marched forward under Slocum. Their uniforms had gotten so torn and ragged from 450 miles of long marches through swamps, jungles, meadows and fields from Savannah to Goldsboro that out of an entire company there would not have been a decent uniform for one soldier. In spite of that, they were burdened with every imaginable item of plunder; further, every company had six or more strong young blacks who did the heavy work and made the camp comfortable for them. Horses and mules by the hundreds, harnessed to every conceivable vehicle from baby buggy to post-carriage, hauled in whatever foodstuffs could be gathered from the land. The veterans of the 23rd Corps were invited to eat with the 15th and other corps. The following provides a true picture of Sherman's army, after it crossed Georgia from Atlanta to Savannah it was a raiding march forty miles wide, and from Savannah through South and North Carolina to Goldsboro, a raiding march 60 miles wide and 450 miles long, which during this march had destroyed everything as if the locusts had been there, so that the crows would have had to carry a bread-sack along in order to feed themselves. It is clearly proven that the enemy had no chance of opposing such numbers, for across the width of 60 miles the Northerners were strong enough on any road to be able to defend themselves from any enemy attack.

As soon as Sherman's army had gathered at Goldsboro and camps and positions had been assigned, Sherman made a quick visit to City Point to consult with General Grant about the coming campaign. The result was that his army marched to the north in order to make use of the Weldon Railroad and the Roanoke River as another base. Sherman also had the satisfaction of meeting President Lincoln at City Point to discuss with him the collapse of the rebellion and the situation for the southern states after the war. Several changes were made in the command after Sherman's visit. The 20th and 14th Corps under Slocum were designated as the left wing. Schofield's 23rd and 10th Corps became the center and the 15th and 16th Corps (known as the Tennessee Army) became the right wing.

Our battery, still stationed in Wilmington, was ordered to hand over our guns, harnesses and other quarter-master articles to the ordinance officers and quartermaster in Wilmington, and to immediately travel by train to Goldsboro. The order was promptly carried out and on the morning of 3 April we arrived in Goldsboro. Here we were told that we would be given the guns and teams of a Negro field-artillery. We presented ourselves in the headquarters of the battery and were informed by the lieutenant in command, that they had received the order, but that the captain had hurried to General Terry's headquarters right away to have the order rescinded if possible. (This Negro battery belonged to Terry's 10th Corps, while we belonged to Schofield's 23rd, and the latter commanded both.) The lieutenant told us that they had been in the service for a long time already, but had never had an opportunity to prove their capabilities and bravery. Since there seemed now a chance to do this, they wanted to get near the enemy once. The captain soon returned with authorization to refuse the transfer of guns and teams to us until further orders. We now camped under the open sky, near this battery, since we hadn't had any tents since the battle of Chickamauga after we had been at Charleston, Tennessee and our gun covers had to be handed in at Wilmington. We were invited several times by the officers of the Negro battery to observe their maneuvers and we had to admit that they were doing their work very well. But their guns were six bronze cannons and after having had rifled. guns for three and a half years, we would just as soon forgo the Napoleonic firecrackers which he had used in the battle of Italy in 1859 and then been sold to the United States.

On 5 April, the stockpiles of army provisions at Goldsboro, Wilmington and Kinston had been piling up so much that confidential instructions were given to have the army advance on the 10th, but on the next day, the 6th, the news came that Richmond had been abandoned by the enemy and Lee was trying as best he could to reach Danville. Sherman now turned his march directly toward Raleigh. The march forward was begun on the 10th and on the 11th the news reached us that Lee had surrendered at Appomattox on the 9th. The day was bright and warm; real spring weather. The column rested after every hour of marching. The troops sat or stretched out on either side of the road. All of a sudden, a staff officer from the front appeared and gesturing in great excitement shouted to everyone as he rode past, "Lee has surrendered!" The soldiers shouted, "You are the man that we have been waiting three long years for and showed their joy like little kids at Christmas, now that they knew the war had ended. A Southern woman, who came to her garden gate with her children in order to ask the corps commander for protection while the soldiers marched past, heard the noise and when she learned the cause of the jubilation, she looked at her astonished children and told them, "Now our Papa will soon be home, for the war is over." (Her husband served in Lee's Southern Army). From that moment on, the march had no military importance, for it was well understood that Johnson only wanted to hold up Sherman here until the Southern leaders could discuss the situation.

On the 13th, Kilpatrick reached the capitol of North Carolina, Raleigh. When he got near the city, he and his staff and followers were shot at by young men. A young German who served Kilpatrick as ordinance officer was severely wounded. The youths tried to flee but were chased, and quicker than one can write about it, they were captured. They were led in front of the General and questioned to which company and regiment they belonged. Since they weren't in the army, but served the state as clerks, a war tribunal was held and after a short trial, all three were condemned to be hanged. They were led on their horses to a tree, a rope put around their necks, their hands tied behind their backs and the horses under them pulled away and the delinquents were hung. It was said that the young women that they were in love with, were the cause of their deed. Since the young men were in the service of the state, they had been made fun of by the young ladies, that they didn't have enough courage to become a soldier. They then declared that they would prove their courage as soon as an opportunity presented itself. Their action was the result of this craziness.

On 14 April, Sherman received, by way of Kilpatrick, the suggestion of a ceasefire from Johnson, and if possible a meeting between both commander to put an end to the war. They agreed to meet in Bennet's House at Durham's Station. On the 17th, just as Sherman was getting ready to go there, his telegraph operator received a message that President Lincoln had been shot on the 14th. Sherman met with his opponent and after a long back and forth, they agreed on the terms for the surrender. Since Sherman had introduced political conditions into the agreement, the surrender agreement had to be approved in Washington, or a refusal sent back. The mood in Washington was such that approval wasn't possible and Sherman was even accused of treason. Had Sherman put something in the protocol about the complete abolishment of slavery, his preliminary document would perhaps not have been so bluntly rejected. With the rejection of the conditions, General Grant was sent to Raleigh to oversee the surrender of Johnson's army, or to take command of the troops against Johnson. As soon as Sherman learned of the rejection of his agreement, he informed Johnson that his army would attack him again in 48 hours. A new meeting was arranged by both generals with General Schofield to be at the meeting, which wasn't the case at the first meeting. Sherman and Johnson were together alone behind closed doors for a long time before Schofield was called in and informed that the two couldn't come to an agreement, for the conditions that Grant and Lee had stipulated could not be carried out here, and if they couldn't come to an agreement here, the second meeting would also fail to produce a result. After Schofield had listened to their explanation, he told them he could perhaps arrange it, and Sherman asked him to put his ideas on paper. While Schofield wrote, the other two paced up and down the room nervously. When Schofield finished writing, he read the agreement of 26th April to both of them. Then Sherman read the document through for himself and handed it to Johnson who did the same. Schofield thought that this was the best that could be achieved, since after Sherman was out of the way with his army, he as Department Commander could carry out the conditions. The conditions as written down by Schofield, were, as Sherman said, signed by both without hesitation and without difficulty.

Schofield gave, in carrying out the conditions, 250,000 rations to Johnson disbanded troops, to prevent the residents of the South from being robbed, also weapons for preserving order, and free transportation to their states as far as it was possible by train or steamboat. The agreement of the 18th which had caused such anuproar and that of the 26th were quite similar. The horses and mules that were in the victor's hands were liberally distributed among the residents of North Carolina. The rulers in Washington insisted that not the least bit of the Rebel government should remain, so that everything should be new from the ground up, but had forgotten that a newly created government would lead to uncertainty and disloyalty on a temporary basis.

The existing government at the time of the surrender could certainly have been of more and greater value in maintaining order if it had been recognized and watched over by the military occupation forces. All the attempts by the government under President Johnson and later the "carpetbagger" government through Congress only resulted in worse government than had ever been the case before. If we compare Sherman and Johnson's agreement with the political history of the rebel states from 1865 to 1877, we see that Sherman and Johnson at that time displayed more statesmanlike intelligence than President Johnson had during his entire time in power. If Sherman had had a military adviser at his side that could have restrained his impulsiveness somewhat, he would certainly have been the greatest general of any time. He looked with disdain on any politician who wanted to give him advice.

The surrender of Johnson's army was formalized at Greensboro in the neighborhood of the Guilford Court House, where General Green in the Revolutionary War had a significant battle with Lord Cornwallis. General Hardee took this part for the southern side while Schofield carried out the conditions for the Union. As soon as it was known that conditions to keep the peace were part of the agreement, about 4000 riders and an equal number of infantry men from Johnson's Army hid out in the brush, because they believed that all of them would end up in northern prisons, but those that stuck with their flags definitely had the advantages, since they received rations and free transportation to their homes.

Johnson gave each of his faithful a dollar from the available gold and silver reserves as compensation for their services in the now totally lost cause. Then they all went by various ways back to their homes, to begin their lives over again in complete poverty.

The Union army marched northward with flags flying, music playing, singing with strong proud voices, filled with hope and happiness of being about to take part in the great parade in Washington, only regretting that they could no longer do that honor for Lincoln in front of the White House. When General Grant arrived in Raleigh, the first division of the 23rd Corps paraded in front of him for review; the Southerners that had served under Lee were already making compliments about the western troops.

Grant was not often seen during his stay in Raleigh, and as soon as Johnson had capitulated, he returned to Washington in order to issue orders for the disbandment of the troops from there. We remained in Raleigh until the middle of May, when we received orders to go to Greensboro by train. A short while after arriving there we were ordered to complete discharge lists for those soldiers whose service period had ended or that would end in three months. This was naturally unpleasant for the recruits of the battery. When the list was complete, I traveled to Raleigh to have it signed by Department-Commander Schofield. I was sent back from there and informed that the whole battery would be sent home in a few days and discharged there, for the last armed enemy under General Kirby Smith had surrendered in Texas. Now every day seemed endlessly long to us and on 10 June we received the following order:

"Headquarters of the 23rd Army Corps, Greensboro, N.C. the 10th June, 1865. Special Field Order No. 52. First Lieutenant Fred'k. W. Fout, in command of the 15th Indiana Battery, is herewith ordered to deliver all artillery or quartermaster objects in his possession to the officer responsible for such things and will then proceed to travel to Indianapolis, Indiana by way of Danville, City Point and Washington, with the intention of discharging the battery out of the service. The Quartermaster Department will furnish the necessary transportation.
J. D. Cox, Maj.-Gen. in Command

Signed: Theodore Cox, Col. and Assistant Adjt.-General"

I immediately began working on getting transportation and on the next morning at 10 o'clock, our train was standing ready. I went to the corps headquarters to say good-bye to the general and his staff. Here Col. Theo. Cox had another job for me. Thirty-six sacks of rebel mail had ended up in headquarters. A lieutenant that had gone north on leave had already been ordered to take them along but didn't have any men with him to act as guards. My name had been entered in the lieutenant's place and the mail-bags were given to me. With jubilation and waving our hats, we left Greensboro toward Danville. Here we had to wait until the next morning, and then we went on to City Point, were we spent the night on the levee. On the following morning we continued on aboard the "Lady Lang" down the James River. On the trip to Fort Monroe, we saw the remains of the steamers "Minnesota", "Cumberland" and "Congress", which had been destroyed by the "Merrimac". Jefferson Davis was sitting then in chains at Fort Monroe, so our curiosity to see him wasn't satisfied. On the next morning, we reached Washington. I had a wagon come right away and had the 36 bags of mail loaded and as quickly as possible hauled it to the post office, and received a receipt for them and returned to my battery at the foot of 7th Street and the Alexandria Landing. A helper of the quartermaster took us to a soldier's home near the Baltimore & Ohio Railroad. Having arrived there, we had a visit from the Indiana state agent in Washington. When I told him that I brought along 36 bags of mail and had delivered them to the post office, he advised me to notify the war department about them, since they originated from the rebels and would be considered contraband. It was now 1:30 p.m. on Sunday and I doubted that I would find anyone in the War Department, but I rode there and in full field-uniform I strode into the old barracks which served as the War Department. After I had passed the guards, I was led by a young blond German into the adjutant's office where I met Colonel Nichols. I told him what I had done and herewith reported my delivery of the mail to the War Department. He asked right away for my receipt and I handed it to him. He went into another room, but soon returned and said I should go in, Secretary of War Stanton was there and wished to talk to me. Being struck by lightning couldn't have hit me more unexpectedly than this invitation. I wished Col. Cox, his bags of mail and the Indiana state agent to go to "Blocksberg", but in military posture I strode forward. To my great astonishment, the Secretary rose and shook my hand. Then he had me sit down in an armchair covered in Russian leather next to him. The Secretary had dealt harshly with many officers, and since I hadn't come to the War Department right away, I thought I was in for similar treatment. I had barely sat down when I was flooded with questions: who I had seen, what they said, etc. It went on like that for almost a half hour. When I told him that Mrs. Reagan and her daughter had been on the steamer with us and had settled in the "National Hotel", he made a note of it. (Mrs. Reagan's husband was the General Postmaster in Davis's cabinet. Finally, Col. Nichols brought me a new receipt and gave I him my hand to say good-bye. He wished us a pleasant journey and happy future for all of us. We had to wait a few more days at the train station for transportation. Finally it we got it and after five days on the Baltimore & Ohio Railroad, we reached Parkersburg, West Virginia. We had to leave the train here because a train carrying soldiers of the 103 Ohio Regiment home had crashed in Ohio.

On the morning after our arrival in Parkersburg, we got transportation on the river steamer "Kate Henderson", a small, wretched, old boat that we were reluctant to board. But we wanted to get home and anything that could get us in that direction was welcome. Everything went well until 3 p.m. A storm suddenly came up near Portsmouth, Ohio and threw the boat on its side. The crew was in desperation but luck was with us and rolled us against the bank and everyone that could, saved themselves as quickly as possible. The storm let up and we went back on board and reached Cincinnati around 11 p.m. Early the next morning we were on the train to Indianapolis. We arrived there around 10 o'clock. A band awaited us at the station and led us with music playing to the market hall. Here they had us sit down at a long row of tables loaded with good food. Two young ladies served each artillery man. In the afternoon was a public welcome by Governor Morton in the shady area surrounding the capitol building. At noon on the

30th, we gathered again, but already many men were missing. I led the men to the courthouse where they were paid their back wages and given their honorable discharge certificates. We shook hands and said good-bye and for many of us it would be the last time we saw each other. Many had tears in their eyes for joy and for sorrow...joy for a happy return home...and sorrow at being separated from one's comrades with whom we have fought shoulder to shoulder for so long and had borne so many hardships together

The Causes of the Civil War

The North and well as the South had different views over two important questions already for many years: the tariff and slavery.

The North was already largely engaged in a factory and manufacturing economy and hence demanded tariffs, while Southern wealth came from cotton, sugar and slaves, hence they demanded free trade throughout the world. The slavery question had been generally settled through the Missouri Compromise of 1820. But when Nebraska and Kansas received territorial governments, the Missouri Compromise was considered not applicable and the question if a state should be a free or a slave state was left up to the citizens of those states, and each territory was free to decide.

This didn't end the conflict, but only served to fan the flames. Both parties, for and against slavery, now went to work on getting a majority of votes. Emigrants from the New England states flooded into the new territories in much greater numbers than those from southern and slave states. When the vote for or against slavery was held in Kansas, the vast majority of the vote was against slavery.

The result of the vote against slavery outraged the southern states and when the Republican Party came into power with the election of Lincoln on 6 November 1860, the leaders of the South knew there was no longer any hope for expanding slavery and immediately started making preparations and plans for separating the southern states from the Union.

The representatives of South Carolina pulled out of the United States Congress on 9 November. On the 11th of the same month, the same state formally left the Union, which was ratified by a public vote on 20 December. This state was followed by Mississippi on 9 January 1861, Florida on 10 January, Alabama on 11 January, Georgia on 19 January, Texas on 1 February, Virginia on 17 April, Arkansas on 6 May, North Carolina on 21 May and Tennessee on 8 June. The western portion of Virginia refused to join the Confederacy and became a separate state in the Union. The war really had its beginning when the Southern batteries in

Charleston harbor opened fire on the supply ship "Star of the West" on 9 January 1861 and it ended with the surrender of Richard Taylor in May 1865.

Respectfully,
Fred'k. W. Fout

www.ingramcontent.com/pod-product-compliance
Lightning Source LLC
Chambersburg PA
CBHW020737160426
43192CB00006B/225